Spectrum of Mind

Spectrum of Mind

AN INQUIRY INTO THE PRINCIPLES OF THE MIND AND THE MEANING OF LIFE

J Michael Yang

ISBN: 0692379495
ISBN-13: 9780692379493
Library of Congress Control Number: 2015902062
HINT Press, San Diego, CA 92129

Dedication

This book is dedicated to those individuals
who love their lives, are honest to their hearts,
and think independently.
They are like prisms in the world.
The light of life shines on them,
and as they experience life, easy or hard,
they refract the light.
The spectrum of mind comes from each individual.
Whoever genuinely refracts the light of life
always leaves behind a unique spectrum of mind.
May your spectrum be the one
that inspires others' hearts.

Table of Contents

CHAPTER 1

Introduction

1.1 A Timeless Inquiry

On a spring afternoon when I was eighteen year old, I just finished the school homework and decided to take a break. I climbed to the fifth floor of a building in my school, stood at a window and quietly watched the natural scene far away. The sunset at the edge of the sky was slowly falling down on a peaceful river. The red color of the sky and the clouds was reflected on the river, rippled by the waves. The sun, the sky, the cloud, the river, the water, and the world were so peaceful. I forgot myself and totally merged with the beauty of Mother Nature. I felt a deep sense about something mythical and eternal. I thought in my mind that our lives are respectful and precious, there must be something meaningful in our lives we should seek to understand. I didn't know exactly what it was at that time, but it is a feeling that frequently comes to my mind along the path of my growth. The sense becomes stronger when I am an adult. Many times, I have just put it aside, since I was too busy with daily life. But the inner voice urging a quest for the meaning of life is always there.

Two thousand years ago, the great Greek philosopher Socrates declared, "An unexamined life is not worth living." In his view, inquiring the meaning of life is equally as important as the living of life. Similarly, thousands of years ago, the great Chinese philosopher and educator Confucius said, "If I hear the truth in the morning, I am willing to die in the evening." In his view, the understanding of truth equates to the living of life. The quest for the true meaning of life proves to be timeless. Today, even though we live in a modern society, after thousands of years of civilization and cultural evolution, after all of the advancement of science and new technologies, and with well-connected social networks, the most intrinsic questions as human beings still remain the same. "Who am I? What is the meaning of life?" There are no other questions as profound as these to inspire great thinkers and religious leaders around the world, from thousands of years ago to now, to explore the understanding of ourselves as deeply as we can. They came up with answers in a tremendous number of forms, including philosophy, religion, art, literature, and the advancement of science. There is no universal answer, and there is no final answer. For an individual, at any given time of civilization, the question is always fresh. Answers from others, whether from older generations or from others in the same generation, cannot substitute for our own journeys. Eventually, one must be awakened to this question and go through his or her own journey to come up with his or her own specific answer. And those questions introduce many follow-up questions and byproducts.

A man's life is short. However, we seek a feeling of eternity. We live in this world for a brief time, but what will we leave behind? Do I come to this world just to experience a regular life and then leave it without understanding it or knowing if there is a purpose for it? If there is a purpose, how do I know about it? And if there isn't any purpose, why are there ethics and values one is told to follow? A deep understanding of the nature of human beings is fundamental to how we perceive ourselves and others. There are two perceptions of a human being. On one hand, anybody is just one of the billions living on the earth, like a drop of water in the ocean. With or without him makes not much difference. There is no significance whatsoever; an individual comes and goes. On the other hand, any human being is indeed a magical creature of nature, inheriting the results of millions of years of human evolution. A human being possesses the power of spirit, the power of rational thinking, the power of intuition to receive hints, the power of love, and the capability of forming a group that can influence the evolution path of a society.

It is this second perception that makes humans special. There is a precious spirit that every one of us has. That spirit is just like a light shining from our minds. This light can be transcendent to a short life. If there is goal for life, it must be higher than the usual goals of earning more wealth or climbing the social ladder. One comes to this world with life from Mother Nature and must seek to understand the meaning of it. Maybe, at the end, the answer is obvious—or perhaps there is no answer—but the journey itself is a precious experience that will enrich one's life and cannot be replaced by any other means. From that perspective, I can understand what Socrates or Confucius declared.

The understanding of ourselves is crucial to our lives. A full understanding of the meaning of life allows one to appreciate the preciousness of a human life, love and respect oneself (and hence love and respect others), and treasure every second of living at a completely new level. In the end, this is a personal journey. You cannot expect there is answer existing just for you. If you are awakening to the question of the meaning of life, it is just the start.

1.2 Where Is the Starting Point?

Where is the starting point to build a truthful, complete understanding about ourselves? This is not a simple question, because it depends on many outcomes of human endeavors, including knowledge and science, philosophy, psychology, and religion. There is no need to start from scratch, since this question was pondered by people living on the earth for thousands of years. However, understanding from early generations can have both truthful wisdom and delusion. How to decipher them, absorb the truthful wisdom, and unwind the delusion? We are not taking anything for granted and will not assume anything to start with. The key approach for the journey is to tear down the facade, instead to look into the foundation behind the scenes. Let's briefly examine the available knowledge and wisdom from these human endeavors.

The advancement of science is the most powerful achievement of humanity. Advancement of psychology, neuroscience, nonlinear science, physics, and chemistry is pushing our understanding of life and humans to a new level. However, so far, science still cannot explain the origin of life, nor can it explain how the value of a human being originated. There is no doubt that scientific advancement reveals many aspects of truth about the physical world, and the methodology behind science profoundly influences the way we think. We should pay sufficient respect to it, but at the same time, we need to be cautious not to be religious about it. For example, modern astronomy tells us that the sun will eventually die out billions of years from now. Consequently, the earth will be destroyed, and any civilization of human beings on the earth will disappear. Essentially, there is no such kind of thing in a universe that is eternal. If that is the destiny of human beings, the sense of eternal is simply a delusion. How much can we trust the scientific prediction? How to extract the value from science and help our understanding of life, but at the same time not be misguided by its limitations? To answer this, one needs to look at the origin of knowledge. In fact, after we deeply examine the original of knowledge, we will realize that knowledge itself is constructed with intrinsic limitations. For example, it is a faulty belief that we can predict the future with certainty; the sum of knowledge of the parts will not give a complete understanding of the whole. Religious belief on science is dangerous. But the methodologies behind science are important in order to understand the human thinking pattern.

Philosophy extracts principles that have not yet been approved. Philosophy has provided wisdom in searching for the principles behind observed phenomena, even though these principles could be just hypothesis. Due to lack of rigorous details and proof, many philosophical ideas leave gaps and incomplete understanding. It is even more risky to generalize these philosophical ideas. Generalization is a natural inclination of humans that frequently happens—a deep thought that is developed well enough to explain certain parts of the world or ourselves is used to explain other parts of the world or ourselves. Generalization simplifies the understanding, and it is philosophy that is best at generalizing abstract concepts and applying them to everything. Metaphysics seeks the most abstract form of principles without considering limitations, hence is far reaching toward a knowledge boundary. But when it is applied to normal life, metaphysics can be out of touch. For a philosopher, the thinking never ends, and he can continue to seek the truth and not fall into any religions, unless he is rationally convinced. But for regular people, life is limited, and the limitations set the boundary. The solution to this boundary may result in falling into a particular religion. This is just like solving a scientific equation—without boundary and limitation, the principle inside the equation is always true and elegant. But when the boundary is set for a real physical problem, the equation yields a finite solution that may not be elegant. Furthermore, it can only interpret the phenomena for a particular boundary condition. Many great philosophers only ask questions and demonstrate the thinking process, the logic, the rationale, but they may not provide answers or solve problems facing a particular group of normal people. For regular life, the boundary can be your family, your parents, your living conditions, the culture you live in, and difficulties you encounter. It can be a real event, or it can be an emotional attachment. Philosophy does not seem to be a starting foundation either to understand the meaning of life. We should search for other potential staring points.

In the attempt to explore a deeper understanding of life, different cultures in the course of their own evolution introduced different religions. Religion answers some of the questions, such as the origin of the world and the destiny of human beings, by assuming a mythical supernatural being. Believe it or not, it is a fact that religions have influenced the evolution of cultures. In Western culture, the concept of God is crucial to most religions that help elevate human life to a new level. On the other hand, in Eastern religions, the focus is on smoothing out the difference between the self and the surrounding world. Different cultures and religions share certain aspects of religious doctrine, but there are also clear and sharp differences. Unlike rational

philosophy, religions set up doctrine and rituals. Rational thinkers may not like these, as they set limitations on a free mind, but religions provide a platform for some groups of people who are satisfied with the doctrine, the rituals, and have found these rituals make them feel peaceful, whereas the rational thinkers may not have that experience. No doubt, there are truthful components to many religions, yet at the same time, they introduce a new set of questions. For thousands of years, people were debating the meaning of God and whether God exists. What is the truth behind a belief system and a religion? One cannot bluntly label religion as superstition, but how do we distinguish valuable religious practices from superstition? Can the foundation of a belief system be consistent with rational thinking? Can it be beneficial to our spiritual life, even at the risk of becoming superstition? Since there are many open questions, we need to search for more fundamental principles to answer these questions.

Modern psychology provides a much deeper and fundamental understanding of the human mind and the meaning of self. For example, the concepts of the conscious and unconscious mind help to explain why a person cannot be completely rational in his or her thinking; it explains why a person cannot completely control the mind, which in turn explains the need for religion. This common origin of religion helps to explain why there is much similarity of religions in many cultures. However, there is a general limitation of psychology—it tries to explain everything *within* the human mind and psyche. A scientific or positivity view explains the similarity of religions in different cultures in different ways—it is simply because it reflects the truth, and the truth is universal and objective, independent of the human psyche. In this scientific view, there exist some laws that are unexplainable or incomprehensive within available knowledge. It is because of this limitation of human knowledge and intelligence that we need a complementary concept of supernatural agency to make sense of the world and of life. It is a reality independent of the human mind. Psychology explores the understanding potentiality of the mind but ignores the objectivity of the values and goals; therefore, it cannot be the sole foundation for understanding our minds.

There are many ways to explore understanding the meaning of life. But each of them seems to reveal only certain aspects of a complete picture. Furthermore, truth and delusion are intertwined in a convoluted way. The difficulty is to unwind the convolution of truth and limitations among the different pieces of answers to penetrate the surface of these understandings, to extract the valuable parts of them, digest them, and finally put them back together into a complete picture.

1.3 Overview of the Book

The searching of the meaning of life is indeed a complex process. The starting point should come from an honest understanding of human beings in every aspect. Particularly, there are two foundations that need to be built before attempting to answer any concrete question. The first one is the origin of knowledge. After all, how can we trust what we understand and the so-called knowledge? How do we acquire knowledge? How does human cognitive capability interact with the external world? What can human cognitive skills do and what are its limitations? If there is intrinsic limitations in acquiring knowledge, any understanding of ourselves will be limited as well. These are the subject of Chapters 2 and 3. Chapter 3 is an extension of Chapter 2 but specifically focuses on the most respectable branch of human intelligence—the scientific knowledge. It surveys several key scientific branches: quantum mechanics, thermodynamics, and nonlinear and complex systems. The emphasis is that the advancements of this scientific knowledge show self-revealing limitations. The methodologies used in these scientific domains are deeply discussed. Readers may skip Chapter 3 if they are not interested in the philosophy of science.

The second foundation is the basic nature of the human mind. The more accurate and unbiased our understanding of true human nature, the more neutrally we can examine the vast varieties of cultures and religions, and the better our capacity to unwind the convolution of truth and limitations. This leads to better chances of synergizing many theories, cultures, and religions around the world in searching for the meaning of life. We will devote a major effort to understand the very basic nature of humans in Chapter 4. It is the core of this book. It describes the nature of human minds, starting from the wake-up of consciousness, the development of ego and free will, and the advancement of intelligence and knowledge. The two most intrinsic tendencies of human mind are extensively examined: the growth tendency and the reconciliation tendency. The worlds human minds interact with and contribute to are categorized. The new concept of the fourth world is introduced as a complementary concept in order to address the human spiritual activities. Finally, an integrated model to describe the development process of the human mind and fully cover the spectrum of mind activities.

Another important point is that methodologies are fundamental in influencing the ways we think and perceive the world and ourselves, and methodologies from the interdomain of knowledge are critical to account for complete understanding of the human mind. For this purpose, after we examine the major human knowledge and intelligence domains, including science and psychology, we abstract the methodology behind each and explore how they influence our thinking and perception. In Chapter 5, I summarized the methodology similarity found from Chapter 2 to Chapter 4. Synergy in methodology provides additional but profound justifications when I discuss in Part II the reconciliation between science and religion, and the mutual understanding of different cultures.

With the above foundations of understanding the origin and limitations of knowledge, the neutral understanding of basic human nature, and the major methodologies one can find through domains of knowledge, we then go back to address the central question of "Who am I, and what is the meaning of life?" A byproduct found in this search is that although cultures religions around the world came up with different ways to address the central question, these cultures and religions are essentially the same in key content—they just used different methods. Abstraction of methodology is the way to find common ground among different cultures and religions.

Part I of the book is devoted to building the foundations described above. Part II applies the foundations in different cultures and religions, and then explains that these cultures and religions are essentially the same in key content but with different methods. The reason this book devotes major effort on religion is because in answering the destiny of human beings, many religions tried the hardest to answer the questions. In Chapter 6, the following topics will be discussed:

- What are the roots of religions? Why do human beings need religions?
- Is the religious belief just true in the psyche, or there is objective reality associated with it?
- To answer the above point, can we obtain support from scientific hints? It is especially encouraged when we realized the methodologies (not the exact contents) are more compatible between science and religion, as mentioned earlier. We won't be able to eliminate myths in a religion. They exist for a reason, but we can understand them with the new hints from advancements of other fields, such as psychology and science.
- Based on the above understanding, it is easier to distinguish what a mature and healthy religion is and how to recognize an unhealthy religion.

The principles on human nature and different methodologies to deal with our natures can also be applied to better understand the culture difference as well. Chapter 7 attempts to provide more understanding on the following subjects:

- What are the fundamental differences of the Chinese culture from the Western culture? It appears that Chinese culture perceiving the world as a connected wholeness, viewing human beings as the center but fully connected part of the world. Western culture was more emphasizing the methodology of understanding the part and then putting it together to understand the wholeness. The nature of Western reasoning methodology makes it inevitable to introduce a supernature when it comes to reconciling the perception of the world as whole.

- Why was religion never a mainstream in Chinese culture, especially in the intellect class? Western missionary tried to spread the gospel to China for hundreds of years but was never able to gain mainstream acceptance by the Chinese intellect class, why?
- In order to gain better mutual understanding and synergy, what can both cultures learn from each other?

Finally in Chapter 8 we come back to the original question on the meaning of life. How do we interpret the meaning of life? How do we manage the fear of death? What parts of the meaning of life can be answered by religion, and what parts are counting on our own responsibilities as human beings?

To construct a complete view of the world, to search for the meaning of life, is really a personal journey that cannot be substituted by another's journey. The complexity of understanding human beings in a complete picture demands every bit of intelligence, knowledge, and hints from all angles. I am not taking anything for granted; I'm not assuming anything to start with. The task ahead is to decipher the existing understanding in the main branches of human intelligence outputs (science, philosophy, psychology, religion, and culture), unwind the convolution of truthful wisdom and delusion, and put together my own thoughts. Maybe at the end, the answer is obvious or similar to some existing ones; maybe the answer is different from my current understanding. I am not attempting to answer all these questions. In fact some of the texts in the book are the record of a searching process and not offering a clear answer. The goal of this book is to push the reasoning to a limit. The next step is up to the reader to choose: are there better answers to these questions? Readers could come up with their own answers. The key is to take on the challenge of discarding any preoccupied thoughts, to bring an honest heart, and to be able to find the answer through your own journey. This process is more important than the final outcome.

Now, let the journey begin.

Part I—The Foundations

CHAPTER 2

Epistemology—The Origins of Knowledge

2.1 Starting Point of Knowledge

The starting point of knowledge is when the conscious of the human mind was developed to a level that humans were able to distinguish self from external objects. The history of mankind's knowledge evolution is concurrent with the evolution of the conscious of the human mind. The conscious mind is capable of awareness of the external environment and the self. When the awareness of external objects is sufficiently focused, it leads to the development of scientific concepts and knowledge. Similarly, the capability to understand the self and interpersonal relationships leads to the development of social value, psychology, and religion. It is the advancement of this self-awareness that makes society and life better and better. Knowledge acquisition is one important step in this process.

Clearly, humans are the starting point of our knowledge and also the end receiving point of that knowledge. Knowledge must be observable by humans with or without observation tools. "Man is the measure of all things," was a credo of Protagoras of Ancient Greece. Originally, it meant that morality is relative. There is no absolute truth and no absolute morality, and hence morality doesn't really matter in one's daily life. However, a deeper meaning of "Man is the measure of all things" is that any knowledge or experiences must start from human nature, and in the end, they ought to be comprehensible and tested by human beings. Particularly for philosophy and religion, this statement implies that in the end, a wisdom system or an ethical system must be practiced by an individual to check if it can really bring peace and happiness, and whether it can motivate a person to live a virtuous life. It is important to confine the power of human imagination to not go too far beyond what humans can experience. This is the typical view of empiricism.

However, such a view has its own shortsightedness. First, an important characteristic of knowledge is that it has its own life cycle. Yes, man is the starting point for any knowledge, but when the knowledge is developed and evolved, particularly when it reflects the truth to some degree and extent, it becomes an independent existence. It also becomes transcendent to one's life and can continue to evolve through others. With continuous improvement from others' thinking, this kind of objectivity of knowledge can remedy the limitations of an individual view of reality. The world of knowledge is similar to the third world that is different from the objective and subjective worlds (Popper, 1). It reflects reality to some degree but cannot be completely accurate because it is a product of human intelligence, though it can transcend beyond an individual's life. It essentially builds a layer of pseudoreality; through it, humans make a connection to true reality.

Secondly, human experience itself can be misled. This can be shown in an example from visual technology. A color picture can be encoded as RGB (Red-Green-Blue) or YUV format. In the YUV format, Y is the black and white component, and UV are the color components. The YUV format is preferred because it is backward compatible with black and white picture signals. Engineers found the non–black and white components, U and V, don't need to be a straightforward conversion of an RBG signal. Instead the U and V signal can be reduced, because the human eye cannot really tell the difference. A 4:2:2 ratio for Y:U:V components is widely used, rather than a 1:1:1 ratio. This example tells us that for satisfaction of the human eye, a good-enough representation of actual reality is sufficient. Further accurate representation is subjected to the law of diminishing returns. A similar analogy applies to our intelligence. We seek the truth using our limited powers of intelligence and describe the outcome of our thoughts with limited language. We may obtain a fairly good representation of the truth. We tend to believe it is a true representation of reality. Further seeking of a more accurate representation of reality suffers diminishing returns, since the outcome may be highly indirectly connected to actual daily life. The key point here is that our senses can be misguided, so purely relying on human senses cannot accurately determine whether our knowledge is the truth. This was vividly described in the famous metaphor of Plato's cave.

We approach the truth in infinite steps. The first few steps are big, but the following steps are smaller, and smaller, and we're never able to approach the end point.

However, this doesn't mean we should give up our effort. Why? Because it is human nature to apply creativity and thinking power to seek truth. Furthermore, even a small step closer to truth tremendously broadens humanity's view of reality; it helps to better avoid superstition and arrogance, and to better understand each other. Essentially, more accurate knowledge of truth makes life and society better. Because of this, it is important to understand where knowledge comes from.

2.2 Source of Knowledge—A Classical Debate

The source of knowledge has been a fascinating debate subject in the history of philosophy. There are many different schools of thoughts. One fundamental question is whether knowledge exists before one actually experiences it.

Rationalism proposed that knowledge could be attained by reasoning alone, prior to experience. There is abstract truth that Plato called "Form" that exists for all objects. Such abstract truth exists independently of whether humans attempt to experience it. What a human experiences is a concrete representation of the abstract truth. The concrete knowledge we attain is just an approximation of the abstract truth; we can get closer and closer to it but are never able to understand the absolute truth. Rationalism says that knowledge simply exists, waiting for us to understand.

On the other hand, empiricism rejects the idea that abstract knowledge exists before a human experiences it. It insists that knowledge can be acquired only through the senses, and after experiencing it. Humans, as the actual carrier of knowledge, must experience it first. Plato's Form, being impossible to comprehend with absolute accuracy, simply does not exist from a knowledge acquisition point of view. Empiricism believes human experience is the single source of knowledge. Knowledge through pure reasoning is not valuable unless it is validated through human experience.

Idealism pushes it one step further, proposing that external objects have actual existence only when they are perceived by an observer. This means not only knowledge, but also the object associated with that knowledge, does not exist if they cannot be experienced by the human mind. In idealism, the human mind is the center of the entire world.

Kant proposed a compromised solution that "we do not receive all knowledge from sensory experience alone, as empiricists claimed. Nor do we comprehend things through reason alone, as the rationalists firmly maintained" (Mannion, 98). While we could know particular facts about the world only via sensory experience, we could know the form they must take prior to any experience. Kant pointed out the mind is the center point that influences the world being perceived. "The mind cannot experience what is not filtered through the mind's [capability]" (Mannion, 98). Since our minds cannot be purely objective, we can never know the true nature of reality. There is an objective world, with a "thing in itself," which cannot be directly known. But Kant believed we had certain intuitive hints to the nature of the thing-in-itself world. For example, "the feeling of awe on a starry night, a spiritual sense of oneness with the cosmos"(Mannion, 98). How do we believe in such a thing-in-itself world? Idealists suggested this needs faith.

Kant's philosophy revealed that to understand the source of knowledge, one cannot avoid examining the human mind itself. The mind is crucial for acquiring knowledge. In Chinese philosophy, Neo-Confucian philosophers Lu Jiu-yuan and Wang Shou-jen shared similar thoughts. They believed knowledge needs to go through the human mind. "The universe is my mind, and my mind is the universe" (Fung, 307). But at the time of Kant and Wang Shou-jen, there was much less knowledge about the human mind as compared to modern times. The dynamics between human minds and the things-in-itself world were not explored in sufficient depth.

As it will be described in later chapters, the human mind is comprised of both the conscious and the unconscious; the mind cannot be clearly separated. With a better understanding of our minds, the knowledge acquisition process can be better modeled. This is particularly important for knowledge about ourselves, about ethics or about beliefs and religion. To understand ourselves, to understand ethical value or a belief, we do not decipher the whole into parts. Instead, using our heart (instead of our brain) to feel it makes sense, we bypass the lengthy and sometimes sight-losing process of pure reasoning and gain the initial knowledge (or belief). Then, through the statistical efforts of multiple people, and with multiple generations' refinement and optimization, such knowledge can establish its own life cycle and become objective, even transcendent, to any particular individual.

2.3 A Source and Receiver Model

In this section, we will use a model to mimic the origination of knowledge. It will also explain why the argument between idealism and empiricism is actually unnecessary. The model is based on the principles in wireless communication. Although the dynamics between the human mind and the objective world are far more complex, we still can gain insight on how knowledge is originated from a simple example.

In a typical wireless communication system, a base station transmits signals in a certain coding format. A mobile device, when tuned to the right frequency channel and instructed to decode signal in a given time slot, can decode the signal and understand the encoded information. In reality, there are many kinds of wireless signals—TV, radio, satellite, cellular communication signals, in space. However, if a mobile device is not tuned to the right frequency or doesn't have the correct decryption code, these signals simply bear no meaning to the mobile device. Indeed, there are wireless signals that none of the existing devices can decode. They appear as noise to the device, and hence the information inside the signals cannot be detected. That's why empiricists insist knowledge should be experienced first through the human mind, just like a wireless signal must be decoded through an tuned device. But can we really claim that information inside these wireless signals still exists? That is the stand of rationalists, who insist that even without the well-tuned device, the information, the encoding, the law still exists in space-time. Both rationalism and empiricism are right, and both are wrong. Each only catches one aspect of the meaning of knowledge. In the language of this wireless communication model, Kant's theory says that while we can only know of the concrete wireless signals that are decodable through tuned devices, we can also know the abstract theory behind the concrete wireless communication, such as the Maxwell equations. The abstract part of the knowledge, although it cannot be directly experienced, can be understood through critical reasoning.

There are a few implications from this simple model. First, we can see it is improper to state wireless signals that cannot be decoded are meaningless or do not exist. Those signals can actually cause interference to a signal that is decodable. Similarly, *there are some truths existing in nature that may not be able to be directly experienced or understood by the human mind, but they do exist and influence truths that are understandable.* Truths can be interconnected in a way that is difficult or even impossible to understand, but it is hard to reject their existence.

Second, knowledge is actually a relationship, a connection, not an end object. *Knowledge is about the relationship between the human mind and an external object.* Just as with understanding any other relationship, one cannot understand a bit of knowledge without also understanding the subjects it connects to. Similarly, to understand certain knowledge, one should look to the source and the receiver of the knowledge at the same time. In this case, the receiver is a human mind, and the source is an external object. Just like the meaning of encoded information can only be translated between a transmitter and a receiver, knowledge is meaningful only when it is put in the context of the subjects it tries to connect to. It is about relationship.

Lastly, as mentioned earlier, the human mind is far more complex than a tuned mobile device. The human mind is comprised of both conscious and unconscious parts, has self-learning capability, and has intuitive capability that is beyond linear rational reasoning. How do these characteristics influence the way knowledge is generated? There must be other limits of knowledge due to these facts. The simple transmitter and receiver model cannot provide hints on that.

2.4 Knowledge Acquisition from a Child's Perspective

Another way to get more understanding on the source of knowledge is to take a child's perspective on the learning process. In a sense, how a child learns mimics the way mankind builds knowledge from the beginning.

When a child starts to learn, experience is the first method for learning about the world around him. He looks, touches, feels, and tastes. The next stage, learning language, is a big step forward. The word for an object has no meaning to him initially. A noun may represent an object, but the actual meaning of that object cannot be explained or defined to a child. Instead, he confirms the meaning of the word through a learning process: first, he hears a parent or someone saying it, then he tries saying the same word and believes the word is related to the object in his mind. Then he gets the response or confirmation he anticipates, thus forming a connection between the word and the object. In the very beginning stage of knowledge acquisition, not only the experience but also belief and faith can play critical roles. And at the end, confirmation is essential to close the loop.

In the next step, the child learns the relationship between two things. There are many possibilities for learning relationship among things. One possibility is that even if the meaning of two words for two objects are not completely or accurately understood, the relationship can be understood and confirmed better than the meaning of objects themselves, hence he can learn the relationship even without accurately understanding the objects. For example, for the statement "Santa Claus delivers gifts on Christmas," the child may not clearly understand who Santa Claus is or whether he really exists, nor does he know much about Christmas, but the connection between Santa and Christmas can be clearly understood. This is particularly true when the connection is confirmed multiple times as he receives gifts on Christmas over several years.

So far, the child learns through experience, trials, and confirmations. Knowledge built at these stages is very fragile. The next step of learning through logic, induction, and analytical reasoning is a powerful leap. For example, a five-year-old child believes there is a Santa who lives at the North Pole and sends gifts to him on Christmas. He believes it because someone tells him so, and he also gets confirmation at Christmas. But a ten-year-old figures out it is not true, even though he also receives gifts at Christmas. He uses reasoning to question whether Santa is real. For example, he can have questions such as, how can Santa deliver gifts to so many kids around the world in one night? By examining hints, he figures out the gifts actually come from parents. Knowledge based on both experience and reasoning is more reliable. Later in the child's intelligence development process, logic and reasoning capability is developed at a fast pace and eventually becomes a dominant thinking skill. At the peak of a person's intelligence, knowledge is examined to the finest possible level. The power of rational reasoning is proved through mathematics, physics, and other engineering branches, to the extent that the situation can go to another extreme of believing knowledge can be attained to explain the whole world.

As we see, a child develops his initial knowledge based on his limited, and sometimes faulty experience, logic, and even belief. But as he grows, experience increases and more reasoning powers are developed; concepts can be refined and connections among concepts can be rearranged. It is an adaptive process. The process continues, and knowledge is refined to better reflect reality. Experiencing, confirming, adapting, redefining, and reconfirming is the most basic process of how humans learn. The third world created by this process is never perfect. It reflects a certain degree of truth, and the process continues infinitely to get closer to the truth.

A child's learning process shows several important aspects of how humans acquire knowledge. First, when a concept is defined and assigned a name, the process has already simplified the nature of how things should be defined. In other words, *in order to define a concept in a certain language, simplification and exclusivity occur at the same time.* Defining a concept means differentiating an object from a chaotic status. When no concept is defined, there are infinite opportunities for describing the object. Once a concept is defined, the object in the knowledge world is differentiated from the rest of the world and relies on relationship to other concepts to be connected.

The process of defining concepts and discovering relationships among objects shows that we simplify things in order to construct a theory to interpret the world in a certain way. Through this process, we can approach some aspects of truth. *Knowledge is always constructed with intrinsic limitations, because simplification and differentiation imply loss of information.* Inevitably, at some point a theory cannot grow any further to explain something better or more things. At that stage, restructuring and rebuilding become necessary. In this sense, knowledge has its own life cycle. There shouldn't be any doctrines that do not need adaptation while mankind's understanding of the world grows and improves. However, there will be switching costs—the pain of going through the process of restructuring a theory. This is particularly true when there are social implications.

It seems quite obvious that knowledge has intrinsic limitations; however, mankind tends to generalize concepts and theories being developed. We keep believing we can attain the absolute truth. No doubt there exists an absolute truth, but mankind cannot fully grasp it or grasp all its aspects. One should abandon dependence on attaining absolute truth as a way to secure certainty. Later chapters will describe that absolute certainty in the future is not true but just a faith. There are other ways to build our foundation on knowledge, without the necessity for certainty.

2.5 Beyond the Limitations of Knowledge

Whether or not there is absolute truth is not a real question. Instead, how the human mind interacts with the thing-it-itself is more a meaningful concern. We can believe there is absolute truth, but in the end, what is important is how we approach it. Since knowledge is actually the relationship between a human mind and the object under study, it should be understood together with the source and the receiver. Let us look at both the human mind and its objectivity.

As will be discussed in more detail later, the human mind consists of the conscious and unconscious parts. The conscious is, in fact, just a tip of the iceberg emerging at the surface of an ocean. There is a vast unconscious part of mind that is not understood. Intelligence and knowledge are the products of the conscious, which is the product of the tip of an iceberg. *The capability of the human mind is vastly underutilized, or should be utilized in a different way, in the search for truth. It is reasonable to expect that mankind should be able to approach truth in many different ways.* Knowledge and intelligence should not be considered as the only ways for humans to approach truth; instead they are only a small part of it. This is where faith and intuition play a role. Using heart and intuition to sense the truth, to overcome the limitations of current knowledge, should be considered as a complementary method to rational thinking.

We already know that knowledge is generated with intrinsic limitations of simplification and differentiation; humans have difficulty attaining the absolute truth (thing-in-itself). It is therefore necessary to utilize the whole capability of a human mind to approach truths. This means that not only experience (as empiricists insist) and reasoning (as rationalists insist), but also faith and intuition should be considered as complementary methods. "Listen to your heart" is ancient wisdom from many cultures. Self-awareness and being honest with oneself is a unique capability humans are able to keep improving, and it is the real subject for religion and belief. *It is more important to approach truth than to just develop knowledge.* The human mind is comprised of many components, including rational reasoning, emotional feeling, and unconscious components. Each can detect and receive different components of the truth, and each should be utilized. Ignoring these capabilities only handicaps us in searching for truth. The mind is so complex. Intelligence and rational reasoning is only one capability of the mind; another capability is intuitive thinking. The characteristics of intuitive thinking are in leaps in logical processes, where certain steps are skipped, but we feel it makes sense based on judgment from the heart. Why this is reasonable? Because you utilize the mind as a whole, instead of just the conscious part; you reason through the wholeness of mind instead of just intelligence. It is a more powerful way to get closer to the truth, since the unconscious part of the mind is sometimes more powerful than the conscious part. This is particularly important for explaining why we have sympathy. When we see someone suffering, we have a similar physical reaction inside our minds as the one who actually suffers it. Being sympathetic motivates us to care about others but also implicitly to care for ourselves. Ethical behavior itself is rewarding, no need to wait for eternal rewards. Acting according to our consciences is beneficial to ourselves in the end, even if it is not easy to explain logically. When you listen to your heart, the total benefit to yourself as a whole, including both the unconscious and conscious mind, is bigger than the benefit just to the conscious mind.

On the objectivity of knowledge, the argument from idealism is that objective truth does not exist if it cannot be experienced by the human mind. This view emphasizes the importance of the knowledge carrier—the human mind. How is the objectivity of knowledge assured? Science philosophers have explored this question in many ways. A theory should produce a prediction that can be confirmed, or falsified, (Popper, *The Logic of Scientific Discovery*, 17) in order to assure its objectivity. In addition to these, knowledge has its own life, because once created, its existence is independent of an individual, hence transcendent to an individual mind. Moreover, *knowledge can be statistically refined over a large number of samples. The statistical synergy of knowledge from individual minds provides additional assurance as to its objectivity. The statistical average can be over a large number of people, or over a large scale of time in human evolution, or over very different geographies and cultures.* It is not uncommon to see cultures from different areas sharing similar teachings. Thoughts from different great thinkers show similar proverbs. Certain truths can only be revealed over a long period of time. If the time scale is large enough, e.g., hundreds of years, an individual may only see a subperiod of the phenomenon and therefore has insufficient evidence to draw a conclusion. In such a case, he cannot experience the truth personally. This is similar to observing a stock index. The overall trend could be upward statistically, but for a short period, one can only see downturns or oscillation.

How does an individual get to know or believe a truth that needs a large scale of sampling? Some media is necessary to carry over the partial truth being understood at a given time for continuous improvement and testing. This media is what we called knowledge. It is a collection of written concepts and the relationships between concepts. The collection records the reflection of human beings' understanding of truth and its evolution. These types of knowledge, particularly for ethical principles, are developed based on large-scale sampling. They have to be tested and experienced by a large number of people, perhaps spanning multiple generations and multiple geographic regions. When they are written down, this knowledge gains independent existence, and they have their own life cycles. Large numbers of people continue to improve it, bringing it closer to reality. Media avoids the shortcoming of a single individual's thinking capacity and therefore lifts the objectivity of knowledge to a new level. In the scenario where large-scale sampling is needed, truth is attained not only through reasoning but also through believing, especially when the knowledge of truth is still in the early stages of its life cycle. One can only either ignore it or believe it, since there is no time to experience it or prove it within one's life-span. Faith plays a necessary role in the search for truth. When faith itself influences the behavior of humans and in return confirms their belief (like positive feedback), the belief itself acts as a seed to generate truth. This will be discussed in depth later.

Knowledge is developed with the intrinsic limitations of simplification and differentiation from the start. Through statistical and continuous refinement, it gets closer and closer to truth. If a deficiency is not within the reach of reasoning and experiencing (via direct personal observation or with tools), the limitation has no direct impact and we may not even be aware of it. The knowledge is considered sufficiently objective until the limitation is uncovered. When the limitation is known, another round of refinement occurs. This is inevitable because knowledge is created with loss of information. When the lost information is needed, the limitation becomes known. Stability of the knowledge life cycle depends on the subjects in question. Knowledge about ourselves is the most difficult and the most dynamic because we are both the subjects and the observers. The time line for attaining objectivity of knowledge is also variable. It is this complexity of process that demands complementary methodologies instead of just pure reasoning, or direct personal experience, or taking extreme approaches, such as idealism.

Life Is Larger than Knowledge

There is another angle to understanding the limitation of knowledge and intelligence. It is well known that by deciphering a whole into parts, understanding the parts in depth, and then putting the parts back together again, you still may not understand the whole. Whenever you decipher a whole subject into parts, you intervene in it and cause loss of intrinsic information. *Existence of an object itself is a truth and must be respected. We can only observe its properties as a whole but not decipher it. The methodology of deciphering the whole into parts has a fundamental fault, although it generates powerful knowledge.* Human emotion and feelings are some examples that cannot be deciphered. These emotional worlds have principles to follow that are crucial for proper interaction among individuals. Love is one of the principles in the emotional world. But understanding love cannot totally come from logical reasoning. Eastern philosophy has emphasized the wholeness of the connected universe. Chinese Taoism put this very well in the famous statement, "The Tao that can be comprised in words is not eternal Tao; the name that can be named is not the abiding name" (Fung, 94). In Western terms, it means that reality can only be experienced but not understood through words and symbols. In reality, everything in the universe is connected and related. And because the self is part of the whole connected universe, life of the self can only be experienced, not worded.

2.6 Belief and Preknowledge

It becomes clear that *the scope of seeking truth is much larger than the seeking of the origin of knowledge.* There are two key reasons for this statement. 1) Some types of the truth may be gained through intuitive belief, especially when knowledge of that truth requires large-scale sampling and is still in the infant stage. 2) The human mind, as the receiver of information, is a complex system containing both the conscious and the unconscious. Rational reasoning is the primary approach for seeking truth but should not be the *only* one. Intuitive belief is another approach. As long as a belief is an intuitive extension after exhaustion of rational reasoning, one has to make a choice—ignore it or believe it. A choice is needed because either it is beyond understanding based on our current intellectual capacity, or there is no time to experience or prove it within one's life-span. Life is more important than knowledge, hence for questions such as the meaning of life, one has to make a choice. Some prefer to be suspicious for their entire life-span, and some take a chance by choosing to believe knowledge not yet proved. Here one may interpret the meaning of being proved in different ways. It can be interpreted as being able to be repeated, or as it being accepted by the majority of society, or it can be explained in a consistent theoretical framework. This stage of knowledge not yet proved can be called preknowledge.

Faith is choice of free will. One should not regard accepting a faith as a weakness due to lack of critical reasoning. On the contrary, belief is an act of a person who is truly understanding the limitations of knowledge and truly honest to his own heart. It is not conflict with the power of intelligence but a complementary method for seeking truth. Through the power of intelligence, mankind's knowledge expanded over the course of civilization. It helps to explain many phenomena and helps increase self-awareness for an individual. A person capable of digesting more knowledge is expected to be more objective. The more objective a person is, the more honest he will be to his heart, which in turn allows him to touch and feel more knowledge in different formats, including intuition. Although intuitive belief is still in the preknowledge stage, it may influence a person's life. Later, some of these beliefs might turn out to be wrong, and some of them can be revealed to be true. A person who is more honest, and with less interference by the self, will have a better chance of getting to the right belief. When we say a person is honest, it implies there is a reality that is not straightforward to be realized or understood, yet it is still in his best interest to set his thinking, mind, and feelings to align to the reality. Otherwise, there will be bias, and it will be hard to recognize the true reality. This is particularly true when the knowledge of truth requires large-scale sampling and is still in the infant state.

2.7 Knowledge and Methodology

In the discussion of origin of knowledge, one lesson learned is that it is crucial to utilize proper methods to approach reality and develop knowledge. If the methodology is incorrect, human intelligence will be misguided. For example, empiricism, rationalism, idealism, etc., are not the only methods to approach reality. Nonconventional methods become necessary. Remember that life is larger than just seeking knowledge. It is more important to attain truth at our best than to just advance intelligence. Several examples were identified and are explained further below:

- How do we handle the knowledge of truth that requires large scale of sampling and is still in the infant state? Statistical sampling can be in the time dimension or the space dimension. In the time dimension, it can mean several hundred years, therefore within an individual's life-span, but you may only experience a portion of a cycle for that truth to reveal itself. This is a strange interaction of individual with statistical truth, because he may not obtain the benefit of following the truth during his life-span. This is similar to the situation when trading stock: follow the long-term trend or follow the short-term ups and downs? It can be a conflict of interest. When there is a conflict of interest, it becomes a matter of choice—follow your current interest or align your life to the truth. Which one is more important? A person with deeper self-awareness most likely will choose the latter, therefore the power of belief is lived out. He may not obtain the current benefit, but he probably has deeper and profounder satisfaction living his life because he feels more deeply and has a heightened sense of life. An ideal life is not only to align your life with external truth but also receive the actual benefit during your life-span. However, this is not controllable by an individual.

- There is another scenario when the proof of a principle depends upon whether one believes in it. This is very typical for ethical principles and is seen very often in religions. For example, many religions teach us to love other people unconditionally in order for the world to become peaceful. If one believes in and follows the teaching, he shows love to others without conditions, even with a loss of certain current interests. And if everyone follows the same teaching, the outcome is proven. If many don't follow it, the teaching becomes insane. Here, the free will of human beings is crucial. Faith becomes a determining factor to prove the teaching. Knowledge or truth about group behavior of humans in many situations depends on the initial faith. Faith becomes a seed for the principle to become truth, a phenomenon similar to positive feedback in nonlinear science.

Methods are the underlying reasoning pattern that influences the ways our minds function. Further, different knowledge domains require different methodologies. It is necessary to abstract methodology from each domain and exercise extra caution when applying the methods to different domains. This topic will be discussed in more depth in later chapters.

Reference

- Fuller, Andrew R. *Psychology and Religion: Classical Theorists and Contemporary Developments* (Lanham, Maryland: Rowman & Littlefield Publishers, Inc., 2008, fourth edition).
- Fung, Yu-lan. *A Short History of Chinese Philosophy* (New York: Free Press, 1997).
- Mannion, J. *Essentials of Philosophy* (New York: Fall River Press, 2006).
- Popper, Karl. *The Logic of Scientific Discovery* (New York: Taylor & Francis e-Library, 2005).
- Popper, K. *Three Worlds—Lecture on Human Values.* (The University of Michigan on April 7, 1978). In the lecture, Popper split the world into three categories. World 1 consists of physical objects and events. World 2 is the mental world, comprising mental objects and events, thoughts, emotions, etc. World 3 is the objective knowledge. It is partially autonomous and independent of World 1 and World 2.

CHAPTER 3

Lights from Science

The discussion of the origin and limitations of knowledge in Chapter 2 is mostly philosophical. To further deepen the discussion in a concrete knowledge domain, it is necessary to examine whether those philosophical statements are consistent with the findings from that knowledge domain. In the history of mankind, there are no knowledge domains than science that unleash the power of human intelligence to the largest extent. The product of the human conscious is best demonstrated in the advancement of science. If scientific knowledge is the best outcome of our intelligence, and still there is limitation in it, it becomes self-evident that knowledge is created with unavoidable limitations.

Further, the methodology derived from science has fundamentally influenced our thinking process. Science frequently provides an innovative view of a particular methodology that cannot be easily revealed in other fields. It is important to examine the methodologies in science and check carefully if they can be applied to other fields. A belief becomes self-evident if it can be explained scientifically, hence it becomes a fact rather than a belief. The advancement of science will reduce the amount of intuitive belief, or increase the quality of process in choosing a belief. Methodology extracted from science is most credible, since science is the best output of human rational thought. By analyzing the thinking process successfully utilized in science, one will gain more understanding of the power and limitations of human rational power. However, it should be mentioned again that rational thinking is only a portion of the capacity of the human mind; there is still an unconscious world that should be studied, and this will be discussed in the next chapter.

There is a tremendous number of areas of scientific study; it is impossible to touch all of them. Since what we are interested in here is methodology derived from science, not the scientific content itself, we will select only a few fields as case studies. This chapter only discusses three fields: quantum mechanics, thermodynamic statistics, and nonlinear systems.

Although this chapter is a natural extension of the previous chapter, readers who are less interested in science can skip this chapter or just read the conclusion at the end of the chapter.

3.1 Quantum Mechanics—The Uncertainty Principle

In classical Newtonian mechanics, an object can have both position (x) and velocity (v), measured accurately at the same time. Since the momentum of an object $p = mv$, an object can have both position and momentum measured accurately at the same time. However, in quantum mechanics, such common sense becomes false. The Heisenberg uncertainty principle says that the standard deviation of position σ_x and the standard deviation of momentum σ_p obey the following relationship:

$$\sigma_x \sigma_p \geq \hbar/2$$

where $\hbar$ is the reduced Planck constant. Since $\hbar$ is a nonzero number, measurement of x and p with zero deviation at the same time is impossible. Reduction of error in one variable is at the expense of an increase in error of the other variable.

There are many different interpretations of this basic quantum mechanics principle. Some physicists thought it was because the observation introduced interference of the quantum system in measurement. Later, it became clear that this relationship is a fundamental property of a quantum system. It is simply due to the wave nature of the quantum system. The two simple concepts, position and momentum of an object, which are well defined and accepted in classical mechanics, collide when they are applied to a quantum system. The wave nature of quantum systems prohibits two concepts to be a quantum reality at the same time.

The Heisenberg uncertainty principle, according to Niels Bohr, implies that *overdetermination* is not applicable to the quantum world. Position and momentum are two concepts used to describe a particle in the macroscopic world without considering the measurement environment (Jammer, Ch. 4). But when applied to the atomic level, they overdefine, or overdescribe the object, because measuring both values precisely is impossible. This idea of overdetermination is very interesting and deserves further examination. As mentioned in previous chapters, a concept is always constructed with some kind of simplification. For example, conceptually, position is a point without size. Speed, conceptually, is an average of distance over a time delta. When the time delta takes the limitation to zero, the speed is precise. For a quantum particle that has wave-like properties, precise speed means precise momentum, which means the wave property is a plane wave function. A plane wave function cannot describe a fixed localization, which is needed to precisely measure position. Both position and momentum together overdescribe a real object. Such simplification in classical mechanics is acceptable because the scale of the object in question is sufficiently large. But when it comes to quantum systems, the scale is small enough that such overdescription is not allowed any more—two simplifications cannot be allowed at the same time. Overthinking, oversimplifying, or overdefining are harmful to understanding a system as a whole. The beauty of the uncertainty principle is that it reveals a limitation of our knowledge within one of the most fundamental sciences—quantum mechanics. It truly shows how sophisticated philosophical thinking can be echoed in a measurable science.

The other side of the uncertainty principle is that although both position and momentum cannot be measured at the same time for a quantum system, both concepts are still valid to describe a property of the quantum system. The two concepts, leveraged from classical mechanics, can still be used to describe a quantum system as much as possible, as long as it is not necessary to measure both variables precisely. The example of the uncertainty principle shows us how seemingly conflicting concepts can actually coexist to provide different perceptions of the same reality.

Bohr's interpretation has philosophically generalized the uncertainty principle. The uncertainty principle reveals the principle of complementarity: *the definability of two concepts and the measurability of such two concepts are incompatible, even though such two concepts are complementary in understanding the system* (Jammer, Ch. 4). Definition of the concept assumes an ideal environment with no disturbance. But with this condition, measurement is impossible. Alternatively, one can set up an environment to measure one variable, but that environment intrinsically disturbs another variable, making measurement of that other variable impossible. However, both variables are needed to completely describe the system. Hence, Bohr concluded that to understand the system as a whole, you cannot decipher the system into parts, then study or measure each part, and finally put them together (Bohr, 199–242). You have to regard the system itself as a reality unit and starting point for building any theory for it.

Bohr's view is fundamental and even revolutionary in the methodology of physics. Historically, physicists thought they could explain the whole world using the most fundamental theory of physics—they would keep improving it. However, Bohr's interpretation of quantum mechanics says physics theory has a fundamental limitation: parts + parts ≠ whole. One can decipher the whole system and study the parts, but when he adds together the understanding of parts, it doesn't come up with an accurate understanding of the whole. This was speculated long ago by philosophers, but when it became a self-evident phenomenon in physics. It became much more convincing, because it is based on real experimental results, not just speculation. That's why the philosophy derived from physics is extremely valuable, as they are closer to the reality and truth.

The risk of overdefinition and the principle of complementarity can be applied to understanding religion and culture, because defining a concept with limitations is generic to any human intelligence activities. *A set of concepts are defined with the best understanding at the time of definition; later another set of concepts can be defined in a separate context, but there could be overdefinition when both are applied to understand the same reality. This problem is not easy to detect.* We need to either unwind the definition of both concepts or apply the principle of complementarity to the unified reality. For example, in religion, the concept of the supernatural and the tendency to personalize it can be overdefined, making it impossible to understand both precisely. One may need to unwind the definition and treat the understanding behind both concepts as a unified entity. The principle of complementarity can also be used when a culture wants to integrate another culture. Using the ideas and concepts of local culture to interpret incoming culture, or vice versa, is the best way to gain mutual acceptance and respect. The focus is neither the accuracy of individual concepts nor whether the concepts come from this or that culture. Instead, the focus is on the same reality and how different concepts provide description of an aspect of the same reality.

3.2 Quantum Mechanics—The Wave Function

In quantum mechanics, the same reality can have multiple representations. At least three mathematical formulations are well accepted to describe quantum principles. The first is the Schrödinger equation:

$$i\hbar \frac{\partial}{\partial t} \psi = \hat{H} \psi$$

where ψ is the wave function of the quantum system, i is the imaginary unit, $\hbar$ is the reduced Planck constant, and $\hat{H}$ is the Hamiltonian operator. The Hamiltonian operator represents the total energy of any given wave function and comprises different terms depending on the initial condition. The quantum system is described using a wave function, and behavior of wave function is completely governed by the Schrödinger equation. By solving the equation, possible states for the quantum system can be derived, and consequently measurable physical variables, such as energy, momentum, and position, can be calculated.

The second, and more rigorous, mathematical formulation is the matrix operators, initially developed by Heisenberg and later generalized by Dirac, Hilbert, Neumann, et al. In this theory, the possible states of a quantum mechanical system are represented by state vectors within a state space. An observable physical variable is represented by a linear operator acting on the state space. Using this abstract mathematical model, one can calculate probabilities of outcomes for concrete experiments. For example, it allows one to compute the probability of finding an electron in a particular region around the nucleus at a particular time.

The third and less used form of quantum theory is called the path integral formulation, popularized by Feynman.

Besides the fact that the quantum principle can be represented by different theories consistently, the other interesting point here is about the interpretation of the wave function. There is no direct mapping of any measurable physical reality to the wave function itself. Instead, according to the well-known Copenhagen interpretation (Heisenberg 44), the square of the module of wave function represents the probability density of finding the quantum system, if measured, in a given location or state of motion. When a measurement takes place, the measurement causes the wave function to collapse to one of the eigenstates that allows one to take a definite value. Quantum mechanics describes the probability of obtaining the possible outcomes from measuring an observable, and this probability information is encoded in the value of the modulus of wave function, not the value of wave function itself. The Schrödinger equation, or the Heisenberg matrix mechanism, describes the behavior and time evolution of an abstract variable—the wave function. However, the physical reality is not associated with the wave function directly; instead, it is associated with the square of its amplitude. In this sense, wave function itself is a calculation tool. The wave function is a complex variable, where the square of its amplitude shows the information about probability, and its phase value is related to the interference of quantum states. After solving the Schrödinger equation based on certain boundary conditions, the wave functions can be derived, and measurable physical variables can be computed from the weighted wave functions. These theoretical computation results are then compared to experimental measurements.

This two-step mechanism from theory to measurable reality is a good example of how an advance theory may take variables or concepts that have no direct physical meanings. However, it is unquestionable regarding the reality of validation of the theory. The finding here is that *a theory that reflects reality doesn't need to take only concepts of variables that have direct physical meanings.* In more simple language, one can consider this as a pragmatic approach—as long as the theory works, it is true. For example, it is not necessary to insist that wave function in quantum mechanics have a direct physical meaning, or that it must be truly existing, before we accept the truth quantum mechanics describes. The truth of quantum mechanics is validated by the fact that it works; that is, it explains well the microscopic world and greatly changes modern life.

If we generalize it, there is an analogy in the methodology between quantum mechanics and a belief system. A belief system (or a religion's tenets), like quantum mechanics that takes wave function as its primary variable, takes certain mythical concepts as core. We don't know the exact physical interpretation of it, just like we don't know the exact physical meaning of wave function. Similar to the two-step approach in quantum mechanics, in a belief system, man takes a mythical concept and meditates or prays on it. The outcome of a single meditation (or prayer) is not deterministic, but has a probability. This is similar to an operator applying to the wave function; you may not be able to predict the outcome, only the probability. The meditation may turn out to be effective in influencing one's mind and consequently alters the individual's behavior. The belief system is hence proven to be true in the sense that it works, regardless of whether the mythical concept has direct physical meaning to it. It is just that the mythical concept has a complicated, rather than straightforward, relation to reality. Many people simply reject such methodology and consequently treat any belief system as superstition.

In summary, whether quantum mechanics theory is true or not doesn't depend on whether the wave function itself has direct physical meaning or not. Instead, it depends on whether the outcome of an average number of measurements on a physical variable matches the theoretical prediction. Similarly, an individual's personal experience or action is like a measurement of putting a belief system into practice, and whether a belief system is true does not depend on the mythical concept, but depends on the average or statistical outcome of a believer's experience or actions. In this regard, finding out the meaning of a mythical concept before you believe it is like finding out the meaning of wave function before using it. There is a similarity in methodology here. This is one of the tasks of philosophy—abstracting the knowledge and methodology from one area and applying it to another area. It is a risky generalization, but it is part of human nature. In fact, the most fascinating modern physics is the interpretation of quantum mechanics. It reminds us that any theory is just an approximate knowledge of reality. Furthermore, it even challenges the meaning of reality at the philosophical level.

3.3 The EPR Paradox and Quantum Entanglement

The interpretation of quantum mechanics puzzled many great scientists for years. Quantum mechanics reveals that even with the most advanced theory of physical science, human understanding of reality is extremely limited and fundamentally different from the classical ways of certainty and being deterministic. The idea of both position and momentum cannot be measured precisely at the same time, and the Copenhagen interpretation is just simply unacceptable as a final verdict to many physicists. There were many attempts to prove that quantum mechanics is an incomplete theory. Among them, a critique from Einstein and his colleagues Podolsky and Rosen (collectively known as EPR) was the most influential one. They designed a thought experiment intended to reveal what they believed to be the inadequacies of quantum mechanics. By studying the EPR paradox and its countercritique, another level of philosophical implication can be examined.

The thought experiment in the original EPR paper is described below (Einstein, Podolsky, and Rosen). It starts with the following assumptions: 1) Quantum system 1 and system 2 initially interacted from $t = 0$ to $t = T$. After that, they no longer interacted. A wave function is constructed to describe such systems. 2) If a physical quantity is predicted *in certainty* without disturbing the system in question, there must be a reality corresponding to it.

With the above assumptions, the EPR paper constructed a predefined wave function to describe systems 1 and 2, and proposed a series of measurements on system 1:

a. At $t > T$, measuring the momentum of system 1 can predict (note that here it is "predict," not "measure") with certainty the momentum of system 2;

b. At $t > T$, measuring the coordinator of system 1 can predict (again, it's "predict," not "measure") with certainty the coordinator of system 2;

c. But since $t > T$, system 1 and system 2 are not interacting anymore, so no matter what measurement has taken place with system 1, the reality of system 2 is the same (undisturbed). EPR said the two wave functions for system 2 resulting from the two measurements must reflect the "same reality." Also, it is not important which step, a or b, goes first. They can take one step at a time, since either way, system 2 is not disturbed in any way;

d. Since both momentum and the coordinator of system 2 can be predicted simultaneously in certainty without disturbing the system, there must be two corresponding physical realities simultaneously;

e. However, the uncertainty principle of quantum mechanics says both momentum and coordinator cannot be *measured* simultaneously;

f. Therefore EPR concluded that there are two possibilities: either quantum mechanics is incomplete, or measurements in steps a and b disturb system 2 when measurement occurs. However, the second possibility violates the locality theory, meaning the signal traveled faster than the speed of light. It is thus more prudent to conclude that quantum mechanics is incomplete to describe physical reality.

The argument in the EPR paper strongly depends on their two assumptions. However, assumption 1 is problematic. If two systems interact between $t = 0$ and $t = T$, then have no more interaction later, how to construct a wave function for such a system? The simple wave function in the EPR paper only describes the state for $t > T$. A complete wave function should describe both $t \le T$ and $t > T$, and in theory it must be derived from Schrödinger's equation, with proper boundary conditions. The simple wave function for $t > T$ is not accurate because it cannot be independent from the conditions for $t \le T$. Therefore, the statement that the measurements of system 1 in steps a and b do not disturb system 2 is questionable. There is an entanglement between systems 1 and 2 for $t \le T$, and such entanglement cannot be ignored after $t > T$.

Such view is further confirmed by Bell's theorem (Bell). Recall that the EPR paradox strives to interpret quantum mechanics based on very general intuitive assumptions (Einstein, Podolsky, and Rosen), namely:

- Principle of local reality: An event cannot be influenced by another event at a distance that occurs at the same time (or, at least, occurs in a time range shorter than the time for the speed of light to travel the distance).

- There exists a definite state of reality *before* it is measured, as long as the reality element can be determined. For example, even though one cannot accurately measure the position and momentum of a particle at the same time, one can measure the momentum accurately and deduce and calculate the position of the particle at the same time, even if the position is not measured. Hence, both position and momentum are reality with a definite state. These states are called *hidden variables*.

However, Bell's theorem says quantum physics must necessarily violate either the principle of locality or the second assumption above (Bell). Under the assumption of local reality and hidden variables, the correlation between outcomes of different measurements performed on two particles that have interacted and then are separated has to satisfy one constraint. This constraint is called Bell's inequality. The same correlation is also computed based on quantum mechanics. However, the calculation outcome from quantum mechanics violates Bell's inequality. The Bell's theorem can be explained as below.

1. First, compute the correlation with the assumption of local reality, where the quantum level object has a well-defined state that accounts for all its measurable properties. Distant objects do not exchange information faster than the speed of light. These well-defined states are sometimes called *hidden variables*. Such a variable is considered hidden because it cannot be accurately measured, but nevertheless represents a physical reality.
2. Then, compute the same correlation under the normal quantum mechanics assumption that hidden variables do not exist. The properties of a particle are not clear, but may be correlated with those of another particle due to quantum entanglement, and their state to be well defined only after a measurement is made on either particle, i.e., collapse of wave function in the Copenhagen interpretation.

Both calculations yield different values for the same correlation definition. Actual physical experiments show method 2 is more accurate, and therefore either the principle of locality or the hidden variable assumption must be refuted (Bell).

Bell's inequalities, due to quantum entanglement, just provide a definitive demonstration that quantum physics cannot be represented by any version of the classical picture of physics. These unusual entangled states cannot be explained by any local theory. However, quantum entanglement is the foundation for present-day applications of quantum physics, such as quantum cryptography. This dilemma once again shows that in one of the most exciting scientific adventures, *scientists are able to develop a theory that can explain all measured data to date, but are unable to interpret the theory itself.* In an entangled particle pair, information between the two particles is exchanged instantaneously, even when the separation distance is large (faster than the speed of light). This fact is especially counterintuitive and violates the fundamental assumption of the theory of relativity. However, the quantum entanglement was eventually verified experimentally (Matson) and recognized as a valid, fundamental feature of quantum mechanics. The focus of the interest has now changed to its utilization as a resource for communication and computation.

This kind of pragmatism is very much like William James's theory on religion (Fuller, Ch. 1). It works, therefore it reflects truth. We cannot interpret quantum mechanics using a classical view. Position and momentum are two concepts derived from classical physics; how can it be certain they are also applicable to the quantum world? A leap of faith is needed to interpret quantum mechanics. We can accept the Copenhagen interpretation that position or momentum has no definite value until it is measured. When a particle is measured, its wave function collapses to an eigenstate. This interpretation is beyond the classical view of the properties of a particle.

Quantum entanglement clearly shows that for an entangled pair of particles, the pair cannot be truly isolated. No matter how far apart they are, they are still entangled. The method of studying the parts, and then putting them together to understand the pair, is an absolute no-go for quantum entangled pairs. *The notion of the whole not being equal to the sum of parts is vividly demonstrated in the scientific research of quantum entanglement.*

3.4 Quantum Mechanics—Measurement

In quantum mechanics, the action of measuring is significant. It alters the state of the object being measured, to a state that is measurable. Measurement in quantum mechanics is a mysterious process in that, according to the Copenhagen interpretation, it disturbs the object being measured and causes the wave functions, which could be a superposition of multiple eigenstates, to collapse into a single eigenstate and then the measurement is certain. This interpretation has been questioned by many other physicists. A complete quantum measurement theory should include the instruments to measure the object in question, i.e., the wave function describing a system comprises both the measured object and the measuring instruments. According to quantum decoherence theory, the measurement process causes loss of the phase coherence of superposition of different eigenstates. Decoherence shows how a macroscopic system comprised of a lot of microscopic systems moves from being in a pure quantum state—which, in general, will be a coherent superposition—to being in an incoherent mixture of states. The weighting of each outcome in the mixture, when measured, is exactly that which gives the probabilities of the different results of such a measurement ("quantum decoherence"). However, it does not answer the question of why the measured outcome is a deterministic value.

From coherence to incoherence means the loss of phase information among these states. Hence, the measurement action in quantum mechanics causes loss of information. Information loss is a familiar fact in thermal dynamics, when considering a large number of particles evolving to a state of equilibrium where the probability of possible microstates reaches a maximum. This is an irreversible process. Decoherence is the process by which information of a quantum system is altered by the system's interaction with its environment (which forms a closed system). It is possible that the system and environment form an entanglement. As such, *a description of the system by itself cannot be made without also referring to the environment (i.e., without also describing the state of the environment)* (Lidar, Whaley, 83–120). From this perspective, the uncertainty principle can be reinterpreted. When you measure momentum precisely, the system (comprising both measured object and measuring environment) becomes decoherent, such that some information related to position is lost. As this is an irreversible process, it is not possible to recover the information needed to measure position precisely.

In thermal dynamics, the second law says irreversible process is measured by the increase of entropy. Entropy is the measurement of information. Inspired by the similarity of loss of information in quantum measurement and entropy increase in thermal dynamics systems, some physicists interpret wave function as describing the statistical property of a large number of identical particles. This can avoid the problem of understanding the measurement process. But the question is what mechanism describes a single quantum particle. This is still an active research area.

The theory of quantum measurement can shed more light on the EPR paradox. When two particles A and B are entangled and described using wave functions, it already means there is coherence information that is intrinsic and should be described by the wave function. A measurement of particle A causes decoherence of the wave function for system A/B. It is an irreversible process and causes loss of information about system A/B (not just loss of information about A), therefore it impacts the measurement outcome of B. *The assumption in the EPR paradox that when A and B are far away, then they are not related, is not sound.* However, exactly how the loss of information of A and B system is communicated to B is not described in quantum measurement theory. This is perhaps not important because the problem does not exist after all—to describe the measurement in A that is entangled with B, one needs a wave function that describes the measured object A/B (not just A) and the measuring environment. It is not possible to separate A and B. *In other words, the statement of "measuring A" for an entangled pair is not a correct statement after all. The information loss in any measurement is about A and B together; it cannot be for just A or B. Hence, the information communication problem does not exist.*

Measurement in quantum mechanics is a profound action, in that it involves both macro and micro worlds. Any further breakthrough in quantum mechanics should examine the measurement itself at the micro level. Quantum decoherence once again shows understanding the whole by studying its parts causes information loss. When one considers the measuring instrument from the macro world as part of the measured objects in the micro world, using the same scientific language to describe both, then it is possible to understand and measure the micro world. But such an assumption itself is not possible to realize. *When an observer in the macro world probes information in the micro world, it causes information loss. Observers from the macro world can only detect collective signals transmitted out of the micro world, instead of using intrusive measurements. An observer cannot be a player at the same time.* This is a classical view from a linear world. Later when we discuss non-linear system, the view is different.

It is a classic problem that when two different levels of the world (or two different cultures) interact, there is no easy way to have smooth communication without altering the coherent existing in one world or the other. The principle that governs one world is very different from the principle that governs the other world. But they are not completely unrelated. In the case of quantum measurement, classical mechanics is very different from quantum mechanics. But classical mechanics is an approximation of quantum mechanics; an observer in the classical mechanics world can only understand language based on collective information derived from the quantum mechanics world. On the other hand, a player in the micro world cannot understand the language used by the observer in the macro world.

The interaction between the classical world and the quantum world can be seen from the difference between photons and fermions. Photons are bosons and can stay in the same microstate, therefore, collectively, the statistical behavior of photons is similar to that of a single photon. The wave property of photons (light) was discovered much earlier in the Maxwell electromagnetic equations. On the other hand, electrons are fermions and follow the Pauli exclusion principle, i.e., no two electrons can be in the same state. Pretty much like a human being. Therefore, collectively, the statistical behavior of electrons is very different from that of a single electron. And the wave property of electrons is much harder to discover until a measuring instrument is advanced to a point that measurement of single electrons becomes possible. The macro world observer can know more about the player in the micro world when observation tools continue to advance.

3.5 Quantum Mechanics—Philosophical Implications

Quantum mechanics fundamentally overturns many concepts in classical mechanics. Even today, there are many quantum mechanics concepts that cannot be fully understood. We simply accept them as fact. It shows us that the world we understand is far more subtle and complicated. For a knowledge branch that best demonstrates mankind's intellectual power, there are still fundamental unknowns and unresolved issues. The correct attitude toward this situation is just to acknowledge there are unknowns, rather than to reject the existence of these issues. On the other hand, the philosophical implications of quantum mechanics are fascinating, as they can greatly influence the methodology through which we understand the world. It is therefore worthwhile to summarize them below:

- The uncertainty principle reveals that multiple concepts can overdescribe objects. These concepts from the classical world are complementary. But when applying them at the same time, they together overdescribe a quantum object.
- Quantum entanglement shows a quantum system cannot be isolated. The whole is not equal to the sum of its parts. The principle of locality is a nonexistent problem for entangled systems, because the statement of measuring A for an entangled pair A/B is a misleading statement.
- The interpretation of wave function demonstrates a pragmatic two-step approach to interacting with reality. It is an acceptable approach, using concepts that have no direct physical interpretation, but still relate to the truth and reality in a nonstraightforward way.

- Quantum measurement and decoherence remind us one more time that a quantum system cannot be understood using the divide-and-conquer approach. Furthermore, *when an observer in the macro world probes information in the micro world, it causes information loss. Observers from the macro world can only detect collective signals transmitted out of the micro world, instead of using intrusive measurements. The observer cannot be a player at the same time.*

- The observer in the macro world can know more about the player in the micro world when observation tools advance. The observer in the classical mechanics world can only understand language based on collective information derived from the quantum mechanics world. On the other hand, the player in the micro world cannot understand the language used by the observer in the macro world.

These implications for methodology can be extracted and applied to help understand difficult problems in other areas. The thinking pattern derived from classical mechanics, such as divide and conquer, deterministic certainty, locality, direct physical interpretation of concepts, etc., have strong influence in other areas of culture and religion. The lessons learned from quantum mechanics can help us refine our methodological thinking.

Quantum mechanics demonstrates how human beings interact with our most intelligent product—scientific knowledge. Originally, we lived comfortably with classical mechanics, as long as we only dealt with the regular world instead of dealing with atoms or particles with the speed of light that are kind of extreme to humans. The knowledge we possess from the classical world is sufficient to provide the stability and certainty we are looking for. However, the quest for absolute truth is an infinite process, yielding infinite knowledge and requiring infinite refinements and breakthroughs. This process yields the breakthroughs and discoveries of quantum mechanics. On one hand, it falsifies many of our comfort zones. In the meantime, it brings to light new understandings of knowledge and methodology that could not be seen before. Scientists now have to live with the fact that we cannot interpret many concepts in quantum mechanics from a classical view. We rely on concepts that have no direct physical meaning, such as wave function. It is like a mythical concept in religion. And we cannot treat an entangled system using the approach of divide and conquer. The ways we understand quantum mechanics are somehow very similar to the ways we understand religion. In some sense, the understanding of quantum mechanics is indeed like a religion, and the classical view cannot fully comprehend it.

3.6 The Second Law of Thermodynamics

The most interesting question in thermodynamics is how to explain the macro behavior of a system comprised of a large number of particles from the collective microstates of each particle. In the typical classical view, the statistical behavior of a thermal system is derived from the summation of microstates of each particle. The microstates determine the macro behavior. Although we already know that it is not a solid methodology to study the whole simply from the sum of its parts, it is nevertheless a first-degree approximation. There is still valuable insight gained by studying the relationship between micro and macro behaviors.

There are several fundamental laws in thermodynamics. The most interesting one is the interpretation of the second law, which states that an isolated thermodynamic system reaches thermal equilibrium when the entropy of the system reaches its maximum value. From a systemic point of view, increase of entropy means loss of information from the initial condition. From a microscopic point of view, it relates to the equal probability of each microstate. Boltzmann developed a statistical theory to derive the macro description of a system from the physical laws that govern a single particle. The theory computes the number of possible system microstates, where each system microstate is a combination of states of the individual particles in the system. The theory also assumes certain constraints for the macro variable. For example, the total energy level of the system is the same for any possible microstate. This imposes a constraint on the available microstate. Then, Boltzmann proposed a fundamental assumption. It says that when the system reaches equilibrium, the number of possible microstates reaches maximum. In other words, the equilibrium state is the most possible state. From there, it can be deduced that entropy is maximized in equilibrium. In later development of thermodynamics, it was shown that the state of equilibrium being the most possible state can be derived from a more general assumption, which states that when reaching equilibrium, the probability of occupying any possible microstate is a constant.

Let's examine the mathematical logic first and then the philosophical interpretation.

Definition of Entropy

The starting point to understanding the second law is the definition of entropy. Precisely, entropy is a logarithmic measure of the density of states:

$$S = -k_B \sum_i P_i \, ln P_i$$

where k_B is the Boltzmann constant, equal to 1.38065×10–23 J K^{-1}. The summation is over all possible microstates of the system, and P_i is the probability that the system is in the ith microstate. Note that here, ith microstate refers to a possible state that combines the microstates of all the particles in the system, hence it is still a microstate at the systemic level. Each microstate still conserves the constraints of a macro variable, for example, the same energy level at the macroscopic level. The fundamental assumption of statistical thermodynamics states that the occupation of any microstate is assumed to be equally probable (i.e., P_i = 1/Ω since Ω is the number of possible microstates); this assumption is usually justified for an isolated system in equilibrium. Then the previous equation is reduced to S = k_B ln(Ω). The most general interpretation of entropy considers entropy as a measurement of uncertainty about a system. The equilibrium of a system maximizes entropy because we have lost all information about the initial conditions except for the conserved macroscopic variables; maximizing the entropy maximizes our ignorance about the details of the system. The qualifier "for a given set of macroscopic variables" above has a deep implication—it sets the condition for calculating entropy.

Furthermore, it can be proven,[1] purely mathematically, that S reaches maximum when Pi is a constant P. The maximum value is S = k_B ln(1/P). If one interprets that 1/P = Ω, then S = k_B ln(Ω), which is exactly the Boltzmann equation. This proof is generic, regardless of what comprises the system and regardless of whether the particles

---

1 For any given x, there is inequality: ln(x) ≥ (1 − 1/x). Now let x = p'$_i$ /p, where p is a constant and p'$_i$ is the probability of ith microstate in any other distribution. Substituting x into the inequality gives ln(p'$_i$) − ln(p) ≥ (1 − p/ p'$_i$). Rearranging the inequality gets p'$_i$ ln(p'$_i$) − p'$_i$ ln(p) ≥ (p'$_i$ − p), the sum of every item of the above inequality over all possible microstates. Σ(p'$_i$ ln(p'$_i$)) − Σ(p'$_i$ ln(p)) ≥ Σ(p'$_i$) − Σ(p) = 1 − 1 = 0; hence, Σ(p'$_i$ ln(p'$_i$)) ≥ Σ(p'$_i$ ln(p)) = ln(p) * Σ(p'$_i$) = ln(p). Multiply the Boltzmann constant on both sides of the inequality: − k_B *Σ(p'$_i$ ln(p'$_i$)) ≤ − k_B ln(p). The left side is simply the entropy of the system in any distribution, S'. The right side is the entropy of the system when the p'i is a constant, S. Rewrite the inequality: S' ≤ − k_B ln(p) = k_B ln(1/p) = k_B ln(Ω) = S, or S' ≤ S. Hence, S is the maximum value.

in the system have weak or strong interactions. That P is a constant means an equal probability of occupation of each microstate. Since the second law says an isolated thermal system reaches equilibrium (the most possible state) when entropy reaches maximum value, and now it has been proven that entropy of the system reaches maximum value when each microstate has equal probability, we can conclude that the second law is the equivalent of stating that *an isolated thermal system eventually reaches equilibrium distribution that any possible microstate is equally possible. This is an irreversible process, i.e., the system irreversibly trends toward equal probability of any microstate.* It also implies that the system can reach all possible states.

In addition, the grand canonical ensemble theory shows that for a given energy level (macroscopic variable), at equilibrium, the average number of particles over *all* possible distributions is the same as the number at the most probable distribution. The reason for this is due to the fact that the distribution probability function is extremely steep; it fades rapidly when it deviates from the most probable distribution, making the rest of possible distributions negligible. Hence, there is no need to assume that equilibrium is the most probable state; instead it can be proven. *The only fundamental assumption of the second law is that under given macroscopic variables, the system reaches equilibrium when occupation of any microstate has equal probability.* Hence, as long as the occupation of any microstate has equal probability, then equilibrium is the most probable distribution.

Interpretation of the Second Law

Having reviewed the physical meaning of the second law of thermodynamics, let's turn our attention to its philosophical meaning. In fact, it is very intuitive to understand. For the given resource or macro variables, a system explores all possibilities and eventually settles down with equal probability of staying in any microstate, and this is an irreversible process. This is similar to a society where a group of humans explore existing resources and experience all possible states. Only when all the possible states are equally probable is it a stable society, i.e., reaches equilibrium.

Interpretation of entropy as the measurement of disorder is sometimes confusing. When S is bigger, there is more disorder (more chaos). An isolated thermodynamic system reaches equilibrium when it is in its most disordered state. In other words, the thermal system is most chaotic when occupation of any microstate has equal probability.

Instead of viewing this as the most chaotic state, there is an alternative way to look at this—a system in a macro distribution where occupation of any microstate has an equal probability reaches its maximum freedom, because such macro distribution allows each possible combination of micro distribution of particles to have the same opportunity. Hence, instead of saying a thermal system reaches maximum disorder, one can say an isolated thermodynamic system reaches equilibrium when it reaches maximum freedom. Entropy is the measurement of freedom. From a systemic point of view, entropy does measure the loss of information of the whole system with respect to the initial condition. But when taking the viewpoint of an individual element of the system, maximum entropy means a maximum of degree of freedom, because equal choices of any possible microstate are available to occupy. Entropy, therefore, can be considered as the system's capacity for freedom. A system that reaches a maximum degree of freedom for individual elements also reaches its maximum potential. But in physics, this is interpreted as the system at its most disordered. The entropy of an isolated system increases because the total degree of freedom is increasing, and potentiality for the system as a whole is maximized. *Increasing degrees of freedom means loss of information and an increase of disorder from the system's point of view.* It is interesting to see how the system's view and individual's view are quite different.

The second law states that the process, from initial state to equilibrium, is irreversible. This irreversibility implies a direction of evolution. It cannot be approved. Instead, it is a given. This is equivalent to saying that *the process to evolve the system from unequal probabilities of occupying possible microstates to equal probabilities is irreversible.* As mentioned earlier, although it cannot be approved, it is very intuitive. This irreversibility is based on many preconditions. If, for the purpose of this thought experiment, the elements of the system have some level of free will or preference, such that the probability of staying in a certain state has higher probability, then the entropy, S, will not reach its maximum value. It appears that internal intelligence would reduce the entropy of the system. But this can be a delusion. Free will does not imply a preference. There is the possibility that even the constituents in a system have certain intelligence, the second law would still hold. That is, for a given macroscopic variable constraint, after sufficient period of evolution, *the system irreversibly trends toward equal probability of occupying any microstate*, regardless the individual constituent has free will or not. For the given macroscopic constraint, the constituents always seek maximum potentiality of freedom, i.e., to explore the available freedom allowed within the constraints of macroscopic variables. This law appears to be so generic that there is a tendency to apply it to other fields.

Paradox of Irreversibility

Statistical mechanics attempts to explain a macroscopic behavior through laws that govern the microscopic world, with help from statistical theory. The irreversibility is a very intuitive assumption, but cannot be easily explained. The laws governing the micro world, i.e., classical mechanics, are reversible. However, macro evolution is irreversible. The irreversibility was initially explained as loss of information when internal elements interact. But why does the information get lost if classical mechanics is reversible? There are many possible answers. The first answer is that the irreversibility is just the nature of statistics. Any observable variable is a macro-level variable derived through statistics. In an isolated thermal system, macro variables that are observable tend to demonstrate a direction (such as entropy increases) when a system evolves to equilibrium. In theory, the variable can go the other direction, but the time to observe such behavior is far longer beyond typical observation time. Hence, it is unlikely observable. It is crucial to realize that *a behavior theoretically possible at the micro level may not be observable at the macro level.*

The second explanation is based on nonlinear theory. In chaos theory, a system's behavior has infinite sensitivity to initial conditions. An infinitely small difference in initial conditions determines the behavior of the system. Infinite sensitivity to initial conditions implies an irreversible direction of a system's evolutionary path. According to Prigogine, the second law is described as a selection criterion—those initial conditions that contain finite (as opposite to infinite) information break the symmetry of the past and the future, and only one direction is chosen, hence the irreversibility (Prigogine and Stengers, Ch. 9). But this explanation relies on one assumption—the direction of irreversibility is determined at a particular moment, i.e., the initial condition. However, irreversibility is true for any given moment before equilibrium; the direction is due to the fact that the thermal system evolves toward the state where every microstate has equal probability of being observed. The argument that because classical mechanics (i.e., Newton's laws) are time reversible, hence the behavior of a thermodynamic system should be reversible, is not logical reasoning. *The root cause of irreversibility is due to the nature of internal particle interaction. All particles are the same; any differentiation, after a sufficiently long period of interaction, will be smoothed out, and eventually causes the observable microstates to have equal probability.* The second law only applies to those systems where internal interactions make all the microstates have equal probability, and such interaction is governed by classical mechanics. Newton's laws are in fact part of the reason for irreversibility. Irreversibility is a language at the system level, while Newton's laws are at the micro level. *Newton's laws can explain how momentum and energy pass from one particle to another particle, but cannot explain why the probability of the observable microstates obeys a one-way direction—from unequal probability to equal probability.* This just means that along with Newton's laws, additional concepts and postulations are needed when it comes to describing thermodynamic systems at the macro level. The direction of microstate probability change is one such new basic postulation.

For other systems comprised of elements that involve nonlinear interaction, with positive feedback, or where an element can hold a difference, some microstates will have a higher observable probability. In such case, the second law will fail. Those are more exciting areas to explore in the future.

Limitations

One should be extremely cautious about applying the concept of entropy to other fields. There are many limitations when applying the Boltzmann theory to nonphysics systems, especially complex or nonlinear systems. For example:

- How to define the completeness of a system microstate? In the original Boltzmann theory, a microstate is defined as a combination of all particles in possible individual states, as long as the total energy level stays the same. Energy level is the only macro variable to constrain possible microstates. When we attempt to apply equal probability to a higher level of substance, such as a chemical molecule or substance with general properties, the number of macro variables to define (i.e., constrain) a complete microstate can be much higher, and it is difficult to define the meaning of microstate. But without a complete definition of microstate, the theory of equal probability cannot be applied.

- Even it is possible to define the meaning of microstate for a complex system, if the elements in the system have intelligence, or free will, the equal probability concept is likely to fail, because the elements may have certain preferences, and therefore the system as a whole may have a higher probability of occupying certain microstates (if you can define them at all). Furthermore, as Prigogine's dissipation theory shows, at far-from-equilibrium states, the behavior of the system is nonlinear (Prigogine and Stengers, Ch. 5). In such states, many behaviors cannot be understood from the linear world. Entropy, as a measurement of information, will not move toward a stable maximum number. The behavior of a system comprised of complex elements may not have a state of equilibrium at all, as the behavior is nonlinear.

- When dealing with an isolated system for a macro complex organization, for example, a society or the world or even the universe, how to define the elements inside? It could be at the atomic level or molecular level, or some form of organic structure, or human beings. The laws governing these various elements are quite different. Further, even if a microstate for such a complex system can be defined, the quantity of elements is huge, so the number of microstates is nearly infinite. It would take infinite time to experience all microstates.

- After all, an isolated system is hard to realize, since a real system (with or without life) is always interacting with the environment. Such interaction may only involve information transmission.

- Even if an isolated system exists, the structure of a complex system can contain many different types of subsystems. Each subsystem can behave differently from the point of view of entropy. Some subsystems are not isolated and evolve to a state with less entropy. On the other hand, an open system evolving toward less entropy may have some subsystems evolving toward increasing entropy.

- Last but not least, the second law only applies to those systems whose internal interactions cause all microstates to have equal probability, and such interaction is governed by classical mechanics. It is linear, no feedback, no free will internal elements. For other systems that are comprised of elements involving nonlinear interaction, positive feedback, etc., some microstate will have a higher observable probability. In such case, the second law cannot be applied.

Summary

In understanding the second law of thermodynamics, we get a glimpse of the difficulty of explaining macroscopic system behavior through laws that govern the microscopic world. It is always more prudent to step back when applying a theory from one field to another.

The evolution from unequal probability to equal probability of occupying possible microstates is essentially a process to even out the difference. When an isolated system evolves to equilibrium, differentiations among various regions from the initial condition are eventually evened out. This is system behavior at a macro level. Entropy is in essence a measurement of differentiation. *When the thermal system reaches equilibrium, entropy reaches its maximum, and differentiation reaches its minimum.*

Although the classical mechanics that govern the movement of each particle is reversible, the irreversibility at a systemic level cannot simply be derived from it. Irreversibility means the system's evolution is a one-way direction. It is very important to realize that when the subject under study moves from one level to the next, e.g., from a microscopic to a macroscopic level, additional postulation or hypothesis is needed. For example, human intelligence can be good or bad, either direction, but a value system that provides guidance to use intelligence cannot be derived from it. This is because values and ethics are at a different level than that of human intelligence. Scientific advancement provides new knowledge, but the knowledge can be used for either good or bad intentions. Directional guidance from a value system must come from another level of laws.

The subject in thermodynamics is an isolated system, where differentiation from the initial conditions is eventually evened out. To maintain differentiation, either the system should be an open system, or the elements inside the system are capable of holding onto the differentiation. The first case is already demonstrated in dissipation theory; for the second case, the elements in the system most likely will interact in a nonlinear manner, or even in a more advanced form of intelligence or life. This is the subject we will discuss next.

3.7 Nonlinear and Complex Systems

Definition of Nonlinear System

The basic difference between linear and nonlinear systems is that nonlinear systems are not subject to the principle of superposition, while linear systems are subject to superposition. In other words, a nonlinear system is one whose behavior cannot be described as a sum of the behaviors of its parts (or of their multiples).

It is such nonlinearity that builds up differentiation, self-organization, and life. Obviously, the world is nonlinear in nature. But because we have developed many elegant linear classical theories (even quantum mechanics) and applied them to change our daily lives so successfully, we tend to perceive the world using models or methodology based on a linear system. We tend to believe a linear description is the first-order approximation of reality. However, in many real life systems, nonlinearity is not merely a second-order term—it is indeed a dominant factor influencing the system's behavior.

A complex system is one that exhibits nonlinear behaviors or other behaviors that cannot be intuitively understood. In this section, we will briefly describe several of these phenomena, but more importantly extract the philosophical implications and methodologies behind them.

Chaos

A system is considered chaotic if the behavior is extremely sensitive to initial conditions. A tiny difference in the initial conditions can lead to totally different system behavior over time. This can be true even when the system itself is deterministic. For a deterministic system, once the initial conditions are exactly defined, system behavior is predictable. However, in most practical situations, the initial conditions can be only approximately measured, and with error, or the system has a large number of variables and we cannot obtain the initial value of all variables; due to the chaotic nature of being extremely sensitive to initial conditions, the behavior of the system is unpredictable. This phenomenon is known as *deterministic chaos*. Weather forecast models are a good example. The number of variables to determine the weather is tremendously high; it is impossible to obtain the initial values of all these variables. Further, the interactions of these variables are nonlinear. It has been shown that even with a tiny difference in the initial value of one of these variables, after a short period of evolution, the weather forecast system shows dramatically different behavior. This is famously known as the butterfly effect (Lorenz, 130–141).

In many chaotic systems, when described in the phase space, the system's behavior usually converges on a localized region called *attractors*. That means for large sets of initial conditions, the system's behavior in the phase space converges on the attractor areas. For a chaotic system, the attractor is called a strange attractor because the dimensions of such an attractor is a noninteger. Although in the phase space, system behaviors converge on the attractor area, in the time and three-dimensional spaces, behaviors are drastically different.

Even though a nonlinear chaotic system exhibits complex behavior, certain order can be born from it. The strange attractor is one example. The attractor is a fractal structure and exhibits infinite self-similarity. Another example is dissipative structure theory (Prigogine and Stengers, Ch. 5), which shows that systems at far-from-thermo-dynamic-equilibrium states (a chaotic state) can produce order when energy passes through the system. However, the mechanism of evolving from chaos to order is not well understood yet. Several mechanisms are suggested (Prigogine and Stengers, Ch. 6): 1) Order can be born from the amplification of noise when the system is far from equilibrium. These fluctuations of the system seed the potential evolutionary paths toward an orderly state. On the other hand, if a system has evolutionary paths includ-ing complex patterns, such as bifurcation or multiple bifurcations, a fluctuation far from equilibrium can lead the system to randomly select a path, hence the behavior of the system is not deterministic. Instead, it can only be described with statistics. 2) Correlation of the system. At a state far from equilibrium, system correlation increases. Local events can impact the entire system. Two seemingly far away components can be correlated. Because of these long ranges of correlation, a small change in a local area can be amplified and propagated to the whole system. 3) Once orders and structures are born, these orders and structures need to be immune from possible noise that tries to reduce it back to chaos. Only structure or orders that are immune from po-tential threats for reduction back to chaos can survive the evolution. Such behavior is similar to the idea of natural selection.

The understanding of mechanisms of evolution from chaos to order is still pre-liminary. At best, it can explain only relatively simple physical or biochemical systems. Hence, it is dangerous to generalize the idea that for more complex systems, order can also be born out of chaos. Nevertheless, chaos theory instills a fresh view on under-standing complex systems and introducing new methodology.

Fractal Structure

A strange attractor typically exhibits a much more complex structure called fractal structure. Fractal structure shows a pattern of infinite self-similarity, i.e., it may be exactly the same at any scale. By magnifying the same fractal structure at an infinite scale, new details and structures always exhibit, yet one may still see the same or similar pattern.

One of the most famous fractal structures is the Mandelbrot set. The mathematics behind creating the Mandelbrot set is relatively simple and deterministic ("Mandelbrot set"): for a complex number C, if the Julia set from complex function $Z = Z^2 + C$ is connected, color the spot representing this C value in the two-dimensional Cartesian coordinate system black; if the Julia set is disconnected, color the spot representing this C value according to how fast Z goes to infinity. The resulting map is the Mandelbrot set, shown in the picture below. The picture on the left shows the initial Mandelbrot set, and the picture on the right shows that after zooming in on a tiny part of the initial set by 10^{12} times, the shape is still as complex as the initial set, and one can see a miniature of the initial shape. We will not get into the rigorous mathematical definition of a fractal pattern or a fractal geometric dimension. The key point to remember here is that in a fractal pattern, no matter how much scale one zooms in, the structure always shows complex details.

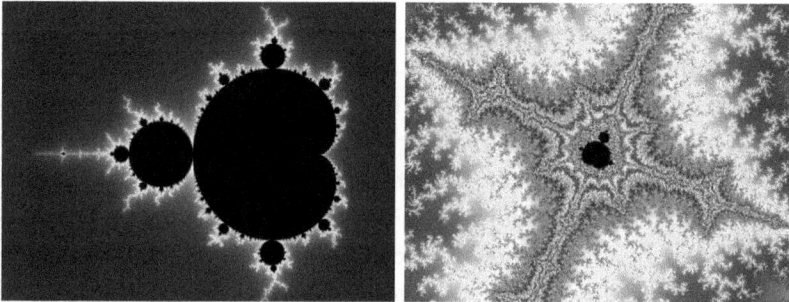

Figure 1 Self-similarity at infinite scale

A fractal line cannot be mathematically differentiable, meaning at any point, the derivative of the curve doesn't exist. In a more understandable way of describing it, consider that on a regular wavy one-dimensional line, at any given point one can always find a small-enough straight segment where the length is approximately equal. But for a fractal line, no matter how small you zoom in, the wavy pattern repeats itself and there is no way to find a small-enough straight segment to approximately measure length.

The simple geometric shapes we are familiar with are just idealized representations of many natural shapes that are actually more accurately represented by fractal shapes. For example, the coastal line and the surface of a mountain are more accurately represented by fractal shapes. The complexity of these shapes is beyond what mathematics can easily describe. Secondly, fractal structures are observed in chaotic systems, such as the Lorentz attractor. This means that even in a chaotic structure, some kind of order (such as self-similarity) can still be there. In other words, more complex order may be born in chaotic systems.

Bifurcation

Bifurcation is one type of chaos phenomena. It refers to the behavior of a dynamic system where a small change to a parameter causes sudden topology change of the system's behavior. Typically, such dynamic systems are described using nonlinear differential equations, such as Hopf bifurcation, Pitchfork bifurcations, or the logistics map. Probably the most famous bifurcation example is the logistics map because of its simple mathematical model. The model is used to study demographic behavior when considering both reproduction and starvation rates (May, 459–467). Specifically, the population ratio at nth year x_n is written as $x_n = r\,x_{n-1}(1-x_{n-1})$ where:

x_n is the ratio of population in nth year, compared to the maximum population capacity the given environment can sustain. It is a number between 0 and 1.

r is the rate combining both reproduction and starvation.

This simple mathematical model is in fact quite intuitive. The first factor in the equation comes from the assumption that the population increase is proportional to the current population. The second factor reflects the assumption that the population growth rate will decrease at a rate proportional to the remaining capacity (maximum capacity minus current population). Obviously, when population increases, fewer resources are available to accommodate more growth, hence the growth rate decreases.

The behavior of this simple nonlinear equation highly depends on the value of r ("logistic map"):

- *When r is between 2 and 3, the population eventually converges to one value.*
- *When r is between 3 and 3.44949 (approximately), for almost all initial conditions, the population converges to oscillation between two values. These two values depend on r.*
- *When r is between 3.44949 and 3.544099 (approximately), for almost all initial conditions, the population converges to oscillation among four values. When r is beyond 3.54099, the population converges to oscillation among sixteen values, then thirty-two, sixty-four, etc.*
- *When r approaches 3.56599 (but is less than 4), it is the end of the period-doubling bifurcation. Instead, it is a chaotic behavior; the population is drastically different with a tiny variation, and there is no more oscillation. Between 3.56599 and 4, there are still some isolated ranges of values of r that show nonchaotic oscillation.*
- *When r equals or is greater than 4, the value is beyond the range of [0, 1] and diverges for almost all initial conditions.*

The bifurcation map is shown in Figure 2 below ("logistic map"). The bifurcation map at the range of 3.56599 and 4 shows fractal structure and self-similarity. For example, if one zooms in on a point and picks only one arm of the value map, the bifurcation map along that arm looks very similar to the entire map. Again, this is another example of the deep connection between chaos and fractals.

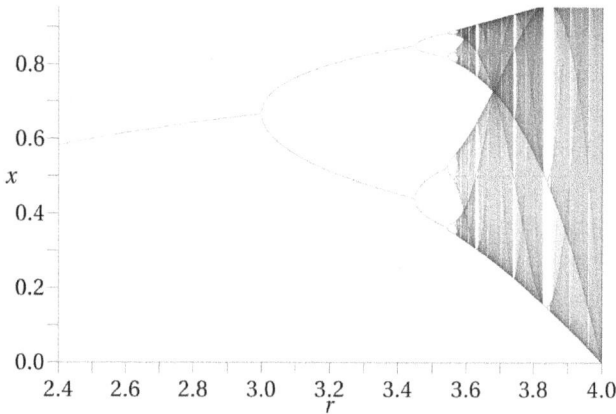

Figure 2 Bifurcation—the logistics map

Self-Organization: Order without Designer

There is order at the system level that is evolving; however, the elements are not aware of it and just follow their own nature at the local level. In a self-organized system, the constituent in a system is acting only for its own purpose, for its own interest, i.e., its behavior is selfish and local or regional, but the end results are beneficial to the system as a whole. It is as if there is a goal at the system level, but there is no designer, coordinator, or invisible hand behind the scenes. For such phenomena to occur, the internal interaction among the elements in the system is nonlinear in nature. The nonlinear internal interaction ensures order at the system level is born out of it.

One such example is the assembly of white ants (Nicolis and Prigogine, Ch. 6). Each ant moves objects randomly, unintentionally. It attaches its own emitting chemical to the object. The chemical attracts other ants to move other objects to the same place. This results in a positive feedback. There is information unintentionally communicated locally, but through nonlinear and positive feedback, the system is self-organized. This example is the so-called ant colony (Gordon, 1–13). There is no one ant acting as central coordinator to give direct orders or to tell other ants what to do. Instead, each ant reacts to chemicals emitted by other ants and leaves behind a chemical trail, which in turn provides stimulus to other ants. Each ant is an autonomous unit that reacts depending only on its local environment and its own instinct. Despite the lack of centralized decision-making, these ants, as a group, exhibit complex behavior.

Self-organization is also behind the theory of the free market. Government regulation is generally considered harmful to the free market. Instead, the free market regulates itself. Any component of a free market, be it an enterprise, a stock trader, or a consumer, just acts in his own interest to maximize profits. The interaction among the market elements are local and have very limited knowledge of a small number of other market elements. Each acts regardless of the overall market behavior. By doing so, the market as a whole still exhibits a number of trends and patterns. Yet there is no leader; there is no one entity that controls the workings of the entire market.

A common trait of self-organization is that the interaction among the constituents in the system is nonlinear. The previous step of evolution leaves a memory that can influence the next step. The elements are not aware of the overall behavior at the systemic level and cannot control the macro behavior. Yet the overall behavior at the systemic level is still born out of micro interactions. Here the nonlinear part of the interactions plays a crucial factor for evolution and laws exhibiting at the systemic level. It was mentioned before that the second law of thermodynamics could fail if the interaction of particles at the micro level is nonlinear. In the classical treatment of describing reality, nonlinear characteristics are typically regarded as a second-order term and are ignored, resulting in only the linear description of the system. Classical Newtonian mechanics is linear. Thus the interactions of particles always smooth out the difference. Possibly, by adding back certain ignored nonlinear second-order terms to classical mechanics, the second law of thermodynamics could fail.

Nonlinear Methodology

As science and technology advanced, we developed many elegant linear classical theories, even quantum mechanics. They were applied to change our daily lives so successfully that we tend to perceive the world using models based on linear systems. We tend to believe linear descriptions are the first-order approximation of reality. The temptation of using linear methodology in seeking the truth about reality is indeed very dangerous. Linear methodology can include, but is not limited to, the following:

- The whole can be understood by deciphering the parts and then adding them together.
- When there is a result, there is always a cause behind it that can be clearly identified and understood—the idea of rationalism.
- We acknowledge there are two sides of the same coin for many phenomena, but only see the interaction of the two sides using a very simple model: either black or white. Only one side plays a dominant role at any given time.
- Determinism. The future can be predicted based on knowledge today. Randomness is just fluctuation that will fade away as time passes.
- Certainty. There is need and desire for certainty, and discomfort with an uncertain world or with uncertain knowledge.
- Order must be designed; it cannot be born from within or self-organized.
- There is always a clear distinction between an observer and the system being observed. Influences between the observer and the observed can be ignored.

We are unaware of most of these assumptions, but they pose great limitations when we try hard to understand reality. In order to gain a deeper understanding of life, self-organization, and many real world scenarios, we need to change our normal ways of thinking using linear models to using more complex and subtle nonlinear models. In this section, some of the methodologies learned from complex nonlinear systems are examined.

Randomness and Determinism

We have seen two examples of how determinism and randomness are coupled together. The first example is the Mandelbrot set. The mathematics behind it is simple and deterministic, but the fractal geometric shape is so complicated, it is impossible to find out the details of the shape. The complex number C can be considered an initial condition for the Julia set, and the overall outcome (connect or disconnect) represents dynamic behavior of the nonlinear system. The Mandelbrot set shows that dynamic system behavior is infinitely complex, depending on the value of C. Even though the system is deterministic in theory, there is infinite sensitivity to the initial value of C, and any observable system behavior in practice is random. The second example is observed from a thermodynamic system that exhibits bifurcation at a point far away from thermal equilibrium. The behavior of the system is comprised of two phases—between bifurcation points, it is deterministic. But near and at the bifurcation point, which path the system evolves toward is unpredictable, since any tiny noise can be amplified and cause the system to choose either direction.

In both examples, randomness is rooted in the fact that the system is infinitely sensitive to the initial conditions, even though the system follows deterministic laws. This is in contrast to typical rational reasoning. Rational reasoning is a type of linear thinking, where cause and effect are always consistent, and there is no randomness or irrational, emotional thinking. However, it is an incomplete approach for decision-making in daily life because we cannot known all the factors that influence the decision-making. Similar to that we learn from bifurcation theory, randomness can sometimes play a crucial role in influencing daily decisions. Complementary approaches, such as emotion or religion, can play a critical role in one's life and decision-making. A complete reasoning methodology should comprise both approaches without conflict, just like linear and nonlinear behaviors of a system can coexist on an evolutionary path, depending on external conditions and where the system is on the path.

Goal and Process Are Inseparable

The phenomenon of self-organization has an interesting implication—goal and process are inseparable. The constituents of the organization don't know the goal; they just carry out the process. But the process determines the outcome. Such a model is crucial to explain the role of human creativity and intelligence in the evolution of society.

In a system dynamic, the system's behavior evolves to a substable state with certain distribution, but the control parameters to reach this substable state may keep changing, resulting in a series of substable states and new distributions. The process repeats, and the evolution continues. In this process, there can be an evolutionary path that cannot be predicted but is self-controlled through nonlinear interactions among the constituents. Furthermore, when the constituents of the organization have free will and faith that influence the selection process, how does that influence the overall evolution? When viewed from a systemic level, the will and decisions of an individual are always local and seem unable to influence overall systemic behavior. In a special environment where that correlation range is long enough, through nonlinear interaction among the constituents, the local will or decision of an individual can cause change at the systemic level. Such a model can also help in understanding the role of a person's will in the development of social ethics. For example, the classical theme of ancient teaching is that one should follow natural laws and not abuse the freedom of will. When it comes to following laws from the external world, such as physics or natural sciences, it is easy to understand. But when it comes to laws for society or ethics, it is difficult to judge what to follow because the collection of wills and choics of each individual together form the social laws and ethics themselves. I need to follow a social ethical value, but my own will is also part of the force forming the social ethical value. In other words, I am a follower but at the same time also a contributor. Actor and audience cannot be clearly separated. The relationship and interaction between individual and the whole cannot be simplified as a linear model. It is hard to separate the goal and the process. The process itself is the goal.

Uncertainty Can Be a Dominant Factor

Classical Newtonian determinism can be shown as inapplicable for certain systems. In a classical Newtonian system (which can comprise lots of interactive particles inside), the laws that govern the system are a set of Hamilton equations in the (p, q) phase space. A system comprised of N particles will have a phase space of $6N$ dimensions, with $6N$ equations. When all variables are known, the solution corresponds to a point in the phase space. The time evolution of the system is simply a trajectory in the phase space. The assumption here is that the exact initial conditions must be known. Let's assume there are two types of initial conditions, and each type will end up with a solution creating very different systemic behavior (Prigogine and Stengers, Ch. 9). However, these two types of initial conditions are mixed up in the $6N$ dimensions of phase space such that they form a fractal geometry, like the boundary of a Mandelbrot set. With such conditions, it is impossible to exactly predict the system's behavior since it is impossible to provide a set of initial conditions exactly. Furthermore, measurement of a set of (p, q) initial conditions precisely is impossible, according to the Heisenberg uncertainly principle in quantum mechanics. A tiny error in a fractal geometry, no matter how small (as long as it's not zero), will end up with a completely different systemic behavior. Therefore, one cannot predict the system's behavior in any way. That's the logic in Prigogine's book to argue that deterministic theory is inapplicable to systems comprised of a large number of particles, and the statistics approach has to be used as a fundamental principle, instead of just considering statistical mechanics as an approximate theory. In this view, statistics methods become intrinsically fundamental.

Since there is a scenario where determinism fails, even with simple systems described by classical mechanics, it is reasonable to conclude that for more complex systems, there will be more scenarios where systemic behavior is uncertain.

Statistics as a Fundamental Approach

For large-scale systems, statistics is the fundamental approach, not approximation. The sum of the parts is more than the whole. We need to study the whole without separating it into parts. If one insists on using classical mechanics to describe the behavior of the whole system, complexity and required information will grow to infinity. Even such a task is possible, the effort may end up with similar results as using the statistical approach in the end. It is for this reason that we treat both approaches as complementary. This is similar to the view of methodology regarding randomness and the deterministic approach. Both are complementary to each other.

Another example is the discussion of irreversibility. Irreversibility simply implies loss of information, and the elements in the system are more and more random. Interaction of the constituents in the system causes information to be more and more evenly distributed. The fact that there is an irreversible direction should be viewed as a law itself; it is a statistical property of the system and cannot be derived from the laws governing the behavior of the elements inside the system.

Chaos theory offers more insights as to why the statistical approach is fundamental. If a chaotic system is infinitely sensitive to initial conditions, observations of the system's behaviors ought to be statistical. One should discard the belief that a statistical approach is just an approximation and aggregation of a deterministic theory.

3.8 Summary

In this chapter, we have examined several fields in natural science to get a deeper understanding of the power and limitations of human intelligence. Quantum mechanics, as the most fundamental physics theory, shows us there are great limitations of the theory itself. Physicists have developed and applied the theory successfully in practice, but have had difficulty interpreting the theory itself. Nonlinear and chaos theories reveal our knowledge and understanding of complex systems is still in the infant stage.

Science—as the field where our intelligence most shines yet still has so much difficulty—shows it is reasonable to anticipate that understanding human beings themselves is going to be more challenging. When coming to the subject of understanding ourselves, different approaches must be used. The methodologies used in studying physics and science cannot be utilized to understand ourselves because the subject under study is extremely different. However, because of the success of natural science in the history of human civilization, the methodology derived from natural science has profoundly influenced our thinking patterns. This will be the case when we attempt to understand other areas, including ourselves.

As explained in the beginning of this chapter, the purpose of examining the natural sciences is not about the actual contents but the philosophical implications. There are two important hints we learned from science:

- First, we have already seen that science reveals its own limitations. The purpose of scientific advancement should be to not only tell us what it can do, but also tell us what it cannot do.
- Second, by extracting the methodologies used in scientific research and the philosophical implications of scientific discoveries, we know the roots of these methodologies and philosophical ideas. Knowing the roots helps us to apply them more cautiously and properly. The achievements and limitations of science, the methodologies and thinking patterns in scientific research, provide a reference for investigating other areas.

In short, the core value of scientific philosophy is in the self-revelation of its own limitations. Scientific discovery reveals more and more knowledge about the miracle of nature. The more we know, the more we appreciate why nature functions the way it does. Without scientific knowledge, we wouldn't know how complex nature is and we'd be less appreciative of it. But knowledge gained through scientific research cannot be generalized to a degree that one can claim to understand everything in the world. Instead, by knowing there are always limitations to scientific knowledge, we know how difficult it is to attain truth about nature. Lastly, scientific knowledge and its methodologies represent the peak of human intelligence; even with the self-revealed limitations, we still deeply trust it. Such a thinking pattern provides a most trusted reference framework for understanding other areas, as we will explore in the following chapters. In other words, *we can argue that we believe in a hypothesis to a certain degree that is comparable to the degree we believe in the scientific theory.*

Reference

- Bell, J. S. "On the Einstein Podolsky Rosen Paradox," *Physics* 1, 3 (1964), 195–200.
- Bohr, Niels. "Discussions with Einstein on Epistemological Problems in Atomic Physics," in *Albert Einstein: Philosopher-Scientist*, ed. Paul Arthur Schilpp (Illinois: Open Court Publishing Company, 1949).
- Einstein, A., B. Podolsky, and N. Rosen. "Can Quantum-Mechanical Description of Physical Reality Be Considered Complete?" *Physical Review* 47 (10) (1935–05–15): 777–780.
- Gordon, Deborah. *Ants at Work: How An Insect Society Is Organized* (New York: W. W. Norton & Company, Inc.).
- Heisenberg, W. *Physics and Philosophy.* (Harper, 1958).
- Jammer, M. *The Philosophy of Quantum Mechanics.* (John Wiley and Sons, 1974).
- Lidar, D.A., and K.B. Whaley. "Decoherence-Free Subspaces and Subsystems" in *Irreversible Quantum Dynamics*, eds. F. Benatti and R. Floreanini, 83–120. (Berlin: Springer Lecture Notes in Physics, 622, 2003).
- "Logistic map," Wikipedia, Web. Jan. 11, 2015.
- Lorenz, Edward N. "Deterministic Nonperiodic Flow," *Journal of the Atmospheric Sciences* 20 no. 2 (1963).
- "Madelbrot set," Wikipedia, Web. Jan. 11, 2015.
- May, R. M. "Simple Mathematical Models with Very Complicated Dynamics," Nature, Vol. 261, Jun. 10, 1976.
- Matson, John. "Quantum teleportation achieved over record distances," *Nature*, 13 (August 13, 2012).
- Nicolis, G., and I. Prigogine. *Exploring Complexity: An Introduction.* (W H Freeman, 1989).
- Prigogine, Ilya, and Isabelle Stengers. *Order Out of Chaos* (New York: Bantam Books, 1984).
- "Quantum decoherence," Wikipedia, Web. Jan. 11, 2015.

CHAPTER 4

The Nature of the Human Mind

The knowledge of humans can be sorted into two categories: knowledge of the external world, and knowledge of ourselves. In the previous chapter, we examined the first category through scientific research, philosophical implications, and particularly their limitations. In this chapter, we shift the focus to the understanding of ourselves: the human mind and the nature of human beings. Before we get deeper into understanding our minds, a basic question needs to first be answered—what methodology is appropriate for understanding ourselves?

4.1 What Is the Proper Approach?

Scientific knowledge is about understanding the external world. When we shift focus to the human mind and the nature of human beings, meaning of life, etc., we need to first seek out and define a set of basic laws and assumptions. The methodology learned from science cannot be simply applied here. The journey of advancing knowledge from basic physics, chemistry, biology, and self-organization, to the origin and meaning of life could take forever or be impossible. Using current scientific knowledge as building blocks for understanding the top goal is simply too rudimentary. It is as though you want to construct a high-rise building. You need steel and bricks, but all you have is mud and sand. Decomposing the understanding of life into physical, chemical, or biological principles underestimates the complexity and undervalues the meaning of life. To achieve the goal of understanding ourselves, high-level building blocks are necessary. We should explore other theories, such as social theory, ethical theory, religions, and psychology.

However, we also ought to be cautious with the approaches taken by high-level building blocks such as psychology, religion, and philosophy. These theories are all essentially built upon the understanding of the fundamental nature of human beings, but they can overemphasize one aspect of human nature. For example, while psychology can help us understand some aspects of the human mind and the inner life of individuals, it usually overemphasizes a single aspect, such as emotions, dreams, childhood experience, or sexuality. This can distort the complete picture of the human mind and become misleading. Some social theories, such as socialism, overemphasize the social and economic aspects of an individual. The idea of social class conflict is tied to specific social conditions. Certainly social standing is part of human nature, but is it the most basic one? Socialism is based on the assumption that social and economic relationships are a person's primary life concerns and motivations. This doesn't seem to be a natural assumption. I don't intend to study this theory in depth here. The point I want to make here is that *an objective and accurate understanding of what is the most basic human nature is the foundation of higher-level theories on humanity and society.*

So what are the proper approaches to understanding fundamental human nature? There are no easy answers, but several basic principles need to be kept in mind:

- We need to treat ourselves as whole beings. Phenomena and behavior observed among ourselves need to be accepted as they are, instead of decomposing them such that they can be explained with lower-level knowledge. In other words, we take the phenomenon, the behavior observed among ourselves, at face value.

- Unbiased observation and analysis are basic requirements for analyzing these phenomena to derive common characteristics. To be unbiased, one should discard any preconceived ideas about culture, religion, or race. Indeed, fundamental human nature should have nothing to do with a particular culture, religion, or anything else of the sort.

- Most importantly, the ultimate source of understanding ourselves is self-examination. A deep self-examination, listening to the heart, is crucial in order to derive the basic building blocks. There is a great deal of different schools of thought throughout history, from Western to Eastern cultures, from philosophy to religions, available for us to digest and analyze. But as the famous ancient Chinese philosopher Lu Xiangshan said, "What book did the great thinkers read?" (Lu, Vol. 36). The ultimate source comes from our own minds, our own understanding, rather than from books.

- No matter how hard we try, there is a risk of overdefinition or underdefinition, and any theory is subject to reexamination once new knowledge is gained. It is very possible that some parts of human nature simply cannot be put into words; they can only be felt and experienced. The fact that we expend effort to understand ourselves is part of human nature. It ties into the value of a thinking creature and the meaning of life: that we basically should contribute to the knowledge base of humanity and to the understanding of truth.

- Lastly, since nature, the human mind, and their interactions are so subtle and are ever evolving along with the human mind itself, the principles behind human nature, if there are any, need long periods of time, maybe many generations, to reveal themselves. So a statistical approach, over time and space, must be applied in order to extract unbiased principles. A human being is both the observer and the observed. Any approach to the study of ourselves needs to remember this dilemma.

In a very high-level view, the nature of a human being can be divided into several categories, from lower level to higher level:

- Psychological, subconscious nature
- Conscious—rationale, reasoning, logic—how humans know about the world
- Emotional, interpersonal relationships
- Ethical, moral, cultural, religious
- Social, economic, political

The higher levels of our nature can influence lower levels but will not be able to determine the lower level. Therefore, a philosophy must be built upon an accurate understanding of the lower level of human nature first. That is where we will start.

4.2 Conscious and Unconscious

The human mind is largely unconscious. Modern psychology tells us that the conscious is just the tip of the iceberg, and the majority of the mind is below the surface of the conscious. The emergence of the conscious is still not fully explained, but it is a generally accepted fact that the unconscious mind is at the root of the conscious mind. Although we are unaware of it, the unconscious mind influences the conscious subtly and constantly. It simply exists and cannot be controlled by the conscious part of the mind.

What does conscious mean? It means being aware of oneself, aware of what happens around oneself, and even aware of the life-span of oneself. *A healthy person can be in a state of mind where he can concentrate on abstract thoughts and not on any part of his body. This should be considered as a miracle and not taken for granted.* The human mind must have gone through a long journey to get to such a state. Most fundamentally, *the conscious means a separation.* This is because the conscious means awareness, and awareness is only meaningful when there is a comparison. Similarly, the conscious is only meaningful when the self is isolated from the rest of world. The mind can enter a state of thinking about something disconnected from the physical self. Hence, by definition, when the conscious exists, isolation is always associated with it. In other words, *the conscious and isolation are two sides of the same coin.* The conscious is a waking up of the human mind; it enabled human intelligence to grow and civilizations to start, but it also led to a sense of isolation, which is a fundamental struggle of humans.

Secondly, conscious means one can behave in a way that is not completely according to pure, natural drive. The conscious can impose some level of restraint on natural drives. However, such control is limited because natural drives can come from the unconscious part of the mind, and as said earlier, the unconscious part of the mind cannot be completely controlled by the conscious part.

Thirdly, conscious also means the capability of expression and cognition. These enable intelligence to begin and grow. The evolutionary path of the conscious of the mind becomes a self-organized behavior. One cannot really tell where the path will lead, but it is clear that it will grow and continue to evolve. It has an intrinsic life. The potentiality of such growth depends on historic accumulation and environmental conditions. If such growth is not unleashed but repressed, the human mind will not reach its potential.

Psychologist and philosopher Erich Fromm deeply explored the meaning of consciousness. In his view, the emergence of consciousness was an awakening of humanity (Fuller, 197–200). Before this awakening, humans were "one with nature, in the manner of animals" (Fuller, 197). There was no sense of separation, a lack of discriminating knowledge of good and evil, and no intelligence with which to understand the world. This tie to nature was broken when consciousness emerged. And the process was not necessarily at the will of human beings. It is an evolutionary step of the human mind. But it is a significant step that is, in Fromm's view, similar to the "emergence of life." This was the beginning of humanity; it signified that humans were different from animals (Fuller, 198). However, the emergence of the conscious also produced the following dilemmas:

- A sense of separation. The development of a sense of self is the same process that creates the sense of separation. It is two sides of the same coin. The more sense of selfhood and intelligence one has, the more sense of separation he will experience.
- Life and death. The conscious mind is aware of its own life-span. It is aware that at some point it shall cease to exist. This is one of, if not the most, controversial dilemma. The more a sense of selfhood, the more awareness of this dilemma.
- The potential of a human mind is tremendous. It has its own life to grow and evolve. However, since a person is a short-lived entity, how to maximize the potential and usefulness of an individual within a short life-span is a fundamental question one shall struggle with.

There are many other difficulties in life, such as social conflicts, cultural conflicts, and financial difficulties, but the above dilemma is most intrinsic. Other difficulties can be solved, either at the current time or later.

In fact, the emergence of the human conscious was so significant, that Fromm interpreted the biblical fall (Adam and Eve eating the fruit of knowledge) as the beginning of human history, a waking up that also split humans from Mother Nature (Fuller, 197). From then on, humans were on their own in finding a way to reconcile with nature. This is called the separation of primary ties.

Facing such an intrinsic dilemma, humans have been searching for answers. There is no easy solution, and mankind has explored many different alternatives. Fromm's next contribution is his investigation of the secondary tie (Fuller, 199). In the course of searching for a solution to reconcile with Mother Nature, human beings turned to idols, be they wealth, power, status, or authoritarian religion. Man is "escaping from freedom," and so is instead developing the secondary tie. In doing so, one loses the real self, the reality of humanity's power.

Then what is the real solution? Psychologists have offered different answers. Fromm thinks humans should fully develop the abilities of love, reason, truth, freedom, independence, productivity, courage, community, justice, and peace. One should devote themselves to unleashing the power of one's capacity for love and rea-soning instead of ignoring it and turning to the idols (the secondary tie). Hence man should be for himself first, not idols (Fromm, Ch. 4). These are wonderful solutions, but they fall short on methods, i.e., the means to achieve these goals. Fromm thinks man can totally rely on himself, with no need for submission to any supernatural en-tity. Essentially, Fromm believed that humans can control their own destinies, which is a very bold assumption. Unfortunately, *since the conscious is just a small part of the human mind, it cannot fully control the unconscious part of the mind. Therefore, the products of the conscious mind, such as reasoning, truth, freedom, independence, productivity, courage, community, and justice cannot fully control the whole spectrum of products of the human mind.* The notion of a completely self-reliant human being is ig-norant of the complexity of interaction between the conscious and the unconscious.

Another psychologist Carl Jung went much deeper into understanding the human mind. According to Jung, the human mind consists of four parts (Jung, 42; Fuller, 67–72):

- Personal conscious. This is the part we usually call self. It is the source of cog-nition, intelligence, memory, expressible feeling, etc.
- Personal unconscious. Unique to the individual, this cannot be observed or expressed. The mind occasionally detects its existence through dreams or other indirect means. It can sometimes emerge into the conscious but is later forced back under the surface.
- Collective conscious. This is knowledge and values shared among all human beings. Similar to the concept of the third world from Popper.
- Objective psyche. Also called the collective unconscious, this is a concept dis-covered by Jung. Jung suggested that within the human psyche, apart from the individual unconscious, there is also a component that is common to all human beings and is a sort of record resulting from humankind's millions of years of evolution. Jung believed this part of the psyche objectively exists, re-gardless of an individual's experience. It is not acquired through experience; it is simply inherited. It is the deepest part of the psyche and the most difficult for the conscious mind to detect.

Jung further proposed many different kinds of collective unconscious, called ar-chetypal images (Jung, Ch. 1). These archetypal images cannot be detected, but they indirectly influence the growth of our psyches and how we perceive ourselves. By definition, the collective unconscious cannot be explicitly studied. Instead, it can only be detected after an individual realizes it during the individuation process, i.e., during the growth of the self (Fuller, 76). According to Jung, these archetypes are like the way, or principles by which, a crystal grows. But the exact look of a concrete crystal is only known after the crystal is actually grown. We know of the existence of archetypal images because a collection of individuals demonstrates certain common traits during their lifetimes.

Jung's view is certainly more reasonable than Fromm's view, because it is more reasonable to believe that the human conscious cannot control the unconscious psyche or the collective unconscious. In addition, the ideas of archetypes and individuation are similar to some of the concepts found in ancient philosophies and modern science:

- Plato's Theory of Forms. Form is what an object really is, and the concrete object is just a momentary portrayal of Form under particular circumstances. Form is abstract, an object is concrete. Archetype is basically the Form of humanity.

- Ancient Chinese Neo-Confucianism. The key Neo-Confucian philosopher Chu-Hsi said, "In the universe, there are *Li* and *Chi*. *Li* is the Tao that pertains to 'what is above shapes,' and is the source from which all things are produced. *Chi* is the material that pertains to 'what is within shapes,' and is the means whereby things are produced. Hence, men or things, at the moment of their creation, must receive *Li* in order to have a nature of their own. They must receive *Chi* in order to have their bodily form." (Fung, 299). In modern language, it says that when a person is born, he has already inherited the principles that govern his later growth. But he also needs the physical material to have the actual form and body to grow from. The meaning of *Li* is close to the concept of archetypes when the subject in study is the human mind.

- The interpretation of quantum mechanics. A quantum system has many potential eigenstates, but the actual state is realized when it is measured—the collapse of wave function. An archetype of the psyche is similar to an eigenstate for a quantum system.

- The self-similarity phenomenon depicted in Figure 1. There can be a miniature of the image of what the universe should be in the human mind. It might not be exactly the same image. The point is that the scope of dimension is not important, as shown in Figure 1.

Jung believed that one goal of life is to live out the archetypal image in the psyche, i.e., the common humanity, and in the meantime differentiate oneself (Fuller, 76). This process helps to reconcile the separation of the conscious from the root of the mind. By searching and connecting to the collective unconscious, one essentially finds a connection to a common network, because the archetypal image, by definition, is common to all human beings. Such a common network may not be expressible. It could be just a sense, or feeling, but it helps to reconcile our sense of isolation and separation. According to Jung, in the process of individuation, the early phase is to fully develop the sense of self—a strong and stable sense of self. But at a later phase, it is more important to reconnect the self to the collectiveness of culture, to a common network that helps to reconcile the separation (Fuller, 78). Although, from Fromm's point of view, this is dangerous because it can introduce a secondary tie to an idol or religion.

In summary, the emergence of the conscious in the human mind was essentially the start of humanity. However, such awakening leads to the separation of the conscious and unconscious, and that is one of the central themes in struggles for human beings. The complexity cannot be underestimated. When it comes to resolving the dilemma of the conscious and separation, one needs to be very cautious and appreciate the complexity of the mind, and not overestimate the power of human capacity for love and reasoning. Fromm's solution of completely relying on ourselves appears to be oversimplified. A humanist, as Fromm called himself, seems to be nervous about accepting something that is beyond the comprehension of human intelligence. The collective unconscious is beyond the ability of human intelligence to comprehend. But accepting something that is beyond comprehension is not necessarily in conflict with the goal of fully extending that intelligence. They are not mutually exclusive; they may just belong to different levels of a domain. Such phenomena have been observed in complex systems. For example, in a self-organized nonlinear system, it is the reality that an individual member is performing actions solely for its own interest, but the action helps the buildup of a structure at the higher domain—for the sake of the whole group or society, though the individual is unaware of that fact. *Truth has multiple levels, and one may not be aware of truth at a higher level. But the truth at the higher level does benefit all members of the same group or society. Accepting something that is beyond comprehension is not a submission of human potential, but helps to guide actions.* Both are not really black and white and can be reconciled.

4.3 Ego, Free Will, and Self

As the conscious of the human mind grows, a new level of abstract form is born. That is the feeling of ego. Ego is primarily the product of conscious. The most prominent expression of the existence of self is free will. Free will is primarily an activity of the conscious, hence may not represent the best interests of the whole. Free will can be developed to a state that it is disconnected from its origin in the wholeness of self, or may not act according to the best interests of the whole. It can choose a course of action that is, in fact, harmful to the whole, but is unaware of it. The center of the wholeness of mind is the Self, as Jung called it. The Self represents the real interests of the mind as a whole, consisting of the conscious (and ego), and the unconscious (Fuller, 76). Free will can cause a conflict of interest with the whole Self, and in many situations the conscious mind is unaware of it. When the ego takes control and free will is disconnected from the true Self, free will can be destructive. When an individual's mind is developed to this stage, it is crucial to unwind the power of ego and free will, to restore the connection between the ego and the real interests of the Self. This will allow the Self to naturally follow the interests of the whole. Here the interest is not necessarily just a personal interest; it can be an interest of a higher order, for a group of human beings.

Development and growth of the human mind hence consist of two main components:

- The growth of the conscious and its representation—the sense of ego and the intelligence associated with it. This force unleashes the potential of humanity. We have to admit that this force is in the nature of human beings, and it cannot be ignored or blocked. Any theory attempting to ignore or undervalue such force is, in fact, against the human nature.
- The reconciliation between the ego and wholeness. The ego and the conscious, after growing to a certain level, will find limitations and need to return control to the wholeness. It is a rediscovery of the root of the conscious and ego. This force is also in the nature of human beings but can be shadowed by free will. It can also be buried by a person's routine activity. However, without realizing the importance of this component and unleashing the power of rediscovery of wholeness, one's personality growth is incomplete.

These two components exist at the same time, although one may be dominant in certain periods of one's life. The dynamic of these two forces is complicated and offers opportunity for deep contemplation. There are many ancient wisdoms and modern philosophies that attempt to understand this dynamic. Some of them place more emphasis on the second force and try to denounce the first force, while others emphasize the opposite.

The myth of relationship among the ego, "I," free will, and self has been extensively examined in the past. Chinese Taoism suggests that the Self is inseparable from the natural environment. In fact, Taoism argues that the truth is unspeakable. The feeling of self is a delusion at large. The modern version of the naturalist shares similar thoughts. In this view, intelligence and man-made laws are far inferior to the natural order and structure of the organism with its natural wisdom. The concept of "I" is an example of a man-made artificial word. One such modern thinker is Alan Watts. In his view, humans are part of a connected field in the universe, but when "I" is a word used to define a certain portion of reality, it is separated from the rest of world and taken as a permanent reality, which is not true. He thinks "I" is just a collection of memories of the past, but the actual self is constantly changing (Fuller, 169–170). *The understanding of "I" from Watts is similar to the understanding of ego from Jung.* Furthermore, society imposes the identity of "I" and the rules and orders that "I" should follow. The original spontaneous mind is no longer trusted (Fuller, 171). Because one believes the permanent ego, which is not reality, one feels insecure and anxious. A separated ego divorces us from the flow of life in the here and now (Fuller, 172). The result is that we turn attention to searching for security from the future, instead of in the here and now. If reality is a river ever flowing on, the belief of permanence as a higher order than change is not true.

In Hinduism, "the infinite and absolute is called Brahman. The infinite, in its hereness and nowness, is the atman. As an object of my knowledge, I am ego. As a knowing object, I am the Self. The Self here and now is the atman; the Self in infinity is Brahman" (Fuller, 177). This idea is similar to many other teachings from different cultures. For example, in Christianity, a human being is made from the earth but with the Holy Spirit infused into it. The human therefore encompasses both finite and infinite elements, and the infinite element is connected with God. The similar view in Chinese Neo-Confucianism believes that a human is born from *Chi* but has *Li* in him. Watts generalizes the concept of self, and it becomes a myth. It connects the human being with governing natural laws. It is supreme, above all things, and hence cannot be fully comprehended by human beings. The individual conscious and existence are now experienced as a temporary point of view taken by the self.

Essentially, the wisdom from these teachings is similar, that there is something transcendent that temporarily lives within the individual. The goal of life is to unblock the constraints of the finite ego and reconnect the transcendent part of life to its original source.

The above description so far deemphasizes the separation of ego and wholeness. By perceiving that such separation is not reality, the corrected understanding is that ego is just a temporary feeling, and there is a path to reconnection with its original roots. *However, what is the original root? It can be a mythical concept and is open to different interpretations and religious inspirations.* This concept is crucial to understanding the human self and the healthy relationship of self, ego, and the world. It is necessary and proved useful, but we cannot fully comprehend the concept—this is much like the concept of wave function in quantum mechanics. The humanist, on the other hand, puts much emphasis on human potential rather than the reconnection of self to its root. Fromm and Maslow were some of the modern thinkers in this school of thought. They believed that individuation and self-actualization are the ultimate goals of human life (Fuller, 76, 134). By living out one's full potential, the anxiety due to separation of self from nature is minimized. Note that here potential does not refer to just self-interest at the expense of others. Instead, in Fromm's view, humans should fully develop the abilities of love, reason, truth, freedom, independence, productivity, courage, community, justice, and peace. One should devote himself to unleashing the power of his capacity for love and reason.

In short, the evolution of the conscious leads to the birth of ego, self, and free will. It unleashes the power of humanity, while simultaneously introducing a set of difficulties related to reconciliation of the ego, self, and wholeness. There are many thoughts and much wisdom in this area. A good model for understanding this is not only important to guiding oneself, but also for consolidating a lot of seemingly conflicting thoughts from different cultures.

4.4 One Life, Two Tendencies

What is the reason for the emergence of a conscious mind? What are the most basic forces in a human life? When a life is born, it is like a seed full of potential. As that life grows, these potentials unfold. Some of them become actualized and some of them remain hidden. Growth of that life is a given and is intrinsic as long as the life is alive. It is an objective orientation that nobody can deny or stop. Aristotle called this tendency, this force or orientation, the actualization of potentiality. It is a natural force of living creatures. However, for every step of growth, for every bit the growth tendency pushes forward, there is always a differentiation associated with it, no matter how small. Growth of life is at the expense of moving away from its origin, at the expense of loss of wholeness, bit by bit. Fortunately, what makes humans different from other living creatures is that we have another tendency: reconciliation. This second tendency is not to stop the first tendency or to reverse the differentiation resulting from growth. Instead, it is meant to find ways to reconcile the wholeness of life, to pose a tension to the first tendency, to provide direction to the force of growth. This is not a straightforward interaction, but a unified life should embrace both tendencies properly.

In this section, we will get deeper into exactly what they are and how they interact with each other. These are the high-level concepts that cannot be easily explained through basic physics, chemistry, or biology. They are hypotheses and need to be tested through personal experience and practice.

Tendency of Growth

It is difficult to define a name for each tendency. Instead, we focus on their characteristics. The tendency of growth is the movement of life, and it has the following characteristics:

- It is very similar to the concepts introduced by Aristotle, i.e., potentiality and actualization. Aristotle believed that humans have the potential to explore all possible capabilities and experiences that a human being can possibly reach. Actualization is the realization of such potential during the growth of an individual. Historically, these concepts had many interpretations and were heavily used in religions. There is no interest here in studying the exact meaning of Aristotle's concepts.
- It is the instinct embedded in the human gene. Its existence is objective, i.e., independent of anyone's will. No one can stop it. It should not be blocked in order for a person to be fully developed as a human being.
- When it is developed to a stage, consciousness of the mind emerges, then intelligence is derived from the growth of consciousness, and humanity starts. Knowledge, science, the capability of distinguishing right from wrong, and in the higher level forms, social systems, are examples of the products of this human potential. It basically expands the conscious space in the world of the human mind.

- It introduces differentiation and separation. This force can be self-centric and rely only on the individual. The more of the potential that is gained, the more achievement one can attain, but the more of a sense of separation and isolation.
- Such a tendency is a natural force without predefined purpose. It keeps growing and evolving but without self-aware goals.
- Borrowing terminology from Chinese Taoism, I name this tendency the Yang component of life.

When the first tendency is dominant at a certain stage of individual growth, especially at a young age, the individual will continuously explore possible options for the given social conditions. The individual keeps learning new skills, creating new ideas, and increasing new desires. This is really in the domain of the conscious. At some point, he may realize his own limitations. It is possible, even within intellectual, logical knowledge, for the complexity of nature and limitations of knowledge to become self-evident. A self-evident awareness of limitations is a sign of return from the growth tendency. An individual capable of reaching his or her limitations should be happy and relieved. What he is capable of is actualized to its maximum extend, be it intellectual capability, leadership, or love. The anxiety of separation and even the fear of death diminish. To continue the growth at the next level, he needs to reconcile with the root first.

Reconciliation

On the other hand, the second tendency, reconciliation, is a force behind the scenes. It is a tendency to reconcile the separation and isolation caused by the first tendency, to pull the first tendency back to its origin, and to unify the mind space expanded by the first tendency. No matter how much someone's first tendency can grow, it cannot lose connection to its roots and origin, and it cannot be a dominant force. This is much like the relationship of the leaves and roots of a tree. The evolution of the growth tendency has produced the following side effects:

- Emergence of the consciousness of mind, resulting in the sense of isolation and separation, starts to bother him.
- Emergence of the ego and free will, which are the natural evolutionary outcome of the conscious mind.

- Rational reasoning is dominant to the point that other cognitive skills, such as intuition and meditation, are abandoned.
- The evolution of social systems and individual social characteristics got emphasized more and more throughout human history.
- Specific cultures, values, and ethics have developed and been adopted, and each always has its own geographic and historical limitations. A selection on a specific set means loss of opportunity for a more complete view. There can be conflict among different cultures and value systems.

Reconciliation is a tendency to reconcile these side effects and restore the harmonious mind state. If the first tendency is aware of its own limits and cooperates with the origin, the individual will be in a healthy, full, and optimal state. Even if the potentiality tendency is unaware of its own limits and is not cooperative with the origin, the tendency for reconciliation still exists but is not aware, resulting in a tension, so the individual is in a suboptimal state. In any case, the ability of unification is intrinsic to human nature. It is this tendency that drives us to search for goals in life and for eternal affiliation. It is a powerful force that makes one's life much happier and makes a life larger. The byproduct of the first tendency is the conscious mind and intelligence, and an emphasis on rational reasoning. On the other hand, the reconciliation tendency relies much more on the intuition of the whole mind, the conscience, and the voice of the heart.

Reconciliation doesn't mean to restore the original chaotic state of the human mind. Reversal of the growth tendency and erasure of the results of evolution of the first tendency are impossible. Hence, reconciliation means to find new and innovative ways of making sense of the wholeness out of the separation. This is what makes us different from other living creatures. In general, there can be many approaches for reconciliation. Two examples are described here:

- Filtering out. Because it is impossible to reverse the growth tendency and erase the results from its evolution, there are always unnecessary prejudices, superstitions, or artificial rules introduced. Those should be removed in order to reconnect to the origin. Removal of the shields to human nature is key for reconciliation. The feeling of wholeness is easier to regain with honesty to the self. However, many times this can go to the extreme of calling for complete erasure of the results from the evolution of the first tendency, which is impossible and misleading.
- Changing viewpoint at a different level. In order to make sense of the separated realities, one can view it from a higher level and attain a common ground.

This can be readily understood in a typical family life where young siblings fight with each other because they only care about their own interests. This is from their own views. But if we take the parent's view, these conflicting interests can be reconciled. A parent's mind-set is the healthy growth of the children in the family as a whole. There is a common interest for the whole family, which is difficult for a young child to understand. The amazing thing about the human mind is that it sometimes can sense the interest of a bigger whole. The human mind can occupy different states: most of the time, it is in the state of looking out for its own interest only, but sometimes it can reach a state that senses the higher-level view. At that moment, the separation is reconciled. Within this approach, two subapproaches exist: 1) Explicitly calling out and describing what the next level is. The advantage here is it is easier to follow. But it is dangerous, because it is impossible to have a complete understanding of what the next-level goal is. 2) Not to explicitly call out what the next level is, and instead to assume a self-organization approach. The next-level interest and goal is there, but we don't know exactly what it is. All we can do is our best to live out the most important values as a human being.

When the reconciliation tendency wakes up, unification becomes a dominant force—the conscious, intellectual reasoning, becomes secondary. A peaceful mind and acceptance of being and the surrounding world become primary. Being sensitive and listening to the heart, a sense of harmony prevails, and the wholeness is connected to something that is transcendent. The boundary between the self and the external world diminishes. The feeling of separation is overcome. Fear of death is also managed. This stage is more likely to be reached after his potential as a human being is fully unleashed in a meaningful way through productive means. *Since the conscious mind and free will cannot be erased or ignored anymore, any reconciliation must integrate them as organic components. This opens up many possible solutions. The values of human beings, the meaning of life, are precisely demonstrated with these efforts. One solution is to integrate the conscious and free will into full devotion to an endeavor that is deemed to be transcendent and, at the same time, of benefit to others or society.* Many religions or belief systems capitalize on this part of human nature but in a very indirect way. For example, in Christianity, the New Testament describes the Kingdom of Heaven, the Tree of Life, the river of life, the eternal. Many religions in the world are divided in what their ultimate vision of the world is, but they all agree that the best way to reconcile with the self is to fully devote oneself to an endeavor deemed to be eternal and transcendent. Whether the something that is transcendent actually exists in reality, or is just a delusion, is a separate question and deserves a much deeper discussion in later chapters. Different answers to this question are found in different cultures and religions.

Both potentiality and unification can have an aggregation effect. That means efforts from each force can be aggregated from a group of individuals. There are media available that facilitate aggregation. For example, knowledge and science, which are the products of potentiality and actualization, are the aggregated intelligence from the individuals of a society. In the same manner, religions and beliefs, which are efforts from the unification tendency, are also group behaviors. The same concepts can be applied to analyze the growth of an individual mind and to the evolution of a culture—the aggregation form. This chapter will focus only on the growth of the individual mind.

The Dynamics Between the Two Tendencies

The dynamics between the tendency of growth and the tendency of reconciliation are central to our lives. It is complex and difficult to describe. But there are some characteristics that we can recognize.

In essence, humans have a tendency toward reaching full growth potential. Such a tendency is crucial at an early age for personal growth. At this stage, one has to temporarily ignore the other aspect in order to reach its full potential for the given conditions. After a certain period, the need for reconciliation will be appreciated as the side effects of the growth tendency start to impact life. The dynamics of potentiality and reconciliation will continue for the whole life of an individual. How much potential an individual can reach depends upon how much he can embrace this dynamics harmoniously. The bigger oneness reached, the more difficult unification is, but when harmoniously unified, it produces a stronger sense of relief and eternality. If a person just wants to stay in a small oneness that is harmoniously integrated, he will live a happy life, even though the space of active mind is small. On the other hand, if a person is pushing hard to reach maximum potential but is unable to integrate with the whole self, he may have a good sense of achievement but won't have a happy life. In Maslow's words, he is still in the deficiency realm (Fuller, 136); or in Jung's words, he is experiencing the great struggle of separation between two opposites (Fuller, 89–92); or in Christianity, he is stuck in original sin, unable to reconcile with God. When a person is able to push his potential to the limit and also successfully integrate the whole self, he experiences a great sense of achievement, relief, and eternality. But to reach this stage requires struggle and suffering of the separation first; it is like a spiral spinning from a small circle to a larger circle gradually. The process of growing is painful and is not guaranteed to be successful.

A typical extreme of this dynamic is that a person is moving at full speed exploring potential, without awareness of the need for reconciliation. This is especially true when the individual is in early stages of life. She needs to develop a strong ego and intelligence. Before the individual's ego and intelligence reach a certain level of maturity, she may not realize the need for, or experience the power of, spiritual unification. Maturity in personal growth is a prerequisite for reconciliation. Hence, when an individual is young, she will not really appreciate the need for spiritual reconciliation; it is just not her focus at that period of life. However, without reconciliation, an individual's life is essentially incomplete and won't bring the full extent of spiritual happiness.

The other extreme of attitude is to deemphasize human growth potential. A person basically withdraws from the pursuit of goals in the secular world, such as money or social position, and instead focuses on spiritual goals. This is an easy attitude to choose, but it is not the optimal one. If the potential is not fully realized, individual growth is stalled, and the reconciliation effort is unlikely to get to a high level. Development of potential expands the space of mind for intelligence and awareness, but it poses more challenges for reconciliation. However, when people with highly developed intelligence and consciousness can successfully reconcile with themselves, they will see and experience a higher level or bigger scope of unification that others can't. The secular world is driven by desires, development of intelligence, and the conscious. Success is judged by power, money, and social position. Nevertheless, it is also premature to bluntly blame people who pursue power and money, because some of these people can possibly integrate at a larger scope.

With the increase of intelligence or the conscious, the reconciliation that was not possible before becomes possible. For example, in times past, men would look up at the sky, the clouds, and the moon, but with the limited knowledge available at the time, they tried to make sense of the unknown with imagination and fable, such as angels living in the moon or considering thunderstorms as an angry sign of God. The reconciled mind space was small at that time. But today, with the advancement of science and technology, we can take an airplane or even a space shuttle. We can view the earth from high above, and the imagination of the old times should be discarded, as they have been proven to be either true or false. Mankind is looking at a much higher level of the unknown to solve, such as if there are other living species in the universe.

A balance must be achieved with conditions allowing both tendencies to reach their possible maximum values: let the growth tendency evolve to its possible full extent, but at the same time be able to reconcile it with the true self. The more an individual is able to unify potential that is more developed, the more fullness the individual will experience. An individual should not refrain from the tendency of human potentiality, even for the sake of spiritual happiness. Instead, he or she should embrace and integrate it. One should live out the full potential of life, but within a boundary that still can be reconciled. To what extent? At what boundary? These are the questions each individual should experience and find answers for. An old Chinese saying, "The most superior hermit is hidden in the big city," describes well where the balance should be. It means a complete individual is fully aware of the value of both tendencies and naturally follows guidelines from the heart. Routine life seems as normal as others, but he or she values every moment of life as a miracle and treats every choice as a subtle balance of potentiality and unification.

The dynamics between the tendency for growth and the tendency for reconciliation have been embedded implicitly in cultures and religions. Humanism tends to emphasize human potential and actualization, while religion tends to emphasize spiritual reconciliation. Both humanity and religion should be able to find common foundation in light of the dynamics between the two tendencies. A religion that is unable to integrate the nature of human potential should not be considered a healthy religion. Similarly, a humanism that knows when and where to give room for religion is also a healthy one. No matter how differently mankind's cultures attempt to embrace these, the key points of the dynamics remain the same:

- Growth of life and actualizing potential are objectives in human nature. As a whole, it is a growth of humanity and cultural maturity in history.
- Reconciliation is intrinsic to human nature and will never go away. But the content and methods evolve as mankind's potential grows.
- This dynamic is not a static or linear one. It is evolving continuously and co-exists in a complex way.
- Reconciliation provides direction and purpose. If an individual pursues potential under the guidance of that direction and purpose, then both natures find value in a harmonious way, in the context inside the specific individual.

However, in the current secular world, an optimal life attitude as described above may not be one that attracts most people. Instead, actualization of potential is a dominating force. This is because society has not yet evolved to a point that it most values the optimal dynamics of potentiality and reconciliation.

A concrete model to describe this dynamic can be helpful to many individuals, as this balancing act is not a trivial task. This is pretty much a matter of personal experience and cannot be described precisely in words. Yet here are a few typical models where the potentiality and unification forces can work together:

- Sequential or periodical model. Most of the time, an individual is driven by exploring potentiality but intermittently dominated by reconciliation instead. This assumes that at any time, the mind cannot be occupied by two different states.
- The yin-yang model. This model can be depicted with the Tai Chi diagram (see Figure 3). One constituent comprises the seed of the other constituent, while both constituents depend on each other and also push each other. Together, when they interact well, life grows. When not interacting well, life suffers.
- Overlay model. Growth potential and reconciliation are overlaid, but on different levels. One will continue to actualize his own potential, but now in a different context, knowing the limits and guidelines. When there is conflict, he knows and follows the voice of his heart and the laws of nature. In this model, one can switch levels of viewpoint and find the balance when there is conflict. He pursues secular goals as other people do but with direction and guidelines from spiritual unification. Spiritual reconciliation is a foundation from a higher level of life in a bigger context, while the actualization of potential is a lower-level life in the context of the secular world. The actualization of potential can be considered as a means to exercise the principles behind reconciliation. Both tendencies in fact serve each other. This is the more realistic model and can establish a more peaceful mind rather than tension due to two seemingly conflicting forces.

Figure 3 The Tai Chi Diagram

However, these models are still too simple to describe the complexity of the human mind. The evolution of growth tendency has produced in the conscious mind intelligence and scientific knowledge. The evolution of reconciliation has resulted in belief systems, religions, and cultures. We need a more refined model to describe how an individual's growth and development of mind interact with these byproducts and in different stages of growth.

4.5 Integrated Model of the Nature of the Mind

In order to put different components of the nature of the mind into an integrated picture, a model can be developed and explained. To describe how the human mind develops and interacts with the world, we categorize the world into four parts: 1) The material world. 2) The human mind—the subjective world). 3) The world of objective knowledge, science, intelligence, and other expressible, objective information referred to as third world (Popper). 4) The world of undetected but objective information, those that can be implicitly embedded in values, beliefs, religion, cultures, or *trends and directions as an emergent effect of human group behavior*—which I will refer to as the fourth world.

The concept of the fourth world can be easily interpreted as or linked to superstition. Before moving on, it is necessary to spend more effort to clarify exactly what it is.

- Among the objective outcomes from the evolution of the human mind, those that can be expressed in language are categorized as the third world. The third world can be considered byproducts of the conscious and intelligence. However, *the mind as a whole encompasses both the conscious and unconscious parts. The activities of mind as a whole product are more than just what the third world consists of. The delta is defined as the fourth world.*

- It is undetected yet by the conscious mind. The third world is a byproduct of the conscious. However, conscious means differentiation. It causes isolation and loss of information. This missing information is undetected. The fourth world is the outcome of the mind as a whole, including the unconscious part it is unaware of or undetected.

- It is objective. The fourth world is different from the individual subjective world (the second world). It is an aggregation and statistical outcome of individual minds. Recall the definition of the fourth world is the delta between the aggregated outcome of whole mind activities and the aggregated outcome of the conscious mind's activities (third world). Since the third world is objective, it is natural to conclude that the aggregated outcome of whole mind activities is also objective. Therefore, the delta, the fourth world, is also objective. It remains to be uncovered. In Chapter 6, we will further discuss how to distinguish a healthy belief from a superstition.

- It is communicable. Since it is not yet detected by the conscious mind, the only way to communicate is unintentionally through the heart, intuition, and feelings.

- As human history advances and the mind evolves, some contents in the fourth world can become part of the third world, meaning they are manifested and become aware. Also, due to the growth tendency, the contents of the third and fourth worlds as a whole will continue to expand.

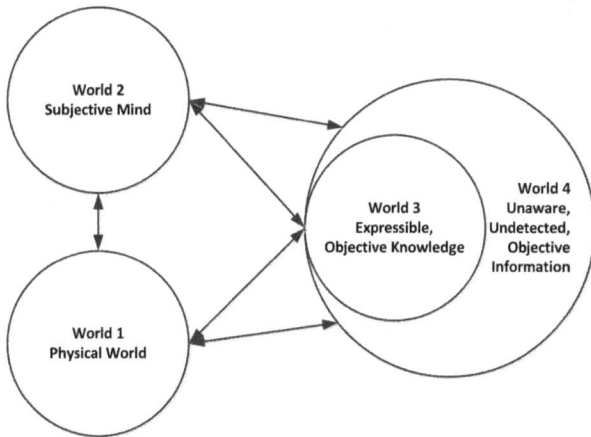

Figure 4 The Four Worlds

The advance of human potential will certainly enrich this world. The fourth world is crucial for the reconciliation process of the human mind. It nurtures the self and oneness of human minds and is an ultimate channel for communication among them.

With the world partitioned into four parts, we proceed to model the growth of an individual's mind. The process can be characterized by internal development and external interaction. At different stages of mind development, there are always internal and external components. Figure 5 depicts key stages of development. The nature of the human mind is too complex to describe with a simple two-dimensional diagram. Figure 5 is just to serve as an approximation to explain the idea.

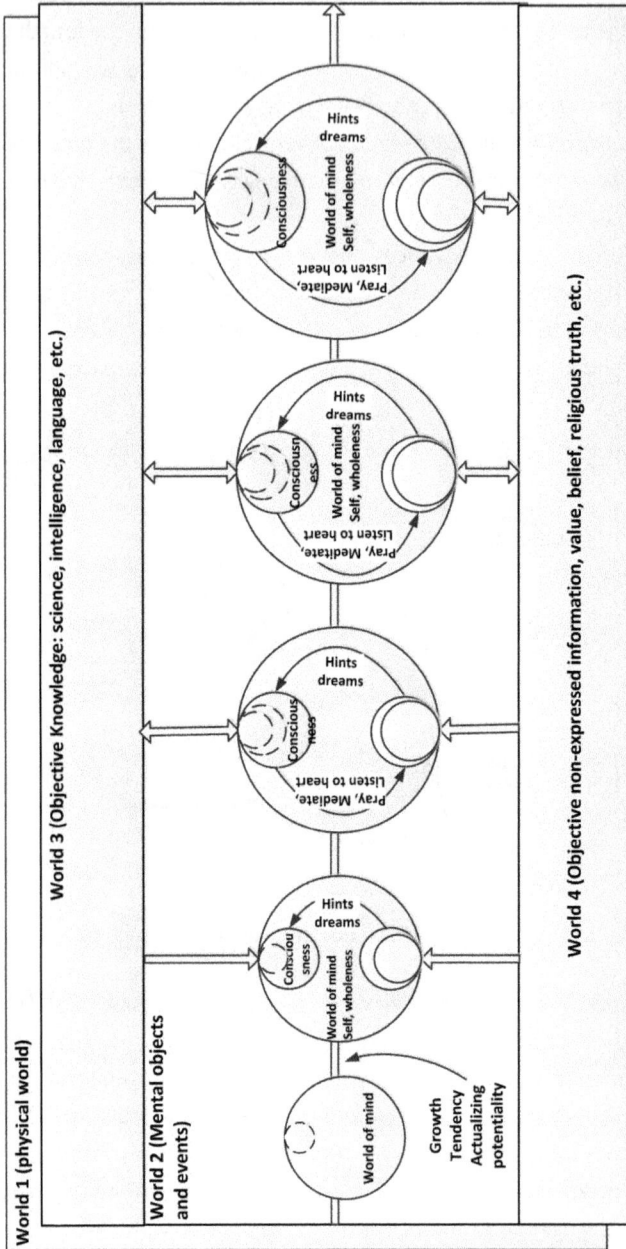

Figure 5 Integrated Model for the Development Cycle of Human Mind

When an individual is born, the mind is full of potential for development but is mainly unconscious. As the individual grows to the second stage, their initial focus is to fully develop potential. The conscious continues to increase and so does the intelligence. The individual continues to gain nutrition from both the third and fourth worlds. The material world is the focus at this stage. People at this stage are eager to pursue all sorts of achievements or status in academics, finance, or climb social ladders. The unconscious part of the mind also gets developed more. In its nature it keep sending hints and probe the conscious part of the mind, but it most likely goes unnoticed. Many people simply stop at this stage of their mind development.

In the third stage, the growth tendency and the conscious are developed close to full potential. It starts to realize its own limitations and begins reconnecting to its root. This is the start of the reconciliation process. An awakening of the sense of wholeness: the conscious mind is more sensitive to signals from the unconscious mind. The conscious submits to the whole self. It gives up control and acknowledges that it's within the boundary of a bigger self. The individual is listening more to the voice from the heart, employing various approaches such as prayer and meditation. The conscious mind intentionally reserves room for the wholeness to take control. The whole self, comprising a large part of the unconscious, can only interact with the conscious through various hints, dreams, or other revelations. The mind is more peaceful, and a sense of wholeness and happiness is felt more frequently. In this stage, the reconciliation mainly occurs internally. Connection to the third or fourth worlds is largely unidirectional, but could be bidirectional to the third world. For some individuals, the connection to the third world at the third stage can be bidirectional. This means that the individual not only gets support from the third world but also contributes to it. This is, no doubt, a very significant achievement as a human being. Many successful people may stop at this stage of mind development.

One should notice that the growth tendency is a nonstop trend, and the tension with reconciliation continues. On the one hand, growing up means the conscious part of the mind getting stronger and stronger, and in charge. On the other hand, the conscious mind must be surrendered to the whole self for reconciliation.

In the fourth stage, internal unification is well developed and the mind of the individual is strong and healthy. The continuous and effective interaction of the conscious and unconscious parts of the mind results in a significant outcome: the connection to the fourth world is bidirectional. That is, the individual not only gets support *from* it but contributes *to* it. As the expression of the mind at this stage in real life, the individual is full of love and is supportive of other people. His or her spirit inspires others in a good way. The unification process occurs not only internally but also externally. Since both the third and fourth worlds are objective and transcendent, meaning its continuity doesn't depend on any individual's life-span, a bidirectional connection to the third world means individuals feel their transcending, but only the conscious part of mind. In the bidirectional connection to the fourth world, on the other hand, the individual feels the transcendence of the self as a whole, hence is closer to the ultimate goal of life. The deepest potential of the mind is lived out by the individual. In reality not many people can get to this stage.

The third stage and fourth stages are not necessarily in that sequence. Some individuals can start having a bidirectional connection with the fourth world earlier. Some may have only a unidirectional connection to the third world but a bidirectional connection to the fourth. And the mind's development does not stop at the fourth stage. The growth potential can continue expanding as long as the internal unification process works effectively. The mind as a whole continues to grow, and the bidirectional connections to either the third or fourth world become stronger and stronger. The mind becomes a mechanism, a channel, to actualize more and more of the potential that can be achieved in a reconciled way.

Potentiality needs to be actualized first in order to complete the internal reconciliation. And the completion of reconciliation doesn't hinder the continuous growth of human capabilities. Indeed, they can both work together to unfold the value of a human individual. If the conscious and the intelligent part of the mind don't fully develop, the connection to the fourth world can be premature, and that can lead to superstition or unhealthy religion. It is important to develop the conscious and intelligence, even though that doesn't guarantee there will be bidirectional connection to the third and fourth worlds, but it is a precondition.

Most people will likely stop at stage two or three in this mind development cycle. That is unfortunate because the full potential of the human mind is not actualized and the full values as a human are not lived out. Each individual needs to make a choice how he or she will pursue the value of life. "Life seeks completeness, not perfection," is very good advice from Jung.

In the above model, the following key assumptions need further investigations:

- The existence of the third and fourth worlds. Are they reality or just a perception? The third world is less questionable. The meaning and existence of the fourth world is a subject for further investigation in Chapter 6. It is objective in the sense that it is transcendent, existing independently of an individual's mind. It must be subjective to certain principles, just as with the principles for the third world, but it will be impossible to explicitly express. It is this dilemma that makes it difficult to study. But there is no doubt that it greatly influences the completeness of our lives.

- The mechanism for internal reconciliation at stage three. Generally speaking, listening to the heart is the best path for guidance, but there are many other concrete ways to achieve this. The methodology can be different, but the goal is the same.
- The mechanism for external interactions. This ties into the answers to assumption one, and it is another subject for further investigation in Chapter 6. There is already much literature on the third world and the mechanism of connection, hence we will not further investigate that.

4.6 Voice of Heart: Conscience

In the model described in previous section, the signal from the unconscious mind is a fundamental communications channel that links both the conscious and unconscious mind. It is a probe from the deepest parts of the mind to remind the superficial mind where the root is. One will experience this as a voice from the heart. When an individual is young, or when he is too immersed in the material world, such voice could be ignored. But it is always there; and at some point it will be heard by the conscious. It is, in fact, one of the most fundamental drives of human beings. This signal triggers the reconciliation process.

Different people have different experiences of the voice from the heart. The more sensitive one is to this signal, the richer spirituality one will experience. Some cherish this voice so much that they regard it as the divine in their hearts. One should always reserve a space in the heart to nurture this communications channel (instead of having it covered up by others). This voice and the reconciliation process it triggers must be addressed properly if a culture or religion wishes to encompass the true nature of the human mind.

The source of the voice from the heart is the deep unconscious, therefore it is not totally comprehensible. If the wholeness of mind follows certain laws that are incomprehensible to the conscious, the voice of the heart gives hints to the conscious. This makes the human mind very unique and different from any other self-organized system. As mentioned in Chapter 3, in a typical self-organized system, any one element of the system acts locally, without being aware of the macroscopic behavior occurring on a different level. But for the human mind, the conscious mind seems to not only interact locally, but also occasionally detect signals from the wholeness and the laws associated with it. *The signal from wholeness may contain information regarding principles at a different level, or the loss information when we acquires conscious knowledge*[2]. This was also described in Jung's theory of archetypes: In the unconscious part of the mind, there are many archetypes. These archetypes are depositions from ancient predecessors in the long history of evolution. The archetypes are part of the collective unconscious and therefore contain information of the common characteristics of human beings. The archetypes, at the deepest part of the mind, constantly send signals to the conscious (Fuller, 73–75). However, the concept of archetypes is just conjecture. It is still impossible to use the concept of archetypes to explain why the voice from the heart provides hints of higher-level law. We will explore this topic deeper in Chapter 5.

Many ethical values and practices are derived from the idea of properly dealing with this voice from the heart. Conscience, for example, flows naturally if we follow the voice from the heart. Honesty is one of the highest values of ethics for the same reason. In order to be honest, one has to detect the signal from the heart and act according to it. When the communications channel from the wholeness to the conscious is suppressed and the voice is not heard, the mind will be in an unhealthy state, since the reconciliation process is broken. In an extreme state, the personality is distorted and unaware. The dark side of the human mind is then exposed, and the individual can become very destructive.

There was a debate in ancient Chinese culture on whether the nature of human beings is sinful or kind. When the voice of the heart is heard, conscience is a natural outflow, and the individual behaves kindly. But if the unification process is broken, the ego is disconnected from the wholeness, conscience is suppressed, and the individual behaves evilly. Kindness is human nature when the ego is unified with the wholeness of self. However, the disconnection between ego and the wholeness is part of the growing process for the human mind. It is also a natural process. There is no guarantee that whenever there is a disconnection, reconciliation will be successful. Hence evil is unavoidable. The issue is not whether there is evil behavior; instead, it is about how it is contained. In the process of containing evil, the power of the wholeness is manifested.

4.7 Interaction of Minds and the Meaning of Love

Since the dynamics of mind development are complex, the interaction between minds can be expected to be complex as well. Since there are two parts of the mind,

---

2 See section 2.5 "Beyond the Limitations of Knowledge".

the conscious and the unconscious, communication methods with another individual will be different for the two parts. In the conscious and intelligent part of the mind, the means of communication is language, logic, and rational reasoning. This has been demonstrated in the success of humanity's revolution—the advancement of science and technology. These are the obvious facets of human communication.

For the unconscious part of the mind, the methods for interaction are feelings, emotions, or through other nonverbal expressions. The human mind as a whole is larger than just the conscious part of the mind, hence these methods of interaction are important for a complete and genuine interaction between two selves. One should see others as a whole self, too. Because both individuals have unconscious parts, their interaction cannot be controlled by the conscious. Hence, the guidelines for interpersonal interaction are sometimes irrational. This principle has a lot of implication for dealing with other people in routine life. One should treat others with love, not just what is right and what is wrong. One would observe other people not only through what they say but also what they do. We influence others not only through what we say, but more importantly, what we do. Integrity for an individual as a whole is the foundation for establishing a good interpersonal relationship.

The principles to govern relationships between individuals, or among groups, are very difficult to establish. The fundamental principle of treating others as a whole sounds easy to follow, but the reality is that this can be fully understood and becomes self-evident only when individuals have developed into the mature reconciliation process. When the underlying reason for a principle becomes self-evident, one follows it voluntarily, without the need for external enforcement. If self-understanding is not in place, a model, teaching, or myth has to typically be utilized to enforce the process.

There are many teachings regarding how to deal with interpersonal relationships. The old saying, "Treat others the way you want to be treated", is just one of them. This is just a minimal common ground to establish a healthy relationship. Essentially, it is similar to saying that a man is the measure of all things, because it uses human beings as reference and criteria. The good part of this teaching is that it is easy to understand and follow. The problem is its relativity. If one has a distorted understanding of himself, he won't treat others well. Good interpersonal relationships depend on a deep understanding of the complex structure and development cycle of the human mind. Once awakened to this understanding, one will realize that a life is really a miracle, and every life deserves full respect; every life should be treated in full as it is. Not only what is right or wrong (which is in the domain of the conscious mind), but also the feeling, the respect, which is somewhat in the domain of the unconscious, must be taken into consideration in how we treat others. Hence, *the fundamental element of love is to respect another's life as a whole, as it is, as what we understand about ourselves.* Love means to respect another's life as a whole, as it is, before making any judgment based on our personal knowledge or experience. It is a precondition for effective communication. With this respect, we can be fully patient and respect the natural development cycle of the mind as it is, and with care when needed. Furthermore, there is a common connection among all of us because of the similarity of the mind's structure and its development process. By caring for and loving others, we also experience happiness, because there is an unseen reward from confirming the principle behind the mind's structure and developmental process.

Besides care and respect, the next component of love is to guide. Note that we choose the word "guide." There are several meanings for this. 1) Since the first principle is to care and respect, one cannot force another individual's behavior and decision, and instead should provide suggestions and recommendations. 2) To guide implies that there is natural law behind the development of each individual. We just need to guide the person we care to follow the natural laws. We should not think we know exactly how an individual should develop or grow. Instead, we respect him and guide him. 3) Very importantly, to guide also means responsibility. If the person you love is deviating from the right direction, i.e., not following the natural laws, it is your responsibility to point it out and guide. But again this must be under the precondition of respect first.

Besides care and respect and guidance, for love between man and woman, there is certainly another unique component of being sexually appealing to each other. That is a natural instinct, and it should still be under the precondition of care and respect.

When two individuals have developed their own mature reconciliation process, parts of their interaction can be through the medium—the fourth world. The advantage of using the fourth world as a channel for interaction is that the foundation is broader. This shared world, instead of an individual, becomes the central point of focus in the interaction. This helps to avoid potential personal conflict such as manipulation, control, or other conflict without a common medium. It is particularly important when a group of individuals is involved. But there is also risk of falling into any form of superstition; it depends upon how mature each person's reconciliation process is, and how he or she perceives the fourth world. This is a very subtle subject to be discussed further in Chapter 6.

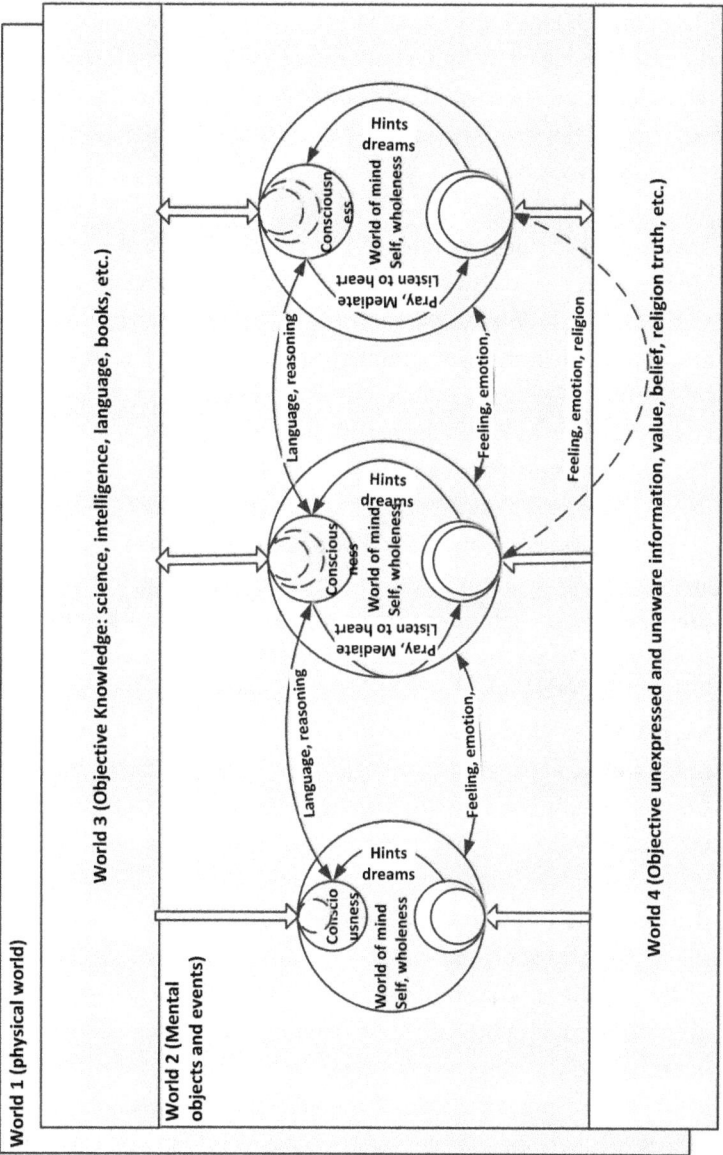

Figure 6 Interactions of Minds

4.8 Aggregation of Minds

The aggregation of mature minds is another important output of human groups. It in turn influences each individual's sense of belonging and consequently the sense of reconciliation. The aggregate outcome from the conscious parts of the minds of mankind as a whole forms the third world. The aggregate outcome from activities from the unconscious parts of the minds of mankind as a whole forms the fourth world. They have several characteristics:

- They are transcendent, not depending on the life cycle of any individual.
- There must be media to carry the information and messages through, generation to generation. For the third world, these are language, writing, books, and, in modern format, any computer storage. For the fourth world, there are other intangible media, such as culture, religious myth, feeling, and experiences passed on from earlier generations.
- They are accumulated, a contribution from earlier generations passed down (through the media) to influence the next generations.
- There are laws governing the evolution of the third and fourth worlds. The aggregation is not a simple sum of the individual minds. Instead, there is natural selection, only those that reflect the true reality will survive and evolve. However, there is a major difference between the third world and the fourth world. In the third world, a major component is knowledge about the external, material world, i.e., knowledge of the first world. It also has a component of knowledge about human beings. The contents in the third world are expressible, hence it is easier to fine tune the objectivity of the knowledge. In the fourth world, however, by definition, not all components are expressible through language. Further, the human mind itself keeps evolving. The objectivity of the fourth world depends upon how honestly our hearts detect the signal from the wholeness and respond to it. It depends on the truthfulness of the experience that is passed from generation to generation. The inexpressibility can also be due to the highly nonlinear interaction between the observer and the observed. Since the interactions between each individual are nonlinear, group behavior is unpredictable. There is no simple model to describe it. But one may get hints from the self-organized system; though each individual may be unaware of the evolutionary path (a myth), the system or society over time will still exhibit a path. It can take many generations

to understand that. But at any given moment, these behaviors are not totally comprehensible by the conscious mind of an individual.

In essence, the aggregation of minds is achieved through the media to carry the products of mind from generation to generation. At a given time, the content of the third or fourth world is the accumulated contents from previous generations, plus the boundary and contour of the conscious (for the third world) and unconscious (for the fourth world) from all individuals in the current generation. As time passes, the boundary expands, and the content of the whole society increases and passes to the next generation.

The difficulty of describing interaction between an individual and the fourth world can lead to some forms of superstition. For example, some believe there is living soul after death, so that the fourth world is just an aggregate of souls. This is definitely a superstition. The connection between an individual and the fourth world is through the media, and the "leftover" of any individual is simply information. By natural selection, only those reflecting true reality will survive and evolve over time. Through statistically averaging out, the "leftover" information is synergized, and no more personal characteristics remain. Imaging a personal soul of someone that can interact with the living is merely a delusion. To avoid falling into such superstitions, an individual's intelligence needs to be fully developed and utilized. This is one of the main reasons that in the early stage of individual growth, the focus is to develop the conscious mind and intelligence.

This principle of developing intelligence first and reconciliation later is not applicable only to individuals. It is also applicable to group behavior, such as culture, because culture is correlated to the aggregation of individual thoughts and experiences over a long period. If an individual can find a way to unify the self or experience harmonization without a supernatural entity, eventually the culture will evolve in a similar way over a long period of time. The developmental path of an individual mind is a miniature model of the evolutionary path of a culture.

When an individual achieves internal reconciliation, the next step of growth is to seek external unification. The existence of the third and fourth worlds provides this channel, because the third and fourth worlds are transcendent. Unification with the fourth world is more fundamental, because the wholeness of mind is more fundamental to the conscious part of the mind. An individual who is able to find a way to unify with the fourth world experiences a complete cycle of mind. As said earlier, not everyone is able to get to this stage.

The goal of an individual's life, besides the biological drives of survival and reproduction, is to complete the mind development cycle, to continue expanding the conscious and potential, while finding successful ways to reconcile with the self and the unconscious. This is from the spiritual growth point of view. The more the self of an individual unfolds, the higher the levels of consciousness and harmony it achieves. By achieving the higher levels of consciousness and harmony, it helps society as a whole unfold the collective boundary of mankind's understanding and unification process, which is transcending in the sense that such contributions will pass on to future generations and society. It is timeless and limitless.

4.9 Reflection Versus Action

The fact that the conscious is only part of a wholeness of the mind has many implications. One of these implications is that knowledge is a byproduct of the conscious. One cannot fully understand the wholeness of mind. Consequently, what we know only represents part of reality. What we don't know is another part of reality. There is a very important consequence of this point: *one cannot wait to understand the whole mind before he or she acts. Acting can be based on the best possible knowledge and intuition, but cannot be based on a complete knowledge or truth, because that is not realistic.* Teachings from many traditional cultures or religions all endorse the importance of action in loving other people. Love is the light of life; it is an action that does not need a full explanation. There is no need to fully understand the reasons behind it before acting, particularly for such action as loving other people.

Life is bigger than knowledge. This is a simple truth, but it is not widely followed. We tend to wait till we have a complete understanding of something before we act on it. But knowledge itself does not represent the fullness of life. The full meaning of life is not totally comprehensible through knowledge. Only putting yourself into action demonstrates the fullness of life. More importantly, acting *consistently* with knowledge is the best way to demonstrate the value of knowledge. Here, I only use the word "consistently" because knowledge may not be able to explain the full reasons for the action, but the action itself should not conflict with known facts. This is particularly important for knowledge about ourselves. The value of knowledge about ourselves can only be revealed when the carrier of the knowledge (i.e., a human being) actually practices it.

A person may have a lot of knowledge but still not apply it to making the most of his life. On the other hand, a person might live a good life but not fully know the meaning. This is seemingly strange, but there is a good justification for it. As explained earlier, the spectra of human minds synergize into a higher level of evolution. But we will not understand the whole meaning of the laws behind this evolution and how it interacts with us. We act with good faith. Knowledge is smaller than life, understanding is from knowledge, but good faith and action are from a real life.

Modern psychologist Frankl put it well with respect to action and reflection. We exist in action, not in reflection, because of the "inaccessibility of human existence to reflection" (Fuller, 238). Because reflection engages the personal center where actions originate, this center of action is held to be inaccessible to reflection. Thus the human foundation of existence is the unconscious: the origin is unable to observe itself—it is a blind spot. The part of the mind that decides whether something becomes conscious is itself unconscious. That existence cannot be fully reflected upon and cannot be fully analyzed. Many fundamental actions of humans, including searching for the meaning of life, worshipping a divinity, etc., originated from this depth of the unconscious, and hence cannot be fully analyzed. Yet it directs humans to transcend to a bigger wholeness, even though we cannot fully understand. But our life-span is limited, hence action is not only needed but becomes more important at some point—especially after exhausting whatever the conscious mind can reflect upon.

Action is more important than reflection when it comes to influencing or caring for other people. This is obvious when we discipline children. Children will be more influenced by the parent's behavior than by the parent's teaching. Another example, based on personal experience: When my five-year-old son didn't show good table manners and was put in timeout, he cried. He basically could not stop his crying himself and kept saying, "Can somebody hug me?" He kept crying until I physically hugged him, then he stopped. Any words, any discipline was useless until I physically hugged him. After that, he silently corrected his behavior. This demonstrates an extremely basic human need—the action of love. It is that simple, the action of love can cure many pains. Words are not enough, let alone just thinking or reflecting.

This simple principle will help us choose a teaching, a cultural practice, or even a religion to believe in. If you have to make a choice of which religion to follow as a result of some boundary limitation, you know there is no perfect choice. But you also have to ask what part of life is more important: loving and curing others' pain, or something else, and which way is more effective. There will be more discussion on religion in Chapter 6, but keep in mind that the action of love is important criteria. Love, in essence, means treating an individual as a whole, as he or she is, before any judgment. Even if one knows what is the right thing to do, simply telling someone else the absolute truth, without introducing the conflict in the unconscious part of the mind, won't solve the problem.

In summary, an individual should be genuine to his true understanding and knowledge. He certainly should act according to what he knows. More importantly, he also acts according to good faith and what he believes, even if there is no complete understanding of it.

4.10 Summary

This chapter focuses on how human beings understand their minds. We started with the question of the proper approach to understanding ourselves. A rigorous methodology is difficult to establish. However, several principles on methodology are observed, including that the whole is larger than the sum of its parts, self-cultivation, self-organization, historical statistics, and geographical statistics[3].

The emergence of the conscious part of the mind was an awakening of humanity. But at the same time, it was the start of separation of our minds from Mother Nature. This was a natural step of evolution that we must accept and face. However, the unconscious part of the human mind remains the majority and the root of the conscious. No matter how much advanced knowledge the conscious can produce, the wholeness of the human mind cannot be completely comprehended by the conscious. In other words, the conscious always remains part of the whole mind.

Along the evolutionary path, two tendencies are intrinsic the development of the human mind. The force that leads to the emergence of the conscious and then leads to the advancement of humanity is the actualization of potentiality. On the other hand, the reconciliation tendency ensures advancement of human growth will not cause a disconnect from its roots. It provides the direction for the growth, and unifies the growth tendency to ensure the integrity of the wholeness of mind. The advancement of growth tendency produces language, knowledge, science, intelligence, and social structure. The reconciliation tendency, on the other hand, is a quiet force behind the scenes. It influences human life through culture, art, music, religion, and in a very subtle way, sometimes undetected.

The dynamics between actualizing potentiality and reconciliation are complex. It governs the development of an individual's mind. To explain the complexity, a model of multiple phases is described. In this model, the two seemingly conflicting tendencies are in fact interdependent and can coexist and be beneficial to each other. The individual must have the growth potential fully developed before it realizes its limitation

---

3 Referred as mega statistics in Chapter 5.

and its root. The self-realization that it cannot be disconnected from its root is an important wake-up call. It starts to voluntarily cooperate with the reconciliation tendency to reach a harmonious state. That completes a cycle of internal unification.

However, reconciliation is not a pure spiritual phenomenon. If that was the case, the theory is nothing more than a psychological hypothesis. External unification is also crucial. Only with external unification can the human mind be considered completely mature. To describe this idea, the concepts of the third and fourth worlds are explained. The third world is a concept borrowed from Popper. It is the product of the conscious and intelligence. It is comprised of language, knowledge, science, philosophy, etc. The fourth world is the product of the unconscious mind and the reconciliation tendency. By definition, it is not fully explainable. It may be revealed through culture, art, music, religion, and myth. Since it is very easily misunderstood, a full chapter will be devoted to it later. The key characteristic of the third and fourth worlds is that they are transcendent. Through connections with them, the human mind achieves a sense of external unification. Only then is the reconciliation process complete.

Human beings are social creatures. Interpersonal relationships are the building blocks for a healthy society. The fundamental principle of building healthy interpersonal relationships is to fully understand the complexity of the human mind and its dynamics, and to treat each individual life as a whole, as he or she is. This is a cornerstone for love and respect. Love and respect are the foundation for healthy interpersonal relationships, and healthy interpersonal relationships are the foundation for a healthy society. Different understandings of the complexity of the human mind and its dynamics are what eventually lead to very different cultures and social systems. Therefore, it is important to go back to the root of the understanding so we can find common ground and reconcile the difference.

When we realize the human mind is complex and cannot be completely comprehended, there is a sense that humans are, in fact, a miracle of nature. One cannot wait for full understanding of oneself before putting oneself into action in accordance with the knowledge one has. This is because any life has a limited time span. We cannot waste time and life to just acquire knowledge but not put it into action. Action is a behavior of living, while thinking is a behavior of the conscious only. And because life is larger than the conscious, action is larger than knowledge. This is particularly true for acting with love and respect.

The dynamics of actualizing potentiality and reconciliation are continuously evolving, not standing still. Life is not about taking a static position one way or the other in regard to growth and reconciliation. Instead, life evolves together with this dynamic. The meaning of an individual's life is derived from the spectrum arising out of the dynamics of actualizing potentiality and reconciliation; and the spectra from each individual aggregate into a flow of light that basically constitutes the evolutionary history of human beings. Current society is just a snapshot of one moment in this evolutionary chain.

<u>Reference</u>

- Fromm, Erich. *Man for Himself: An Inquiry Into the Psychology of Ethics* (New York: Henry Holt and Company, LLC, 1947).
- Fuller, Andrew R. *Psychology and Religion: Classical Theorists and Contemporary Developments* (Lanham, Maryland: Rowman & Littlefield Publishers, Inc., 2008, fourth edition).
- Fung, Yu-lan. *A Short History of Chinese Philosophy* (New York: Free Press, 1997).
- Jung, Carl. *The Archetypes and the Collective Unconscious* (London: Princeton University Press, 1990).
- Lu, Jiu-yuan. "Collected Works of Xiang-Shan," Vol. 36 "尧舜之前何书可读？" 陆九渊,《象山 全集》卷36.

CHAPTER 5

Methodologies

The previous two chapters have examined two very different domains of human mind activities: how human beings understand the external world and how we understand ourselves. Although the subjects are very different, there are similarities in some of the methodologies being used.

Methodologies from one domain, in concrete form, are generally not applicable to another domain. But a certain level of abstraction can be found to be applicable across domains. This level of abstraction is a type of metaphysics. *Often, truth is revealed as methodology itself, not the concrete content.* Due to this observation, it is useful to examine and summarize the most important generic methods. The purpose is to present them for reference, and we'll reexamine whether they can be applicable in later chapters.

5.1 "The Whole Is Larger than the Sum of Its Parts"

In plain language, this quote from Aristotle states the principle in a way that's easy to understand. In modern language, this principle is termed as emergence or synergy. Basically, it means that the interactions of the constituents of a complex system produce a coherent effect that cannot be derived from simple summation of effects from each individual element. Phenomena at the systemic level (macroscopic level) cannot be reduced to the microscopic level.

There is debate among the scientific community whether irreducibility introduces mystery, since the cause of a macroscopic phenomenon cannot be explained. Irreducibility means something is born from nothing. If the whole is larger than the sum of its parts, where does the delta come from? The delta cannot be traced down to the behavior of the constituents. This leaves room for mystical hypotheses to be invented and easily goes into a nonscientific domain. Vitalism is one such example. It claims that living organisms contain nonphysical elements or are governed by principles that are different from the physical world. Such ideas have been rejected in mainstream science. We should distinguish two statements here:

1) First is Aristotle's statement itself. Is such a statement just a hypothesis (even though it is a very sound assumption), or is there scientific fact? There are definitely scientific facts. In Chapter 2, we discussed the irreversibility of the second law of thermodynamics (moving from unequal probability of microscopic state to equal probability), and such irreversibility cannot be derived from the interaction of its elements. The language used to describe phenomena at systemic level cannot be simply derived from language that describes microscopic phenomena. They have to use different terminology. Quantum entanglement is another example showing that entangled particles cannot really be studied separately. A separation of entangled particles causes loss of information that cannot be recovered. One more example can be seen in nonlinear science. In deterministic chaos, even though the behavior of constituents is deterministic, the systemic level behavior is unpredictable, due to extreme sensitivity to initial conditions and the inability to obtain accurate initial values for the variables. With the advancement of scientific knowledge, it is more and more clear that the notion of reducing macroscopic phenomena to microscopic principle is just a special case.

2) Secondly, to explain the delta between the whole and the sum of its parts, hypotheses can be introduced, but they cannot be claimed as scientific hypotheses unless they strictly follow scientific methodology. Vitalism introduced a nonmaterial force that has been rejected by the mainstream scientific community. A more cautious approach should assume that the force or principle to explain the delta still comes from the material world, but we do not understand it with our current knowledge.

The fundamental reason that the whole is larger than the sum of its parts is due to the limitations in the way we acquire knowledge. When the whole is separated into parts to study, there is always loss of information. The loss of information cannot be recovered by adding the understanding of parts into a summation. Therefore, to describe the behavior of the whole accurately, a new set of concepts and principles need to be added. They still should strictly follow scientific methodology if they want to be considered scientific. However, when using the scientific method, the time it takes to prove new concepts and principles can be too long—beyond the life-span of an individual, so that people can choose to treat them as philosophical ideas or even religions. This is completely acceptable, as long as they don't call the new concepts and principles scientific.

When the same principle is applied to understanding human beings, it is seemingly more obvious. For example, we cannot reduce the principles in psychology to just neurobiological dynamics. To describe human behavior and the principle of human mental development, new language and new terminologies are needed. Sometimes the consequence of the emerging principle is not obvious. For example, the mind consists of two parts, the conscious and the unconscious, but the whole of the mind is larger than the sum of both parts, and the conscious will never completely understand the whole. Consequently, the life that represents the whole is larger than the knowledge that is the byproduct of the conscious. This consequently implies that action is more important than reflection. It is acceptable to acknowledge there is something one cannot fully understand before putting it into action. These observations are all rooted in the same principle of emergence. As another example, there are many interpretations of the statement "Man is the measure of all things." One meaning of this statement is that we need to treat the individual as an inseparable unit when measuring other human behaviors. Because of this inseparability, it has to be a human himself, not any other form of reduced knowledge or entity, who measures human behaviors.

5.2 Differentiation and Unification

Reality is a continuous field. Everything is connected directly or indirectly. When one attempts to understand that reality using language, there is always a dilemma. When a concept is defined, there is differentiation. When some parts of that reality are named, a simplification occurs. Now part of the continuous field is isolated, and this part is expressed as an atomic entity. There is a boundary now associated with it, and its connection with objects outside the boundary becomes the focus of communication. When there is differentiation, there is isolation. When there is isolation, there is need for reunification when the dynamics change among the concept and the objects outside the boundary.

When a concept is created with one dominant aspect, there are always conditions associated with it. When the condition or environment changes, the foundation for the concept that makes that concept valid and dominant is now invalid. The reason an entity is successful in a given environment can be the very reason for the entity to fail when conditions change. We see such phenomenon in social development, a person's life journey, or even a company's success or failure. When conditions change, the forces inside the ecosystem redefine their own meaning or their interrelationship. To reflect the new reality, a new concept is created to accommodate the new condition. This is a continuous evolution. The dialectic method from Hagel states a similar idea. The Chinese version of such methodology was stated by Lao-tzu: "Reversion is the movement of Tao." The only situation that can avoid such a cycle is an existence that does not depend on external conditions and is absolutely static. Such an existence is unimaginable; most of the time it is termed as supernatural or a concept of void (emptiness).

The uncertainty principle in quantum mechanics shows that the concepts of position and velocity of a classical object cannot be simultaneously defined for a quantum system. The concepts of position and velocity are a version of simplified definitions (i.e., differentiation) for a classical object. It works properly to describe the reality at the macroscopic level, but at the microscopic level where quantum effect takes place, these concepts must be modified and follow a very different set of quantum mechanical laws. The root cause of the dilemma of differentiation and reunification is not due to the language, but due to the change of dynamics in the reality. Concept and language simply reflect the reality. This is particularly true when it comes to the human mind. As described in Chapter 4, when the evolution of the human mind reached the point that consciousness emerged, the differentiation of the human mind occurred. The chaotic state of mind was completely changed. This was a reality, not a language dilemma. When consciousness emerged, the sense of isolation also emerged. They are the two sides of the same coin. Reunification is needed because consciousness only exists and is meaningful with respect to the unconscious. They cannot be separated.

When one component of the reality is dominant, it stands up and is differentiated from the rest of the wholeness. But this differentiation is only meaningful with respect to the rest of the wholeness. The standing up of a part of reality doesn't mean the rest of the reality disappears. Both sides coexist. Moreover, the dynamics between both sides define the meaning or value of the standing part, and reveal an aspect of the reality as the wholeness. The change of this dynamic introduces new understanding and new knowledge of the wholeness. The classical Tai Chi diagram depicts this dynamic quite well (refer to Figure 3).

5.3 Proxy to Reality (Metareality)

There are many situations where it is necessary to borrow a concept to solve a difficult problem, to reach the reality, even though the borrowed concept itself may not represent an actual physical reality, or it does not really matter whether the concept itself represents an actual physical reality. This methodology utilizes a proxy to reality. The entity that the borrowed concept represents is termed metareality.

This can be first easily explained with a simple math problem most middle school students know. There was an old man who was going to die. He had seventeen lambs and three children. In his will, he wanted the oldest child to have half of the lambs, the second child to have one third of the lambs, and the youngest child to have one ninth. After he died, the three children were puzzled on how to separate the lambs. They then asked a wise man. The wise man brought one more lamb. Now with eighteen lambs, the oldest child got nine, the second child got six, and the youngest got two. The wise man got the remaining lamb back. The problem was happily solved. In fact, the wise man could have brought just a virtual lamb made of paper and still solved the problem. Whether this extra piece is real or not is not crucial for the problem.

More seriously, the idea of proxy to reality is best demonstrated by the concept of wave function in quantum mechanics. There is no physical reality represented by the wave function, but it is a fundamental concept in describing the microscopic world through the Schrödinger equation. No one questions that the concept of wave function greatly helps us understand the reality of the atomic world.

The methodology of using proxy to understand reality is more important when it comes to the study of complex systems. Some scientists are pragmatic in this regard and are comfortable with this approach, but some aren't. It is a matter of different paths to the same goal. In the example of the seventeen lambs problem, one can continue to cut one of the lambs infinitely in order to solve a problem, or just borrow one and solve the problem elegantly. To reach a mountain top, one can climb the mountain foot by foot or just take a helicopter to the top. To describe the atomic world, physicists can use the concept of wave function or leave the puzzle unresolved. The choice is easy to make.

However, the borrowed concept cannot be arbitrary or pure conjecture. *It must be somehow connected to a reality that is measurable.* This is the critical distinction between a scientific approach versus a nonscientific approach. The reason to borrow a concept that is proxy to reality is due to the complexity of describing the reality under study. The situation is like a puzzle unresolved without a missing piece. By introducing the missing piece, the puzzle is solved with a *measurable* outcome. Therefore, even though the exact reality behind the borrowed concept is unknown, or the reality behind the borrowed concept is immeasurable with current knowledge and tools (hence termed as metareality), the method is still justified because the concept helps to solve the problem in question with a measurable outcome.

To look at this approach from another angle, when knowledge is generated and concepts are created, reality as a whole is separated. There are always simplifications associated with that. The reality as a whole is distorted or simplified to focus on concepts that are measurable. When it comes to a complex reality, it is highly possible that some parts of reality can be measured but other parts cannot be easily measured. However, the connection between the immeasurable part of reality and the measurable part cannot be described. A concept could be immeasurable due to the currently limited knowledge or tools. By introducing a concept that is a proxy to the immeasurable part, the reality as a whole can be better described. More outcomes of the measurable concepts can be detected, as we observe in the case of wave function in quantum mechanics. The concept of the Higgs particle in modern physics is a perfect example. The concept was initially introduced to explain the particle model. No one knew the actual reality behind it when it was introduced. After more than half a century, the reality behind the hypothesis was confirmed with the help of powerful computers that run complex data mining. The approach of using a proxy concept is also used in Jung's theory of the archetypes in the psyche and the concept of the fourth world in Chapter 3.

In summary, the approach of using a metaconcept as proxy to reality is not an irrational one; it is observed in modern physics and psychology. The key criteria to distinguish whether it is a scientific approach versus a nonscientific approach is whether such concept is connected to another concept that is measurable, and the connection (relationship) to the measurable concept can be clearly described. As long as such a relationship exists, what exactly the reality behind the metaconcept represents becomes less important, or even irrelevant. It can be revealed at a later time, even a very long time, but one should not stop using it as a result of suspicion.

5.4 Polymorphism

Polymorphism refers to the fact that a reality can be described with multiple theories. Why is this? As mentioned before, when humans create concepts and develop knowledge, there is always simplification, abstraction, and isolation associated with the process. It is very likely the same reality can be described by different models. If each of the models is a complete set of descriptions, these models are equivalent to each other.

This is the case for quantum mechanics, where the principles can be described with Schrödinger's equation, Heisenberg's matrix, or the Feynman's path integral, and all these descriptions can be shown to be equivalent.

But a complex situation is that the multiple models are not exactly equivalent—they are just reflecting the reality from different angles. It is similar to the intersection of a three-dimensional object with a two-dimensional plane. Intersecting at different angles on the same object yields a different two-dimensional shape. For a complex reality, due to the limitation of language, it is highly likely that multiple theories just describe different aspects of the same reality. In order to consolidate these different views of the same reality, a new language or a new perception must be developed first. This is particularly true for understanding the human mind, culture, or religion because of the complexity and the length of time required. To obtain the statistical view of the same reality, one should discard the notion of exclusivity of a particular culture or religion. An open mind with respect for other cultures and religions is a precondition for consolidated understanding.

A consolidated understanding can also be derived by searching the underlying root of the multiple representations, or through looking from a higher level of the same reality. Once the common root is identified or a higher level of perception is attained, the previous multiple representations can be explained in a bigger context and in a consistent way. To understand each variance of the different methodologies used to achieve the same goal, an objective, open-minded attitude—rather than in a preconceived mind-set—is a precondition.

5.6 Megastatistics

In a typical statistical study, a representative sample of population is observed and measured. The data collected are analyzed, then inferences are drawn about the population represented, accounting for randomness. The inference can be the correlation between two observed variables about the population. Inference can also extend to forecasting, prediction, and estimation of unobserved values associated with the population being studied. There are intrinsic limitations of the statistical approach. For example, correlation between two variables doesn't immediately imply there is a causal relationship; the sample may not be truly representative of the population, causing the inference bias. Nevertheless, the statistical approach remains a powerful tool given the fact that surveying the entire population to draw a conclusion is impractical in most situations. A method of inferring a relationship of variables at a systemic level by studying only a sample of the population is attractive and practical.

However, when applying the statistical methodology to infer potential principles of human social behaviors, particularly to study values, ethics, or culture, additional difficulties arise. Two new difficulties are mentioned here. First, the constituents of the population are human beings who have free will, complex minds, intelligence to acquire knowledge, and alter their behaviors based on the knowledge. Traditional statistics doesn't yet deal with systems with such constituents. Second, it is extremely difficult to find a representative sample due to the complexity and variety of individual minds and the tremendous geographical differences. It is also difficult to determine how long the sampling period should be. An ethical value is most likely formed after many generations. If we want to observe the sample over time to derive a statistical conclusion on the impacts of this ethical value, how long of an observation period is considered sufficient?

The problem of applying the statistical methodology to infer potential principles of human social behaviors can be stated as the following:

- Assume there is a hypothetical value that can be developed among the population. Let's also assume such value is beneficial to the population. The benefit should be observable by statistically surveying a sample of the population over a period of time. The statistical inference is given as criteria for accepting such value.
- The constituents of the population (i.e., individuals) know about such value and can choose to either follow it or not follow it.
- If all individuals choose to follow it, the value will be prevalent among the population. It is also easy within a short time to observe whether there is a benefit of this value as claimed.
- However, because the benefit of the value is a systemic level variable and may not be directly experienced, an individual can choose not to follow it.
- Because not all individuals follow the value, the statistical observation results of the benefit may turn out unconvincing. This in turn provides feedback to the population to potentially discourage an individual to follow the value.
- The above steps can get into a cycle, and eventually the hypothetical value will not be accepted.

If the value is indeed beneficial to the population, how can it become prevalent and accepted by a majority of the population? Here is the place where a belief can contribute to the process.

Assuming there is a group of individuals within the population who firmly believe in the value and the benefit it will bring. Their decision on whether to follow the value will not depend on feedback from the statistical observation. We can further classify two types of belief here. The first type is that these individuals consider the belief as absolute truth; it is a predestined truth, with no room for doubt and no need for approval. Let's call this absolute belief. The second type is a statistical belief. In this case, there is no need to assume a predestined absolute truth. The believers assume the benefits will be ultimately statistically self-evident, but the sampling process will take a long time, such as many generations. Therefore, even if the benefit of the value may not be observed or confirmed in the current generation, it doesn't mean the value itself is invalid. The benefit of the value will be statistically proven if the sampling period is sufficiently long and the samples are geographically diverse. Is there a more quantified model to describe the second type of believing process?

Bayes's theorem can be borrowed to more precisely describe the above thoughts. Bayes's theorem deals with updating inferring probability given new evidence. In its simplest form, it can be written as:

$$P(H|E) = \frac{P(E|H) \times P(H)}{P(E)}$$

where:

- H denotes a hypothesis (or belief), E denotes an evidence after observation.
- $P(H|E)$ is the probability of H (or the degree of belief in H) given the evidence E.
- $P(E|H)$ is the probability of E given the hypothesis H is true. This is also called *likelihood*.
- $P(H)$ is the prior probability of H (or the degree of belief in H). In many cases, this is just a constant.
- $P(E)$ is the probability that evidence E will occur for all possible hypotheses. It is also called *marginal likelihood*.

Bayes's theorem has the following mathematical properties:

- When $P(H) = 0$, $P(H|E) = 0$. That is, if the prior degree of belief is null, the posterior degree of belief is always null regardless of any new evidence.
- Similarly, if $P(H) = 1$, $P(H|E) = 1$. That is, if the prior degree of belief is 1, the posterior degree of belief is always 1, regardless of any new evidence. This is the first type of absolute belief mentioned earlier.
- If $(P(E|H))/(P(E)) > 1$, $P(H|E) > P(H)$. That is, the evidence favors the hypothesis, and the updated degree of belief with the evidence is larger than the prior degree of belief.
- If $(P(E|H))/(P(E)) < 1$, $P(H|E) < P(H)$. That is, the evidence discourages the hypothesis, and the updated degree of belief with the evidence is less than the prior degree of belief.

Example: In a city, there are only green taxis or blue taxis. Green taxis are 60 percent of the total, and blue taxis 40 percent. When a taxi is involved in an accident, witnesses report the color to the police with an accuracy of 90 percent. On a particular day, a taxi is involved in a car accident. A witness reported it was a blue taxi. What is the probability that the taxi is indeed blue? Before the witness report, it is natural to assume the probability that the taxi involved in the accident is blue is P(accident taxi is blue) = 0.4. With the new evidence from the witness, intuitively, the probability should be higher. Let's check with Bayes's theorem for P(accident taxi is blue|witness reports blue). It is known that P(witness reports blue|accident taxi is blue) = 0.9. P(witness reports blue) = P(accident taxi is blue) × P(accuracy) + P(accident taxi is green) × (1–P(accuracy)) = 0.4 × 0.9 + 0.6 × 0.1 = 0.42. P(accident taxi is blue|witness reports blue) = 0.9 × 0.4 / 0.42 = 0.86. Therefore, with the new evidence from the witness, the probability increases from 0.4 to 0.86. If there is a second witness who also reports that the taxi in the accident was blue, we can update the probability again. Now the prior probability of a blue taxi being involved in the accident is 0.86 (hence the probability for a green taxi involved in the accident is 0.14). The updated probability will be P(accident taxi is blue|2 witness reports blue) = 0.9 × 0.86 / (0.86 × 0.9 + 0.14 × 0.1) = 0.98. If, however, the second witness reports the taxi in the accident was green, the updated probability is 0.1 × 0.86 / (0.86 × 0.1 + 0.14 × 0.9) = 0.4. Reports from both witnesses cancel out the updates to the probability.

The above example of consecutive observations can be generalized in mathematical form. Assuming multiple observations yield multiple evidences, $E_i \in \{E\}$ where $\{E\}$

is the evidence space. Iterating the Bayes's theorem sequentially for all the evidences, the degree of belief is updated as:

$$P(H|E_1, E_2, \dots E_n) = \prod_{i=1}^{n} \frac{P(E_i|H) \times P(H)}{P(E_i)}$$

Noted from the example of a taxi accident, the calculation of $P(E_n)$ depends on the prior probability $P(H|E_1, E2, \dots E_{n-1})$. In theory, when the number of observation is sufficiently large, the degree of belief may approach a stable value P_f, which is given by:

$$P_f = \lim_{n \to \infty} P(H|E_1, E_2, \dots E_n) = \lim_{n \to \infty} \left[\prod_{i=1}^{n} \frac{P(E_i|H)}{P(E_i)} \right] \times P(H)$$

Most literature on applications of Bayesian inference is based on the assumption that the *likelihood* can be objectively determined. However, in reality, this term is subjective, or at best it has a probability distribution. If the evidence is based on measurement, there is measurement error associated with the evidence, hence the likelihood cannot be completely determined. Let's consider an example of using Bayesian inference on human ethical development:

- Let H denote a hypothesis of the famous teaching "Treat others the way you want to be treated, and you will be well treated."
- Let E denote evidence that an individual experiences he is well treated.
- $P(H)$ is the prior probability that H is true (the degree of belief in H). Before any evidence, it is fair to assume $P(H) = 0.5$. The teaching is equally true and false without evidence.
- $P(E)$ is the probability that evidence E will occur for all possible hypotheses, i.e., the probability of an individual reporting he is well treated by others regardless of the hypothesis.

Since there is evidence that an individual experiences he is well treated by others, intuitively one would expect $P(H|E)$ will increase. But it really depends on the value of $P(E|H)$: given that the teaching of "Treat others the way you want to be treated, and you will be well treated" is true, what is the probability one will be well treated by others?

There are many factors here, even if an individual treats another person the way she wants to be treated, it is possible that the other person does not perceive the same value. Or for any of many other reasons, the other person doesn't treat the first individual well in return. It is natural to assume the value of $P(E|H)$ is subjective instead of objective. And because it is subjective, there is a possibility that a subjective factor (such as a belief) can influence the probability density such that $(P(E|H))/(P(E)) > 1$, which leads to the increase of value $P(H|E)$. If the belief of an individual can influence the value of $P(E|H)$, a bias factor C can be introduced to represent this. The posterior will be instead updated with $(C \times P(E|H))/(P(E))$. If the bias $C > 1$, it will increase the $P(H|E)$ compared to without the bias. This updating process can be iterated over a long period of observation with $E_i \in \{E\}$. Mathematically, the modified posterior probability is given by:[4]

$$P'(H|E_1, E_2, \dots E_n) = \prod_{i=1}^{n} \frac{C_i \times P(E_i|H) \times P(H)}{P(E_i)}$$

$$= \left(\prod_{i=1}^{n} C_i \right) \times P(H|E_1, E_2, \dots E_n)$$

The net impact of the belief can be expressed as a mathematical form:

$$\Delta P = P'_f - P_f = \lim_{n \to \infty} P'(H|E_1, E_2, \dots E_n) - \lim_{n \to \infty} P(H|E_1, E_2, \dots E_n)$$

$$= \lim_{n \to \infty} \left[\left(\prod_{i=1}^{n} C_i \right) - 1 \right] \times P(H|E_1, E_2, \dots E_n)$$

In real life, infinite evidence is impractical. As long as sufficient sampling leads the update of $P(H|E)$ to an acceptable value, it is reasonable to accept the hypothesis as true. However, it is also difficult to quantify what sufficient sampling means. It depends on how fast $P(H|E)$ increases. It can be within the life-span of an individual, but it can also take many generations to get $P(H|E)$ to the acceptable level. *Therefore, in a particular person's life-span, one may only experience a fraction of a time period needed for the hypothesis to be confirmed.* This is a strange interaction between the individual with the hypothesis, because he may not obtain the benefit of following the hypothesis during

---

4 A more rigorous mathematical treatment of the problem is needed.

his life-span. *It is a matter of choice: following the current interest or trying to align your life to the potential truth behind the hypothesis, which one is more important?* A person with deeper self-awareness most likely will choose the latter, therefore the power of belief is lived out. He may not obtain the current benefit, but he probably has deeper and profounder satisfaction because he feels a deeper sense of eternal existence. In order to sustain the belief in the hypothesis, people may rely on a supernatural. There is a rational reason behind it, but the hypothesis takes a long time to be proven. To detect the potential truth behind the hypothesis before its probability reaches an acceptable level, a person has to be very objective and honest. "Honest" here implies there is external absolute reality or existence, and you have to set your thinking, mind-set, and feelings to align with it, as best you can. When you are able to do that, you can bypass the process needed for the probability of the hypothesis to reach an acceptable level.

The sampling to test a hypothesis is not only based on feedback from individuals, but also comes from demographic and geographic data. The time scale can be long enough that historical data is needed. The demographic scale can be large such that populations of different groups around the world must be surveyed. The geographic scale can be large such that different major cultures are considered. Plus, with the difficulty of the subjective nature of the term *likelihood*, testing a hypothesis is very difficult and a new model of statistics is needed. Such an extended approach to statistics is termed *megastatistics*.

5.7 Nonlinearity

Methodology is about the thinking patterns of the human mind. The thinking patterns of the human mind were greatly influenced by the evolution of science and technology. This is because the advancement of science and technology provides strong confidence. Through scientific knowledge, we are able to explain the movement of the solar system; control atomic reactions; and to predict, for example, the bending of light near the sun. The confidence is so high that we start to generalize this thinking pattern beyond these successes. Some of these thinking patterns are described in Chapter 3, but they are highlighted again here:

- The whole can be understood by deciphering the parts and then adding them together.
- When there is a result, there is always a cause behind it that can be clearly identified and understood.

- Acknowledge there are two sides of the same coin for many phenomena. But only see the interaction of the two sides using a very simple model: either black or white; only one side plays a dominant role at a given time.
- Determinism. The future can be predicted based on knowledge today. Randomness is just fluctuation that will fade away as time passes.
- Certainty. There is a need and desire for certainty; we are uncomfortable with an uncertain world or with uncertain knowledge.
- Order must be designed; it cannot be born from within or self-organized.
- There is always a clear distinction between the observer and the system being observed. The influence between the observer and the observed can be ignored.

However, with the advancement of studies on nonlinear and complex systems, the above methodologies have proved to be incorrect or to have limitations. New methodologies were developed for nonlinear and complex systems. The new thinking pattern may be used as a reference for other fields, such as social sciences. At the very least, one should avoid using the linear methodology whenever possible. Nonlinear methodology has been discussed in detail in Chapter 3. Important aspects are captured here again:

- Randomness is not just noise of a deterministic mechanism. Instead, both are playing important roles in describing complex systems. Randomness and determinism are complementary. This is seen in the chaotic system where the behavior can be infinitely sensitive to initial conditions.
- Uncertainty can be a dominant factor. Certainty and determinism are just a special case of nature. Humans have a tendency to seek certainty and deterministic futures. However, the drive for this tendency is born of the need for a sense of safety or a feeling of control. Unfortunately, certainty and determinism cannot be the basis for most complex systems, especially social behavior. We need to discard such drive and the dependency on certainty and determinism for the sense of safety and control. Instead we should acknowledge that uncertainty is the basis for real life.
- Self-organization without an intelligent designer. Even though the future is unpredictable, and uncertainty is the basis of real life, it doesn't mean everything is random and ad hoc. The mechanism in a self-organized system provides hints to how a constituent in a self-organized system interacts with

systemic behavior. There can be higher level (system level) processes that are influencing systemic behavior, but that are beyond the comprehension of each constituent's intelligence. The self-organized system follows an evolution path that depends on each step of interactions among the constituents in the system, but which the constituents are unaware of this evolution path. The fundamental point here is that the constituent itself is both an actor (influencing) and a follower (being influenced). The interaction is reciprocal and not easy to describe in linear format.

- Goal and process are inseparable. For a complex system such as a society, because the element (a human being) is an actor (influencing) and a follower (being influenced) at the same time, the individual will not be able to know the end goal (or the final destination). In such a situation, the goal and the process are inseparable. *The society's destination and evolutionary path exist but are unknown to the individual, even while the destination and path depend on each step of interactions among the individuals.* The individual knows the society as a whole is evolving and depends on the effort of each step of interaction, but he doesn't know the exact destination. All he can do is influence the next step. "Do your best," and "Focus on the here and now," are the most valuable teachings in such a situation. In fact, this becomes the responsibility of an individual in a society. The underlying reason for this is a nonlinear logic: goal and process are inseparable. It is an important methodology for future reference. In a conventional thinking pattern, one would want to know the goal before taking action. But this is not always possible. He or she will either have to adapt to the new thinking pattern and become comfortable with it, or make up a goal and go for it. The latter approach of making up a goal is like trying to fit a complex nonlinear process into a linear thinking pattern. Many people prefer this approach because it is easier to follow. The problem is that in order to intentionally separate goal and process, the goal is set subjectively, instead of naturally revealed. Hence, it is difficult to get people to accept the goal naturally. For a similar reason, cause and effect are not always separable. The conventional view that an effect is always due to a cause, and both effect and cause are two separable sequences, is not always true. We have to get used to such nonlinear logic.

Part II—The Applications

In Part I, the focus is on how human beings acquire knowledge of the external world and how much human beings know of themselves. Methodologies behind the knowledge creation and their influence on our thinking habits are summarized at the end of Part I. These understandings form the foundation for further understanding of higher-level activities of huma minds. In Part II, the focus will be shifted to the application of the foundation from Part I to these higher-level human activities, particularly with regard to belief, religion, and culture. The understanding of these higher-level activities eventually will help to answer the ultimate question of the meaning of life as a human being.

CHAPTER 6

Philosophies of Belief and Religion

6.1 Belief and Religion

t is difficult to define exactly what belief is and what religion is. There are overlaps among the definitions of philosophy, belief, religious practice, and religion. Further, historically, religion has been misused or practiced incorrectly, such that it has a bad image. Although it is not an easy task to clearly define these concepts, we can at least list the major characteristics of each concept, as shown in the table below:

Concept	Main characteristics (Not a definition)
Science	Knowledge or inference that can be proved or falsified through observation, measurement, or induction.
Philosophy	Ideas, perception, inference that are based on rational thoughts. These ideas may or may not be able to be proved or falsified, but they are nevertheless results of rational thoughts.
Belief system	A belief system can be based on a philosophy, but also add assumptions, hypotheses, or psychological feelings that cannot be derived through purely rational thinking. A belief can be based on deep feeling or voice from the heart.

	Note that a belief can also be derived from a logical extension of rational reasoning, due to the limitations of rational knowledge. This is a critical distinction between a belief and a superstition. A belief can sometimes be justified due to the methodology used. A belief system can be just personal experience, or can be practiced as organized social activities.
Religion	A belief system put into practice through organized social activities, rituals, and worship. The level of rational reasoning decreases as compared to just a belief system. Similar to a belief system, some of the religious practices can be justified as methodological extension in order to deal with complex concepts. Religion can be theistic or atheistic.
Theism	Religion based on the existence of a supernatural God. The supernatural becomes the center of the whole belief system.

There is no conflict between rational reasoning and belief. As explained in Chapter 4, rational reasoning is related to an individual's self-awareness. As a human increases self-awareness, she intuitively touches or feels the external reality. This is just like a circle that keeps expanding in a plane; the larger the circle (meaning the more knowledge that is inside the circle), the more the circle will touch the unknown boundary. The more one knows, the more unknown one faces. Sooner or later, the limitation of intelligence is reached. At this point, one can decide to just believe what the intuition reveals without further rational explanation. Therefore, the more the consciousness of an individual, the more she may intuitively touch the truth, and the greater degree she derives a belief. It is a logical extension of human intelligence.

The expansion of knowledge in the history of our civilization helped to advance the explanation and control of the external world, and it also helped increase self-awareness for an individual. The deeper a person is aware of the self and truth, the more knowledge that will be revealed. Before intuitive thinking becomes knowledge— meaning it can be repeated or approved and communicated among individuals without doubt—we have to leverage this preknowledge. The intuitions exist and influence us and we cannot ignore them. Hence we *rationally* choose to "believe" them. Some of these beliefs can be wrong and some of them might be revealed to be true. A person who is more honest, more self-consistent, and in harmony with the self—the more truth he can touch and feel, especially when we talk about the truth of complex systems. Practically, there are two components for a belief:

- Rational component. A belief is only needed when rational reasoning is exhausted. The end of rational thinking is the start of a belief. Without this step, the belief is more likely a superstition. Therefore, when human intelligence advances, the bar of this component will be higher. This component distinguishes a belief from a superstitious idea.
- Psychological component. It has to be accepted by the heart comfortably. To reach this level, it first must pass the rational criteria mentioned above. Secondly, it must feel synchronization with the inner voice of the heart. The belief must be consistent with other personal values.

Both components are very personalized, because each individual's level of intelligence is different, and each individual's approach to listen to the voice from the heart is also different. The two together determine whether an individual can truly believe a hypothesis. Religion is an organized belief system adding many rituals. Because rituals and organization are added by humans, there are factors of human intention here. It is not only logical to state that these human intentions cannot hold truth forever, but it is also natural to raise concerns about the risks of misuse of such intentions and malpractice of the belief system underlying the religion. The reason that religions are organized was for people to feel connected and for the belief system to be spread among larger populations and passed down from generation to generation. There was success in that such method, which attracted more believers. But is organized activity a necessity? A natural, unorganized belief system can also be shared without purposely organizing it. People can still feel connected once they share experiences and thoughts. A genuine belief system is a combination of philosophy and psychology at work in real life; it is deeply rooted in an individual's sincerity and honesty to the heart. The believer acts by listening to the inner voice of the heart, instead of just following rules and guidelines set by cultural or moral teaching. People can feel connected if they all listen to their hearts, because there is common ground in such voices, as explained in Chapter 4 when discussing the fourth world.

An important justification for the value of religion is that due to the complexity of the human mind's process, the journey to understand how the process works is difficult for many people and can take a long time. Religion utilizes organized belief or moral teaching in an attempt to shorten the process by introducing methods beyond the comprehension of rational thinking at a particular historical period. Western religion introduced a God, while Eastern religions emphasized self-awakening, but the purpose is similar: a rebirth of the self and sensitivity to the inner voice, an awakening to realization of the meaning of life. As mentioned earlier, a belief has two components, a rational component and a psychological component. These two components are very personal. Religion addresses the needs of a shortcut process by introducing *additional* methods such as personalized supernatural or other organized belief system. These additional methods or concepts introduced by religion are supposed to get people to reach the state of "true belief" more easily, either from the rational angle or from the psychological angle. In short, a belief is an intuitive extension of our intellectual limitations, and a religion is the irrational extension of our intellectual limitations. Because a belief system and a religion are sometimes difficult to separate, the two terms are interchangeable in this chapter.

When a belief or religion is perceived as a methodological extension of our intellectual limitations, there are several important implications. Firstly, there can be many methodological extensions to shorten the self-awakening and reconciliation process; they do not necessarily mutually exclude each other. Many religions can coexist. Second, once the methods introduced by religion become a norm, there is a complicated convolution of the methods and the end goal of self-awakening and reconciliation. It becomes very difficult to separate both. When the intelligence of mankind advances, the threshold to reach a belief increases too due to the rational component of a belief. The methods introduced by religion must evolve as well. However, most religions are not evolved. This causes an incompatibility between the method and the end goal. The advancement of human intelligence alters the threshold to reach a belief, but it doesn't change the need for self-awakening and reconciliation (one of the end goals of religions). The truth behind religions are coupled with the methodology used in ancient times in order to achieve the state of belief. Methodology must be changed for the same end goal, as modern people can't accept the methods used in religion. *Unfortunately, most religions reject the idea of change because the method and contents are so convoluted, they are afraid a change of method would deteriorate the foundation of belief. The result is that people discard religion altogether, including the truth and underlying teachings, which is an unwise choice.*

It is important to understand the truth behind religion and separate that from the methods used to enforce the teaching. This will not only help to recover the truth behind religions but also allow possible reconciliation among different religions. It is also important to realize that the drive for belief and religion is deeply rooted in the human deficiency in self-control of our intellect or other limitations, and in our need for reunification to Mother Nature,. The need for belief and religion will not go away, regardless of advancement of human intelligence. If the understanding of belief and religion is inaccurate and incomplete, and if we don't have an objective attitude toward beliefs and religion, it is highly probable that we will, sooner or later, fall into some forms of immature religion. Less awareness means less control of risk mitigation. If there is no guidance or deep understanding, and one just takes a simple, extreme view, then our potential and needs are not well addressed. We ought to be able to distinguish which are good beliefs and which are bad ones.

The goal of this chapter is to decipher the truth behind belief and religion. Major efforts include the following:

1. First of all, it is important to examine the root and origin of belief and religion. If these roots and origins are timeless, that is, intrinsic to humans regardless of the evolution history of the mind, then they should not be ignored and should be addressed in one way or another. Religion is one of the ways to address these intrinsic needs of human beings.

2. Decouple the contents of a belief system from the methodologies used in the belief system. Religion can provide a platform to channel the intrinsic needs but can also purposely or accidentally manipulate such needs. A religion can easily fall into superstition. Therefore, it is important to carefully examine the major methodologies utilized by religions. Some of these methodologies are acceptable as they are consistent with those discussed in Chapter 5. By doing so, the need to rely on myth is reduced—although it is impossible to eliminate it. As time passes, in some situations, the methods remain acceptable and the content needs to evolve; in other situations, the content remains acceptable and the method needs to evolve. It is possible that even though one may not agree with the method used, he still believes in the content behind the method. Furthermore, by decoupling the methodology from the content, it is easier to distinguish truths that are intrinsic to human beings, versus rules and rituals that were added by religious institutions. This in turn helps to detect potential malpractice of a religion.

3. Based on examining the origins of religion and decoupling the contents and methodologies, the criteria to distinguish a good religion from a bad religion can be established.

This chapter will not focus on the exact contents of any belief or religion. It is more important to examine the truth behind a belief or religion, rather than the religion itself. Hence the discussion in this chapter is generic to any religion.

6.2 The Psychological Roots of Religion

A belief is a hypothesis that cannot be fully explained by rational reasoning, but it guides an individual's decisions and actions. Why do humans need a belief system or religion to support our value systems, to guide our behaviors? What is the value of a belief? Is such need a permanent phenomenon or a temporal behavior that can be eliminated as knowledge advances? To answer these questions, one will need to explore the origins of a belief system, and subsequently, a religion. There are multiple aspects of such origins, namely, the psychological, rational, and methodological aspects.

Psychological Root

The most intrinsic need for a belief system is rooted in the development process of the human mind, which is discussed extensively in Chapter 4. This psychological root is not just a virtual contemplation, because the development process of the human mind is real.

As discussed in Chapter 4, the awakening of human consciousness was a breakthrough in the evolution of our intelligence (Fuller, 197–200). But at the same time, it was a separation of the conscious part of the mind from the wholeness of the mind. The conscious cannot exist without its root—the wholeness of the mind. Because of this fundamental relationship, the conscious part of the mind, after developing to a certain level of maturity—stage three in the model of mind development cycle—will seek reconciliation with the wholeness of mind. This tendency is a permanent need, regardless of how advanced human intelligence becomes. A mature mind must go through this phase for a complete cycle. But in reality, many people are unaware of this need for reconciliation, the need is buried by the busy routine of life. A prerequisite for reaching stage three of mind development is that the conscious must acknowledge its own limitation as only a part of wholeness, and the intellect must acknowledge its root from the wholeness of mind that comprises both the conscious and the unconscious. It must not position itself as a dominant force in the bigger picture of the whole mind. This is not an easy step. *As long as the intellect attempts to understand a hypothesis, the mind will not enter a genuine believing state for that hypothesis.* Because this step can be painful, an irrational approach can be easier than the rational approach to help people to get through this step.

It is the nature of the human mind that we tend to overthink, overly rely on our intellect, and overstretch our will. This tendency can get us lost, making it difficult to follow natural laws, know where our limits are, refrain from willfulness, and follow the inner voice. Religion provides a practical approach to remedy this deficiency. In a theistic religion, by acknowledging and believing in an external superior existence, the mind can have dialogue with something that is superior to itself. This remedies the tendency of overthinking, overreacting, or being too willful. The result is that the life of the mind is more balanced and more harmonious. At this point, sometimes the existence the mind is communicating with becomes less important, because it has already produced a positive impact on the health of the mind. Different religions may use different methods, but the essence is the same. People who don't realize the importance of having something the mind can submit to, are more easily get into situations of fighting with their own egos. Their intelligence, their self, can become a hindrance when dealing with other people or situations that are out of their control.

It is quite logical to realize the need for a religious approach when dealing with psychological processes such as the reunification of the conscious mind with the unconscious mind. A rational approach comes from the conscious part of the mind. Using the conscious part of the mind (rational approach) to understand the unconscious part is by definition contradictory, because when the unconscious part can be rationally understood, it becomes conscious. Since it is impossible to understand and control the unconscious part using conscious rationale, it leaves room for a religious approach to fill the gap. The above reasoning implies that a belief system that can fill up the gap will have the following characteristics:

- A belief is a hypothesis that cannot be proven through rational reasoning.
- A belief system is to connect the conscious to the whole. However, the unconscious part of the mind is subtle to detect. It requires sincerely listening to the heart in order to function well.
- Since the conscious self cannot completely understand the wholeness, it can borrow virtual concepts (such as the supernatural) to help the dialogue

- between the conscious and the whole self. It needs such a concept that is bigger than itself in order to submit to the whole mind.
- The interests of the conscious and the unconscious will not always be the same. There can even be hidden conflicts of interest. A belief system guides the resolution of conflict.
- The principles for the conscious part can be written down and easily passed to future generations, but the principles for the unconscious part can only be experienced. Therefore, practicing a belief system is a very personal experience and difficult to pass around or share with others. This is one of the reasons that organized belief systems (i.e., religions) are needed.

Many possible belief systems can fulfill psychological needs. Two examples are discussed here.

- In Christianity, original sin is a concept describing what happens when a person's mind doesn't follow the truth. This can be due to the difficulty of understanding the actual needs of the unconscious mind, or that the conscious part doesn't realize the truth or doesn't want to follow it due to a temporary conflict of interest. The root of original sin is in the emergence of consciousness that is separate from wholeness, which is intrinsic to any human being. How to solve the problem? In Christianity, God is the supernatural entity that solves the problem. God, for the conscious part of the mind, represents the external absolute truth; and for the unconscious part of the mind, God is a useful entity to help manage the mind. Believing in an eternal existence that is much bigger than the self surely helps to let the mind follow it.
- Taoism introduced a concept of Tao, a superior but invisible force that the human intellect cannot comprehend. It governs how things develop and interact. The human intellect must follow Tao.

Carl Jung's Theory

The idea that a belief system or religion links the conscious and the unconscious was proposed by Jung. Jung believed that the symbols used in worship and the mythical nature of religion are manifestations of the unconscious to the conscious (Fuller, 84–88). Religions around the world are meant to solve the same problem: redemption from the conflict of opposites through a meditation symbol and unification of the opposites. Myth is unavoidable in religion. According to Jung:

- As long as there's an unconscious part of the human mind, there will be a need for religion as the connection between the conscious and the unconscious.
- Consciousness will never be able to understand the unconscious. Therefore, myth is necessary as symbol (or language) to represent the unconscious. Consequently, myth is a must for any religion.
- Jung opposed any attempt to purge mythical elements (such as the virgin birth and the resurrection in Christianity) from a religion. Because the function of religion is to keep people connected to the conscious and the unconscious, which is represented by "eternal myth," to prove this eternal myth with a scientific approach is meaningless unless religion is no longer needed. That is, a religion without myth is useless (Fuller, 87). "God is neither an idea in need of proof nor an object to be blindly believed in" but a fact in the psyche (Fuller, 81). There is no need to believe in it because it is an experience, a fact in the psyche.

Jung gave a very detailed mapping of Christian religious symbols to his psychological concepts. In his theory, the Father represents the unconscious of the world. The Son is the religious symbol for the conscious. Resurrection means the reconciliation. The Christian doctrine of the Son being separated from the Father, crucified, and resurrected basically reflects the maturing process an individual mind must go through (Fuller, 89–93). Jung's theory on religion is an excellent example of how religion reveals truth in psychology, but in a very indirect way.

Essentially, Jung attempted to establish a philosophical and psychological foundation for religion. He looked beyond religious rituals and viewed them as symbols reflecting the psychological structure of the human mind. He also explained why religion needs to be based on myth. This is crucial to resurrecting religious practice in the modern age. Religion has a lot of values in human life, particularly in dealing with psychology and the mind. But because of its ties to myths and miracles, it leaves a lot of people unable to believe, and hence they cannot experience the benefits of the practice of religion. Now, by providing a philosophical and psychological foundation and explaining the relationship between the unconscious and the conscious, Jung's theory can bring more people to have stronger and healthier minds and interpersonal relationships and positive goals in life, which can help to fulfill the primary benefits of religion.

In the Jungian theory, there is a component of myth. This is inevitable when any theory wants to fully account for the unconscious, unless the human mind is becoming totally conscious. The unconscious of the mind is incomprehensible to the rational mind; one can infer what it does but not what it is. Therefore, any theory on the unconscious cannot be explained by any other theory. It has to make some assumptions, and because of this, we expect there will be many different theories on the unconscious. Other approaches, such as statistical methodology, should be added to obtain truth about how the unconscious interacts with the conscious. Jung's theory is nevertheless a profound start toward minimizing the possibility of religion becoming a superstition or misleading practice.

One of the myths in Jungian psychology is the concept of the collective unconscious. How to understand the meaning of the collective unconscious? First, let's examine the meaning of a collective conscious. In Jung's language, the collective conscious is all the knowledge of mankind. Human reasoning has a lot of limitations, and individual effort to reach the truth is practically impossible. But through statistical effort, or collective effort from all intellectual minds, knowledge is closer to reality. The word "collective" means using a statistical approach, especially the megastatistical approach (see Chapter 5). This analogy can be applied to understanding the collective unconscious. It is "collective" because it is not specific to a particular individual. Instead, it is a depository of millions of years of experiences of human beings. The collective unconscious is revealed through a concept called archetypes. Archetypes are common experiences of the human mind, the statistical average of unconscious minds, and hence it is a social and systemic phenomenon. Based on the methodology analysis in Chapter 5, laws that govern systemic behavior may not be able to be derived from laws that govern the constituents. Hence, a new concept must be introduced. According to Jung, Western religion essentially projects the archetype as God, which is a symbol manifesting the archetype in the conscious part of the mind (Fuller, 80). It is from this common ground that each individual can share experiences and develop relationships. In Western religion, this is through worship and prayer with a group of people, such as in a church. It becomes necessary to share the experience to achieve the statistical effect so people can be closer to the archetype—the God in the psyche.

In the Jungian theory, the archetype is a static concept. We don't know what it is and can only know it through experiences like dreams, an "oceanic feeling," or religious experience. But how does such a concept, derived from millions of years of deposition of human experience, govern modern minds that discover new knowledge and undergo lots of new experience? Archetypes, if they exist, should be evolving some-how as time passes. Rather than calling this mythical concept archetypes, I would call them laws for the unconscious, or truth for the unconscious. Such kinds of laws have similar characteristics as the laws of science and nature. They exist regardless of whether you believe or not. In the conscious world, we approach truth through knowledge and the statistical effort of intellectuals. Similarly, we can try to understand how the laws of the unconscious affect us through methods such as religion, medita-tion, dream analysis, etc., and statistically as well. The archetype as an entity is static, but the way we understand it can change as time goes by. By definition, there is always a component to the archetype that cannot be comprehended. The portion that we understand can change, but the whole may be unchanging. As any of the concepts for metareality, there can be multiple interpretations for it.

The concept of the collective unconscious not only can be used to explain the unification of the individual self, but also can be used as a connection channel be-tween individuals. As explained in Chapter 4, the principles of interpersonal relation-ships are not completely driven by the conscious. The unconscious plays an important part as well. The concept of love is a manifestation of such a principle. Love is not purely rational. Love is superior to justice because justice mostly comes from the con-scious world, but love comes from the world of wholeness. This is essentially the core of Christianity and many other religions. *Consequently, the highest moral in human relationships is love, not justice, because love encompasses both justice and a feeling of well-being for the individual.*

The concept of archetype for the unconscious can be extended to the external world. There is always a big portion of the external world that is incomprehensible to the human mind. But we will have to deal with it, and in fact that part of the world is connected to the parts of the world we understand. We don't know what it is, but we can infer what it does. This is very similar to the quantum mechanics interpreta-tion of wave function. It is possible that quantum mechanics is dealing with a portion of reality that cannot be described with current knowledge, but that part of reality still interacts with the observable part of reality and produces observable results. The quantum entanglement effect, for example, reveals certain aspects of this unknown part of reality. A concept to describe such metareality is needed. These concepts for metareality, either the archetypes in the psyche, or unknown parts of the world, are often collectively referred to in Western culture as God. There will be more analysis on this in a later section.

Summary

Religions are built upon the understanding of human beings. A human has both a conscious and an unconscious. On one hand, humans are the only creature on Earth that has such an advanced conscious mind. Through it, humans have developed language, built scientific knowledge about the external world, and also recognized that life is limited and we shall die in the end. On the other hand, the human mind is a combination of both the conscious and the unconscious. A complete and harmonious life will have to take good care of both components of the mind. They are not disconnected. Both can drive each other equally. The conscious mind functions through reasoning, logic, and language. It differentiates the human mind from a chaotic, undeveloped state. The unconscious mind, however, functions with complementary methods. Religion is one such tool. Both rational and irrational approaches are needed for a complete mind to function well.

The psychological roots of religion originate from the intrinsic dilemma of the emergence of consciousness. A symbol can be introduced to reflect the metareality that is necessary to help the reconciliation process of the separated mind. This concept, be it called archetype, "image of God in the psyche," or the self, essentially means your mind is not only occupied by the ego, but is also driven by a set of principles that governs the self as a whole. As described in Chapter 4, the psychological development process of the mind follows its own set of principles, progresses through each stage. How to make the process easy to follow even before we fully understand it is the subject of many religions. Religious practice usually introduces symbols or personalized figures that help a person to follow the principles quicker and more easily. Behind the scenes of many religions, the psychological foundation is similar. People following a religious practice can feel the benefit of following a correct psychological development process, hence can emotionally attach to the symbol or figure afterward. This is all good for the development of the mind. However, one should not expect that these symbols or figures can alter the external world in your favor. That is superstitious thinking. We will discuss this point further in the next subsections.

6.3 The Rational Roots of Religion

It is a typical misconception that any belief or religious practice is based on irrational reasoning. If a belief or religious practice is based purely on irrational reasoning, it is just a superstition. However, a mature and valuable belief system is an *extension* of rational reasoning. It is an intuitive reasoning used when rational reasoning is exhausted. Therefore, to determine whether or not a belief system is pure superstition or an *extension* of rational reasoning, we will need to know the limitations of rational reasoning, including the limitations of the byproduct of human rational reasoning—knowledge. Not only that, we also need to understand the limitations of rational methodology itself and the limitations of human cognition. It is this need to reach the limitation before taking an intuitive belief that lays the rational foundation for a belief or religion. If there is no limitation from human knowledge and human cognitive capabilities, there is perhaps no need for any intuitive belief. All the myths in religion would be explained sooner or later. Unfortunately, that is not the reality. The limitation of rational reasoning is precisely a root for belief and religion.

Limitation of Knowledge

The limitation of knowledge has been explained in Chapter 2. The key points are summarized here:

- The universe is infinite, so the intellectual power required to understand everything in the universe is infinite. However, human life is finite, and the sum of human intellectual power, plus the power of observation tools and lab facilities, is always finite. Hence it is impossible to accomplish the demand of understanding everything in the universe. The more we know, the more of the unknown that is exposed to us.
- Because there are always limitations to what we can know, the next layer of truth is blocked by the current knowledge. This is like a typical scenario on a mountain. When you are on a mountain and look up at the peak, you think it is the top of the mountain. But when you climb up to the peak, you see another higher peak in front of you. The previous mountain peak blocked the view of the higher peak. Only when you climb up the first peak will you see the next one. The process through which humans acquire knowledge is very similar to this. So it is absurd to think that what we know now is everything and to deny the existence of deeper and higher levels of knowledge, just like denying the existence of the higher mountain peak when our view of it is blocked by the mountain peak we are currently on.

- The human cognitive process has fundamental limitations. To define a concept, there is isolation from the surrounding reality and a loss of information occurs. Knowledge is always constructed with the intrinsic limitation of simplification and differentiation, which implies loss of information. The creation of knowledge is always associated with some degree of loss of information. The lost information, however, may still interfere with and impact real life, even though it is not in the domain of human knowledge. A reconstruction of knowledge may be able to recapture the lost information. But when the lost information is in fact part of reality, how do we deal with it? Just ignore it or believe it?

- The objectivity of knowledge is always in question. Although knowledge is developed with the intrinsic limitations of simplification and isolation from the environment, through statistical refinement, if the limitation is not within the reach of our experience (such as through direct personal observation or with tools) and reasoning, the limitation bears no direct impact and we may not even be aware of it. Knowledge is considered sufficiently objective until a limitation is unveiled. There can and almost certainly will be other dimensions not under consideration when the concept or theory was created in the first place. When the limitation is known, another round of refinement occurs. This can be an infinite process. At any moment, our knowledge is always an approximation of reality. It is just a better approximation as time goes by.

- As discussed in Chapter 3 with respect to complex nonlinear systems, the behavior of complex systems is unpredictable, even though the laws governing the microscopic components is deterministic. This deterministic chaos is just another example of the limitation of human knowledge.

- The discussion on megastatistics in Chapter 5 shows that for principles that can only be revealed with sampling over a large-scale time period, one may only experience a fraction of a cycle for the hypothesis to be confirmed in his life-span. A choice is needed: keep a suspicious attitude for life, or just believe in it without final confirmation.

- Knowledge is a byproduct of the conscious part of the human mind. By definition, the conscious mind won't be able to fully understand the unconscious. When it comes to understanding the human mind itself, rational knowledge is intrinsically deficient. This situation is also true when it comes to understanding and handling interpersonal relationships.

Because of these limitations of human knowledge, there is a deficiency in our ability to rationally understand the external world or understand the self. When a limitation is reached, intuitive belief becomes valuable. There is no conflict between belief and rational knowledge; rather, they are complementary. As a person's rational knowledge increases, and the deeper a person's awareness of the self and truth, the more truth will be revealed and intuitively touched. After exploring the limits of rational explanation, the person can choose to believe these intuitive ideas even though they cannot be considered knowledge yet, meaning they cannot be approved and communicated to others without doubt. This form of preconception is called a belief. Some beliefs will be wrong and some may later be found to be true. A person who is more honest, more harmonious with the self, can intuitively touch more on the external precursors to knowledge. Hence the more a person's knowledge, and the more honest, the more intuitive precursor to knowledge this person can potentially touch and choose to believe.

Belief must be genuine. To be genuine, one must be honest. To be honest, one must realize his own limitations. Hence, *a genuine believer is also a rational believer.* Honesty is required to avoid bias. No bias implies there is external absolute reality or existence, and one has to tune his thinking, mind-set, and feelings to align with it as best he can. One must listen to the heart and acknowledge honestly the limitations of humans; only then is the door opened to belief in something.

The limitations of knowledge force us to make a choice: do we only live with proven and accepted knowledge, or are we open to intuitive precursors to knowledge that have yet to be proved? A person can certainly choose to ignore any unknown information that is in fact influencing us and stay suspicious of any unproven hypothesis. Alternatively, a person can take the risk of believing an intuitive hypothesis and then act on it. There is a risk that the hypothesis is wrong, but there is a larger return if the hypothesis turns out to be right. The individual will have a larger scope of life experience and hence more rewards. This is in accordance to the typical economic principle: higher risk means higher potential return. At the minimum, knowing the limitations of knowledge and the limitations of humans will keep us more alert to this deficiency. With this perception, one will be wiser in his view of the world and the actions he takes.

The end of rational reasoning is the beginning of belief. However, the end of rational reasoning is not a static point. It can advance as human knowledge increases. A belief can become fact with proof, and hence there is no longer a need to believe in it. It can also be discarded due to negative proof. At the same time, the advancement of knowledge reveals more unknowns, and new beliefs are needed. The boundary between knowledge and belief shifts as time goes by, but the pattern remains the same.

The Dilemma of Actor and Observer

One of the evolutionary outcomes of consciousness is that humans have free will. Free will is part of one's ego. The ego seemingly can do what it wants to do freely, but in fact there are boundaries everywhere. An obvious example is that everyone must follow scientific laws. When one jumps from a tree to the earth, he will always fall down to the ground instead of bouncing upward. But when it comes to ethical rules or social contracts, it is not so obvious what boundary the free will should be confined within. To find out where the boundary is, a person needs to pause and observe those around him. Here, observing means both knowing the external social laws and reflecting the internal mind. However, a person cannot be an actor and an observer at the same time.

To see why there is a dilemma in being both actor and observer at the same time, one should realize that ethical rules or social contracts are conventions derived from self-organization and have taken into consideration the free will of individuals. They benefit the social group as a whole but may have conflicting interests with an individual. An individual is always acting in real life, i.e., making choices based on his or her own best interests and the known rules. A choice made without knowing the rule could be different from a choice made knowing the rule. But the rule itself may depend on the actions of each individual. This interdependency makes it impossible to objectively observe the rule. In a simple mathematical term, this situation can be expressed as

$$L = \bigcup_i F(T_i, P_i, C_i)$$

where L is a rule or law. The right side of the equation is a statistical function (expressed as the big U) of a group of individuals within a geographic area at a given time. C_i is the choice from the ith individual in the group based on his or her free will; T_i, P_i are the time and place when the individual makes the choice. However, note C_i itself is influenced by L. It depends on whether the individual knows the law and how he or she reacts to it, and it can be expressed as $C_i = G(T_i, P_i, L)$.

The F-function represents observation, while the G function represents action. The two functions are interdependent. The question of whether it is possible to observe and act at the same is translated into whether there is a converging solution for both L and C_i. If there is no such converging solution, it means that for a given set $\{T_i, P_i, C_j\}$, one can obtain a solution for L, but this value of L gives a new value for C_i. The new C_i value gives a new solution of L, and the looping continues forever. It cannot reach a converging solution. If there is no converging solution, it means that the free will of humans will never be able to align to an external ethical law. There is infinite conflict. How do we resolve this dilemma? One solution is to believe a set of rules that is independent of human free will, meaning these rules are given upfront and human free will cannot influence them. The origin of such rules is similar to the irreversibility of a thermodynamic system: they cannot be derived from laws governing the microscopic elements. These prior laws are hence based on rational belief. They help to avoid the dilemma of infinite looping. This gives another rational root for belief and religion. Many religions come up with a set of teachings and request humans just simply follow it.

The above discussion on the dilemma of observing and acting is based on the relationship of free will and external ethical law. There is one more intrinsic dilemma regarding the identity of self. As pointed out by Watts, the ego as a known object cannot know the self, the knowing object (Fuller, 176). Watts's idea is methodologically similar to Jung's theory if we map the finite ego to the conscious and map the infinite self to the wholeness consisting of both the conscious and the unconscious. The idea of the infinite self temporarily residing in the finite ego, the realization of the true identity, is similar to the process of listening to the voice from the heart. The connection between the finite and the infinite, between the conscious and the wholeness, is restored and that transforms an individual's life. The dilemma of observer and actor can be understood through another angle: observation is an action from the conscious, but action is from the wholeness of life, the true self. Since life is larger than the conscious, we come to the conclusion that human beings cannot know the true self. Humans can only be the observed object and cannot be the observing object of the infinite self. If that exists, it must be the ultimate knowing object. This is a great subject for religion to ponder and explore.

Limitations of Rational Thought

For philosophers, the rational thinking never stops. He will continue to seek truth and not fall into any irrational belief unless he is rationally convinced. But for regular people, life is limited. This limitation sets the boundary, and the solution to this boundary may result in falling into choosing a particular belief and religious practice. Life is larger than just rational thinking. Hence, choosing a particular religious practice is more important than rational reasoning. This situation is similar to solving a calculus equation. Without boundaries and limitations, there is an infinite number of possible solutions. But when the boundary is set, the equation has a finite solution and a finite set of observable outcomes. Now it can only interpret the phenomenon corresponding to that particular set of boundary conditions.

Many great thinkers asked questions and demonstrated their thinking capabilities, the logic and the rationale, but they may not solve problems that normal people are facing. It is at this point that religion steps in and sets up some boundary and some format. The rational thinker may not like this, as it sets limitations, but by doing this, religion provides a platform for some group of people to worship and find satisfaction that the rational thinker may not be able to find. For normal individuals, the boundary can be family, living conditions, culture, and difficulties encountered. It can be a real event and can also have an emotional attachment.

In a religion, the attitude toward myth is a testing point of how to place the role of rational thinking. Myth, by definition, cannot be explained by rational thinking. It is not important the exact content of the myth. More important is whether one is willing to accept the irrational thinking. It is a symbolic step to believe in a myth. Because if everything is explainable through rational reasoning, it means the capacity of rational reasoning can encompass the anything and hence it is larger than the mind, which is not true. Only when one voluntarily recognizes this limitation, that he is willing to let irrational thinking play a role in life. Which myth to believe is actually less important.

The complete and highest potential of individual experience is like climbing a high mountain. A positivist, who insists the only reliable source of reaching reality is through rational thinking, is like a traveler who insists on relying only on himself, climbing the mountain step by step with his own feet. For the religious, the belief in myth is like taking a helicopter. In the end, perhaps both reach the top of the mountain. But it's very likely a positivist may not reach the top during his life-span. As human development evolves and knowledge accumulates, a successor positivist can start to climb the mountain from a higher place, but the religious can take a helicopter from that higher place as well. One can see the ground for religion is different now when compared to predecessors. The religious one has the advantage of reaching the top of the mountain in his life-span by taking the risk of believing in a certain facet of the supernatural, while a positivist takes no risk of errors but limits his experience potential during his life-span. As time goes by, the experience of a positivist improves, but nevertheless he will not reach the top as the religious person does. This explains that religion is never obsolete, but the ground changes. Unfortunately, the reality is that religious theory rarely evolves as time goes by.

Different people have different criteria to move from rational reasoning to belief. The criteria relates to a person's experience, knowledge, reasoning capacity, and emotion. A person should really exhaust his reasoning capacity before choosing a belief, otherwise it is easy to fall into superstition. As pointed out by Jung and Watts, religion is a way of reconciliation of conscious and unconscious, finite and infinite; it is a very personal experience. When personal issues can be explained, taken care of, or harmoniously handled through rational thinking, then the rational approach should be used, instead of overemphasizing the necessity of religion. But when confused, struggling, puzzled, and the limitations of rational thinking are felt, then it is appropriate to rely on religious belief. In other words, a mature individual should know in general the guidelines of when to be self-reliant and when to let go of the ego.

The attitude toward the religious myth is an indicator of how a person understands a religion. On one hand, if a myth is taken as it is without exhausting the critical thinking, it is just a superstition. On the other hand, if an individual, after exhausting the critical thinking, is willing to incorporate a myth concept into his otherwise strictly rational reasoning, it signifies that his view of the world has a leap. The new view covers a broader spectrum of mind. Indeed, the actual content of the myth concept is less important in this regard. The methodological leap is more significant. The root of this step is actually the limitation of rational thought itself.

6.4 The Root of Religion—Beyond the Psyche

There is no doubt that human psychology is one of the most fundamental roots for the origin of religion. But the origin of religion is far more than psychology can explain. Particularly, there are two drivers that cannot be simply viewed as psychological phenomena or reducible to psychological drives: 1) Seeking a connection to a certain transcending existence. This existence is not just inside the psyche but is reality independent of the psyche. With increasing scale of transcendence, this can be: a) Social connection, such as a group of people sharing similar belief. b) The fourth world. c) Infinite, eternal existence. 2) Seeking the meaning of life.

These are beyond the psyche because there is the possibility there is reality associated with them.

Seeking Connection to Transcending Existence

As discussed in Chapter 4, the awakening of human consciousness was a breakthrough in intellectual development, but at the same time it was a separation of the conscious part of the mind from the wholeness of the mind. The conscious will never exist without its root—the wholeness. Because of this fundamental relationship, the conscious part of the mind, after developing to a certain level of maturity—stage three in the dynamics of mind development—will seek reconciliation with the wholeness of the mind. This tendency is a permanent need, regardless of how advanced human intelligence becomes. Without such connection, humans feel insecure. Such insecurity is deeply rooted and must be addressed in one way or the other. It is a fundamental drive to assure certain connections exist. Such connection should have two important properties:

- It is transcending, that is, it does not cease because the life cycle of a certain individual ends. Instead, it connects multiple individuals with common ground and continues with its own life cycle, independent of an individual's life cycle. It is like a flowing river with its own life; anyone who wishes to connect to it can do so.
- Such connection cannot just exist in the psyche. If it is it just in the psyche, it cannot be transcending. However, what is the reality such connection is reflecting? The carriers of such connection are humans, but the connection continues even when an individual carrier's life ceases, passing on with other carriers from generation to generation. The content in the connection is information. What is the reality that the information is reflecting? It must be the principles and laws behind how things are developing, how the human mind functions, and how human beings interact. It must be the deepest laws that govern the world, but it cannot be fully expressed. This is similar to the concept of Tao in Chinese Taoism, or the Word in the Bible (John 1:1).
- Since the deepest laws cannot be fully expressed, the only way to justify the existence of such transcending existence is through the ways humans interact with it. The methodological justification is discussed extensively in a later subsection.

In real life, such connection can be addressed through different levels. At the surface, it can be realized through regular social connection. Human beings are social creatures. At a minimum, there is family, relatives, then friends, then there are many bigger circles of social connection, such as religious affiliation, political party, etc. Social connection helps to reinforce the messages shared within the group. There is a fundamental reason for it: in earlier chapters we stated that understanding of humans cannot be reached with the reducibility approach. "Man is the measure of all things," hence the only way to prove whether a message can be accepted or not is through resonation with another person. Social connection provides such a channel. However, there is a loophole here: multiple individuals accepting a belief doesn't mean the belief itself is truth. We will come to this point later.

At a deeper level, the social connection is not sufficient to meet the desire of seeking a connection to transcending existence. Social connection is still temporary. Philosophers, theists, and many cultures have all come out with different concepts to describe an eternal connection that can address this human drive. Unfortunately, it is the deepest laws that govern the world but cannot be totally expressed. However, the human mind can intuitively touch the existence of such deepest-level laws. This is because we are part of the creation of such laws, so there is a seed inside us. Such process can be better understood through the nonlinear methodology described in Chapter 5: self-similarity and self-organization.

Because such connection is so subtle and difficult to express, religion provides a practical approach to remedy this deficiency. In theism, by personalizing an external superior existence, our minds are allowed to have dialogue with something superior to itself, and thus the mind can totally submit to the supernatural. This effectively helps to nurture the seed inside the heart to get in touch with the eternal laws and build the connection. The result is that the life of the mind is more balanced and harmonious. When this occurs, whether the entity with which the mind is communicating exists becomes less important, because it already produced a positive impact on the health of the mind and the life of an individual.

Contrary to Western religion, which introduced a personalized supernatural entity, Eastern culture put more emphasis on the inseparability of human beings from Mother Nature. The superior and ultimate laws in Mother Nature are infinite and inexpressible. We humans are simply part of nature, and any separation is artificial and unnecessary, as it causes feelings of insecurity. In Chinese Taoism, Lao-tzu said, "The Tao that can be comprised in words is not the eternal Tao; the name that can be named is not the abiding name. The Unnamable is the beginning of the Heaven and Earth; the namable is the mother of all things" (Fung, 94). Human intelligence is secondary, hence it is unwise to exercise excessive free will and intelligence. According to Lao-tzu, the most important ethic for humans is to "follow nature." Taoism didn't introduce a personalized supernatural entity.

Alan Watts interpreted Taoism from the perspective of a Western philosopher. He believes reality can only be experienced but not through words and symbols. Because the self is part of the whole universe, life can only be experienced, not explained (Fuller, 172). Watts's view is similar to the wisdom of "following nature" in Taoism. However, Watts went too far on this because the laws and knowledge have their own life cycles and objectivity. Describing a natural law is not a one-time job. Instead, it should be kept refined, and most importantly, it is statistical truth that matters, i.e., it should be experienced and affirmed by many individuals in order to filter out untruths. There is extensive discussion in Chapter 2 on the limitations in the process of generating knowledge. Nevertheless, the key point here is that because one believes the permanent ego which is not reality, it causes us a feeling of insecurity. Ego separates us from the flow of life, and we search the future for security. In Watts's view, feeling oneself to be a permanent and separate ego means permanent anxiety and misery. A logical need of a permanent existence, God, is also a consequence (Fuller, 174). Watts's view on the inseparability of "I" with nature is similar to the idea of another famous Chinese philosopher Chuang-tzu, who once dreamed of being a butterfly. He couldn't distinguish whether it was he who dreamed of being a butterfly or the butterfly who dreamed of being him (Chuang-tzu). The ultimate goal of life is living in such a way that one cannot remember the difference between himself and the rest of world. This is certainly an ideal world but difficult to achieve.

The Western and Eastern methods are very different in addressing the human desire for connection to transcending existence; both have their advantages and disadvantages. When we deal with this difference, we should keep in mind the following points:

- Emphasizing the indistinguishable boundary between ego and the rest of the world ignores the fact that actualizing potentiality is a natural force of the human mind. Human intelligence will keep advancing, no one can stop it, so any philosophy discounting this force is incomplete.
- Emphasizing the inexpressibility of the ultimate law (e.g., Tao) is one side of the story. How to connect to it is another side of the story that cannot

be ignored. It is easy to come up with a mythical concept. But if it is completely out of the reach of humans, it becomes impractical to follow and not valuable.

- Introducing a personalized supernatural entity helps to solve the above two deficiencies, but it introduces a new problem in that the personalized part is man-made, constructed from the human imagination. Hence it contradicts the original goal that the supernatural should be superior to and independent of any human mind.

- Clearly there is a methodological difficulty here, even though the goal is clear. Methodological refinement is necessary. *The framework from Western religion can be a better starting point. For example, one possible solution is to introduce a concept as proxy or agent to reality. This is a metareality, as described in Chapter 5. Metareality in this context is similar to the supernatural, retaining its infinite and mythical characteristics. The emphasis is on the interaction between the human mind and the metareality, and such interaction should evolve over time instead of being static and unchanging. Essentially, it is the concept of the fourth world in Chapter 4.*

Since the Western and Eastern methods are very different in how they address the human desire for connection to transcending existence, it is necessary to devote more effort in the next chapter to further the discussion. The difference is interesting and contains hints for a deeper understanding of how our minds deal with the roots of belief and religion.

Since there is a mythical aspect to the metareality (i.e., the fourth world), there is inevitably risk that it will be misused as superstition. What would be the criteria to distinguish a healthy human interaction with it versus a superstitious one? In other words, how to ensure the understanding of the fourth world does not fall into superstition? We outline the following criteria:

- Even though the metareality cannot be totally comprehended, it must be able to be experienced by an individual.

- The outcomes resulting from interaction with it must be observable. Interaction here can be many different things: prayer, meditation, dreams, etc. The outcome is the behavior of the individual.

- Although rational thinking cannot explain such interaction, there is a minimum criteria involving rational reasoning. *Even though the mythical experience cannot be explained by human intellect, it should not conflict with the intellect. In other words, although the human intellect cannot say yes to a myth, it should also not say no to the mythical concept. A mythical experience must be appearing neutral to the human intellect.* This is a rather strict criteria. It basically says the mythical experience cannot be explained but also does not conflict with our deepest knowledge. For example, the concept of Tao, or impersonalized God, belongs to this category. It cannot be proven, but it also doesn't conflict with our intelligence. Same with the intelligent designer. From our current knowledge, we cannot prove it, but we also can't rule out the possibility. On the other hand, the idea of resurrection of a physical body doesn't pass this criterion. It cannot be proved and conflicts with our knowledge.

This criterion doesn't conflict with the principle that the conscious cannot fully explain the wholeness of the mind. The part conscious intelligence cannot explain is not purely delusion. We still believe there is reality behind it, hence it cannot be arbitrarily explained or become the basis for superstition. For many ethical rules, there could be a biological reason for them that we don't fully understand yet. We assume an individual has incentive to avoid conflict and pursue harmonious relationships, which is best for the mind as a whole, though not in the best interest of the rational part of the mind. Ethical behavior itself is rewarding in the current life, even at the biological level, but in a very subtle way that is hard to explain. That's why many religions or cultures rely on some form of mythical symbolism to convince people to live an ethical life. Until there is a good model to describe the benefit of an ethical life, such mythical symbolism seems helpful and practical.

This is particularly true for interpersonal relationships. It is already impossible to understand the wholeness of the mind, so it is even more difficult to rely on the conscious mind to handle the interaction of two or more minds. *To build the common ground for humans to establish healthy, loving relationships, it is even more important to realize there is common connection, common property, that all humans share and link to. It is the realization that all humankind shares the same property in this world and are connected that leads to the conclusion that we should love each other.* As discussed in Chapter 4, the fundamental meaning of love is to respect another's life as a whole, as it is, the way we understand ourselves. With respect, we must be fully patient to respect the natural development cycle of the mind as it is, with care when necessary. Furthermore, there is a common connection among all of us because of the similarity of the mind's structure and its development process. By caring for and loving others, we experience happiness because there is an unseen reward and benefit to reinforcing and solidifying the principles behind the mind's structure and developmental process. This is, in fact, beyond the psyche.

Seeking the Meaning of Life

Seeking the meaning of life is also a basic human drive. Very often, it is linked to the seeking of connection to transcending existence. Viktor Frankl believes that humans can transcend our own limitations, and it is this sublimation that makes our lives meaningful (Fuller, 224–226). The sublimation is connected to the search for transcending existence.

Frankl proposes that the origin of the search for the meaning of life cannot be fully analyzed. This is based on his theory of the "inaccessibility of human existence to reflection," which is similar to the idea that the observing object cannot be observed (Fuller, 238). The point is that searching for meaning is originated from this depth of the unconscious, and hence it cannot be fully analyzed. It directs humans to transcend to a bigger wholeness, even though we cannot fully understand it.

But is the meaning of life just a psychological question, or is there reality beyond the psychology? Frankl thinks meaning is objective, not subjective. And since the ultimate meaning originates from the unconscious's bigger wholeness, the unconscious's bigger wholeness has the property of objectivity as well (Fuller, 230–231). This is slightly different from mainstream psychology, which holds that the unconscious is purely a facet of the psyche. Frankl defines the meaning of the unconscious's bigger wholeness: it refers to the objective principles that transcend an individual's life—that is similar to the concept of the fourth world. We have shown earlier that it is methodologically acceptable to assume the fourth world is objective. The unconscious psyche is capable of connecting to it, although the human intellect cannot fully analyze it.

Frankl thinks everything has meaning, even death. The meaning of death is so that one has a sense of urgency to do something meaningful. Without death, nothing will be done effectively (Fuller, 232). Death is like setting the boundary of an equation so that there is a concrete solution, a meaning to be found.

The search for life's meaning is an important subject for religion. The root of the search is from the deepest part of our minds, and it connects to the search for a transcending existence. That in turn connects to the question whether a transcending existence is objective or just a figment of imagination. The answer to this question is beyond the psyche. However, the meaning of life does not necessarily need religion to provide an answer. We will discuss more on this subject in Chapter 8.

Building Productive Relationship

A person cannot just be satisfied with the perfection in his or her own psychological development. Interaction with others and social life are intrinsic to human nature. No matter how perfectly one cultivates his own mind, it must be tested with the interaction of other people. The minds of others are the mirror to your mind. A mind untested with others is not a complete one.

As described in Chapter 4, "Interaction of Minds and the Meaning of Love," there are certain principles one must follow to build productive human relationships. Unfortunately these principles are not easy to understand and follow because it requires a person to have a well-developed mind in the first place. Religion can help in this circumstance. Certainly there is nonreligious support also available for building productive relationships, but building productive human relationships and building high-standard ethical values are extremely subtle and difficult. Historically religion played an important role here.

It is arguable that building productive relationships is really outside the psyche because a healthy and well-developed psyche is a precondition. But it is still categorized as outside of the psyche because there is objective and transcending outcome that can result from the productive relationships for human beings and society as a whole.

Summary on the Roots of Religion

The nature of the human psychological structure, the limitation of human intellect and reasoning, and the intrinsic drive to seek connection to a transcending existence are the primary roots for a belief system and religious practice. These forces are deeply rooted in the human mind and will not become obsolete regardless of the advancement of human intelligence.

The needs are there objectively. A mature and healthy belief system or religion must be built upon addressing these needs. Russell claims that religion is built upon fear (Russell, Ch. 1), which is an oversimplification. It is in fact crucial not to ignore these needs in order to have a complete life.

An individual needs to find a personalized way to follow the psychological development process described in Chapter 4 in order to have a complete journey of mind and to maximize the value of the human mind. Without that, the development of the mind is not complete. In this regard, just as Socrates said, "An unexamined life is not worth living," and as Jung said, "Life seeks completeness, not perfection," it is logical to say that *a life without a belief system or religion is incomplete.* We need to treat the mind as a whole and respect it, own it, nurture it, with either rational or religious thinking as needed. Then we will have a happier, more harmonious life. It is better to address the roots discussed in this chapter in one way or another than to simply ignore them.

6.5 Methodological Foundation and Its Justification

In the analysis of the origin of belief and religion, it becomes clear that the foundation for the legitimacy of a belief sometimes comes from the methodology itself, not necessarily the content and implementation of the belief. This is an important statement. A belief is a complementary method to rational thinking. In order to see this clearly, it is critical to separate justification of content of a belief from the justification of its methodology. A healthy mind always has some sort of belief, no matter the content of the belief. Many times it is easier to accept the methodology of a belief than the content. However, in typical religious practices, the methodology and content are inseparable. It is sad to see people reject a belief or religious practice altogether due to the fact that the content of the belief does not make sense to them. So we need to study the possibility of decoupling the methodology from the content. This separation will let us trim the unnecessary parts of a belief system, allowing us to better see the truth behind the religious practice, which can ultimately help unify the seemingly conflicting belief systems in the world.

Regardless of the actual content, in general, religious practices have the following common framework:

1) Belief that there is a reality that is beyond the comprehension of human intelligence. There is an order or law that is higher than that which we see in the secular world. There is a self that is larger than the ego we understand, and it is our goal to live out of this larger self. Whether such metareality is true or not cannot be completely answered.

2) Belief that such metareality has an impact on our daily lives. There are certain methods, direct or indirect, for interaction between the human mind and the metareality. Such interactions influence us such that our behaviors adhere more to the values the metareality represents. How the interaction occurs is not clearly understood.

3) Since the metareality has positive impact on a believer's life, after a long period of practicing and experiencing, it becomes an integral part of the believer's life. It is less and less important to seek rational proof of the existence of the metareality. The importance of proving the existence of the metaconcept is less than the importance of having the positive impact on the believer's life. This is a pragmatic attitude toward religion, and it is commonly believed. Because of this pragmatic justification, the initial step of believing is crucial. It is acceptable not to seek complete proof, since 1.) it is impossible; and 2.) it becomes less and less important as the believer practices the religion longer and longer. This methodology also implies that religious experience is highly personal. Personal experience is an integral part of belief and cannot be replaced by the experience of others.

The initial belief in a concept of metareality, the experience of a positive impact from the connection between the individual and such concept, and the pragmatic justification for the initial belief based on the actual outcome, are the most important methodologies a belief system relies upon. The justification of this methodological foundation are, interestingly, more obvious than the justification of the content of a belief system. This can be seen by comparing the methodological foundation with the key methodologies derived from scientific study and the human mind, which were summarized in Chapter 5. We will examine one by one whether they are compatible with the approach utilized in a belief system or religion. If they are compatible, it tells us that there is similarity between the way we engage in belief and religious practice and the way we understand science or psychology. If they are not compatible, it helps us to detect potential superstitious practices.

Methodology Justification—Concept of Metareality

We extensively discussed the roots of religion earlier. Religion comes from intrinsic needs of human psychological development, limitations of the human intellect, and belief in the potential existence of the fourth world. In order to deal with these needs, the first step in a belief system is to introduce a concept that has capabilities beyond human beings and which is not completely comprehensible with our intellect. This can be a supernatural concept of God, or it can be a nonhumanized existence, such as Tao or the concept of void in Buddhism.

Why is this concept needed? This can be explained through the roots of religion. The psychological root calls for the concept of a wholeness, a self, in order to complete the unification process. The limitations of human intellect calls for something that is more capable than our intellect in order to describe and understand the incomprehensible. The existence of the fourth world shows that there is a possibility that the law behind mystery, wonders, and the incomprehensible maybe indeed generated through a nonlinear, self-organizing process. However, it is best and most easily understood if such a process can be described with conventional terminology that is more aligned with our regular linear thinking logic. All in all, a concept of supernatural agent is necessary and also extremely effective at helping our thought processes and psychological development. Even though we don't know the actual meaning, it is necessary to interact with the law behind the scenes. It's a bridge between the conscious and the unconscious, the comprehensible and the incomprehensible.

This method is similar to the concept of metareality explained in Chapter 5. In the scientific world, the reason for borrowing a concept to serve as proxy to reality is due to the complexity of describing the reality in question, it is a missing piece to solve a puzzle that would otherwise be unresolved. By introducing the missing piece, the puzzle is solved with an outcome that is measurable. Therefore, even though the exact reality behind the borrowed concept is unknown, or the reality behind the borrowed concept is immeasurable with current knowledge and tool (hence termed metareality), we are still comfortable using it because it helps solve the problem at hand with a measurable outcome. This is exactly how the concept of wave function is widely used and accepted in quantum mechanics, even though the interpretation of wave function is not fully agreed upon among physicists.

A deeper reason for the justification of accepting such a concept lies in the fact that when knowledge is generated and concepts created, reality as a whole is differentiated. There is always an associated simplification. Differentiation is associated with isolation. Reality as a whole is distorted or simplified to focus on concepts that are measurable. When it comes to a complex reality, it is highly possible that some parts of reality can be measured, while other parts cannot. However, the connection between the immeasurable parts of reality and the measurable concept can be described. By introducing a meta-agent concept, reality as a whole can be better described, and there will be more outcomes of measurable concepts that can be detected, as we observe in the case of wave function in quantum mechanics. Another example is the concept of the Higgs particle in modern physics. The concept was initially introduced to explain the particle model. No one knew the actual reality behind it when it was introduced. It was after more than half a century that the reality was confirmed by the help of powerful computers to run complex data mining.

As can be seen, the idea of introducing a concept, or symbol, to reflect a reality that is not yet completely understood, or will be never completely understood, as a dialogue object for a complex system is not a strange method. It is used in many different fields, including in science. The risk is that since there are many unknown aspects of such concepts, components that are pure speculation can be arbitrarily added. In fact, this is unavoidable because such a concept is supposed to link the comprehensible and the incomprehensible. There is room for anyone to arbitrarily add something based on his or her own understanding. It is an intrinsic dilemma. By definition, a concept such as metareality must encompass certain aspects that are mythical and incomprehensible, but the human mind is genuinely uncomfortable with such a black hole and is inclined to fill the void with prior experience or knowledge. Therefore, there are many interpretations of God and multiple viewpoints on Buddhism and Taoism. It is apparent that *the methodology of introducing the concept of metareality in a religion is not an issue as it is compatible with the similar method in many other fields; the issue is instead in the interpretation of the content.*

Is there a fundamental principle here to determine whether the concept of metareality is legitimate? The borrowed concept cannot be arbitrary or pure conjecture. It must be *somehow connected to a measurable reality.* There are many interpretations of the wave function, including the hidden variable theory. But experimental measurements don't match predictions from the hidden variable theory. The same criteria can be applied to distinguish a healthy belief versus a superstitious one. In other words, the reality behind any metareality must be able to show its representation in the secular world. The interaction between human beings and such metareality is observable. We are not calling for a rigorous standard typically seen in scientific research, because the scientific approach as a byproduct of intellect cannot be applied to a belief system that is dealing with the human mind as a whole. However, we are asking that the metareality be at least partially observable or representable in the secular world. Eventually, this translates into how effectively the belief influences the lives of believers. There can be many interpretations of a metareality, but the ones that work for an individual must genuinely influence the believer's life. Equally important, an interpretation that works for one individual may not work for another.

In summary, introducing the concept of metareality in religion is not only necessary, but is also justified in methodology. As Jung pointed out, myth is a necessary part of any religion and it is productive. It is not productive to downgrade God to the level of just superhuman. Still, most people are not ready to believe until there is confirmation of some level of reality associated with such a concept. However, one risk of introducing such a concept is that it can mislead people to think it is an outside entity. But it can have two components, one is inside the psyche and the other is to connect to external existence.

Methodology Justification—Megastatistics

The typical human thinking pattern is not accustomed to indirect, multilevel inference. We are more comfortable with direct experience and linear logic. However, for human society, the evolutionary pattern is complex enough that simple direct experience and linear logic are insufficient. If there is any law behind the evolution of human society, it will not be easy to understand and experience. The phenomenon of megastatistics is a good example.

For an ethical value to become prevalent, it typically needs many generations of being taught and practiced. Presumably, the ethical value should bring an ultimate benefit to each individual of the society when it is prevalent. If it is not a common practice in a society, those who start to help others but don't receive reciprocal help will certainly feel that is not fair. This initial group of people starting to help others needs a belief to continue the practice. When more and more others feel the benefits and do the same, the overall benefits will eventually prevail, but it may take time—even many generations. The initial group of people may not be able to experience the benefit, though they believed in the ethical value in their lifetimes. To enable this group of people to practice the value, it must come from the strength gained from a true belief. This can be either belief in a supernatural entity that directs them to do it, or belief that there is benefit in an afterlife or next cycle of life—if their belief system includes an afterlife or next cycle.

Belief in the supernatural or an afterlife seems ridiculous, but it helps to fill the deficiency caused by practicing an ethical value you may be unable to benefit from in your lifetime. The content of such belief (the supernatural or an afterlife) is hard to justify, instead there is better way to convey the same message through the justification of the methodology. This is what we have already discussed in Chapter 5 with respect to megastatistics through Bayesian inference.

Recall that the probability of a hypothesis H with given evidence E is expressed by Bayes's theory:

$$P(H|E) = \frac{P(E|H) \times P(H)}{P(E)}$$

Let's consider an example using Bayesian inference on human ethical development:

- *H* denotes a hypothesis of the famous teaching, "Treat others the way you want to be treated, and then you will be well treated."
- *E* denotes evidence that an individual feels he is well treated.
- *P(H)* is the prior probability that *H* is true (the degree of belief in *H*). Before any evidence, it is fair to assume *P(H)* = 0.5. The teaching is equally true and false without evidence.
- *P(E)* is the probability that evidence *E* will occur for all possible hypotheses, i.e., the probability of an individual reporting he is well treated by others regardless of what the hypothesis is.

Since there is evidence that an individual believes he is well treated by others, one would intuitively expect $P(H\ E)$ to increase. But it really depends on the value of $P(E\ H)$: given that the teaching of "Treat others the way you want to be treated, and then you will be well treated," is true, what is the probability one will be well treated by others? There are many factors here; even if an individual treats another person the way he wants to be treated, it is possible that the other person does not perceive the same value, or for one of many other reasons, he doesn't treat the first individual well in return. It is natural to assume the value of $P(E\ H)$ is subjective instead of objective. And because it is subjective, there is a possibility that a subjective factor (such as a belief) can influence the probability density, such that $(P(E\ H))/(P(E)) > 1$, which leads to the increase of value $P(H\ E)$.

Because $P(E\ H)$ is subjective for human behavior, a belief can influence the value of this parameter. This eventually increases the value of $P(H|\{E\})$ to an acceptable value beyond doubt, and the hypothesis becomes a norm of society. When this has occurred, the initial belief that helped to establish the norm becomes less important. The initial belief is hence a sufficient condition to establish the norm but not the necessary condition, meaning there may be other means to achieve establishment of the norm. The initial belief accelerated the process. The impact it introduced is real. The content of belief is what we referred to earlier as metareality, and we don't fully understand it. It produces a real impact, and once the norm is established, it could be hidden again.

Once again, it can be seen that the methodology of a religious practice is justified, even though the content of the belief cannot be fully understood.

Methodology Justification—Nonlinearity

The most important methodological concepts abstracted from the study of complex and nonlinear systems includes: 1) Uncertainty of the future. 2) Self-organization. 3) Goal and process are inseparable. We will study whether typical belief systems utilize these methods.

A belief in the destiny of human beings influences an individual's selection of ethical values. Many religions use a better future life as the goal for convincing a believer to choose certain ethical values. Even at the philosophical level, a belief in the destiny of humans can influence one's attitude toward life. For example, if one believes that in the end the earth, the universe, and all human society will be destroyed based on some scientific predictions, what is the point of making the environment better for our children, preserving the good values in a culture, or even exploring the space outside Earth? If there is an end of the world, what one should most care about is the pursuit of all the happiness one can get in this life. It is indeed crucial to examine whether such a belief in the destiny of human beings has solid ground.

It is certainly depressing to believe that in the end, human beings and all our cultures will be destroyed and disappear. However, nonlinear and chaos theories tell us that determinism and certainty are impossible. One cannot predict the future of a highly nonlinear system with current knowledge. The earth, the universe, and even human society are far more complex than a nonlinear system. It is prudent to conclude that we cannot simply predict the future of these systems, particularly the future end of humanity and our cultures.

But what then is the proper stance regarding the destiny of human beings? Since it is unpredictable, can we just ignore it? Humans tend to search for their destiny. It is an intrinsic quest in the deep part of one's heart. Ignoring it is not a good option.

Because the future is scientifically unpredictable, any choice would be just a belief. The question is, what can you sincerely believe that will truly influence your life? What are the criteria for determining a belief is a good one? A healthy belief system should include the following characteristics:

- The belief should be based on human nature and address the root of belief as discussed earlier in this chapter, for example, a deep desire for certainty, to be loved, and to survive. Meanwhile, *it should not conflict with the intellect. In other words, although the human intellect cannot say yes to a mythical concept, it should not say no either because the possibility is not zero.*

- Believe in the creativity and adaptability of human beings in the attempt to survive. There will be solutions to problems humanity is and will be facing. Efforts to extend survival of human beings are always encouraged and needed. Such efforts can include: better knowledge and understanding of nature, of the self; better ability to cope with nature (but not through controlling it); better relationships among ourselves; belief in a "life flow" of humanity throughout history, and one should attach or contribute to it to make oneself more valuable.

- The belief should be constantly checked. It is a dynamic, rather than static belief, and takes into account that there are limitations to the intellect of humankind. We constantly seek for hints and guidance to adjust the content of the belief.

In Western religion, the uncertainty of the future is reflected in the doctrine that there is a generic God, but one cannot predict the behaviors and actions of God. In Christianity, there is a belief in the second coming of Jesus Christ, but one cannot predict when this will happen. The behavior of God is unpredictable; it is a sin to attempt to think on God's behalf. The doctrine that man will not and should not predict God's will, or God's actions, is consistent with the notion that the future is uncertain. Uncertainty is normal; it is certainty that is exceptional.

If we just stop here at the fact that the future is unpredictable, we fall short of manifesting many other important hints from nonlinear science. An uncertain future does not imply there is no direction to the future. Instead, in many cases, the future of a complex system has a direction, a trend, an evolutionary path, but the elements inside the system are unaware of it. Furthermore, such direction, trend, or goal is inseparable from the actions of the constituents in the here and now. It is reasonable to assume that the future of human destiny, the direction of society, and the goals of individuals would exhibit similar characteristics. That is, the direction, the goal, the evolutionary path exist, but we are not aware of it. Furthermore, such direction, goal, or path cannot be separated from our daily routine and our many decisions here and now. The direction, trend, or future destiny of humanity cannot be explained at the microscopic level, similar to the principle of emergence. The behavior exhibited in an emergence phenomenon cannot be traced to or explained by laws governing the microscopic level, even though in our daily routine it is difficult to sense there is any higher-level trend of human group behavior. All we know is that the interactions between human beings and group actions (the force at the microscopic level) can influence such trends and directions (the phenomena at the macroscopic level).

In plain language, there is a trend of human social behavior that can be understood as the river flow of life. It is something that is larger than the meaning of an individual life. A person who attaches to it will feel a sense of transcendence. The significance of the river flow of life is that it provides hope, a sense of transcendence, lifting the spirit of individuals who believe in it, and empowering them to live life with a larger scope of meaning. Such an idea is embedded within and capitalized on in many religious doctrines. For example, in the Bible, Jesus Christ described it as the Kingdom of Heaven. Whoever believes in Jesus is connected to the Tree of Life, and whoever spreads the gospel is sowing the seeds of the fruit of that tree. It is a very powerful message that provides hope and empowers whoever believes in it to live a life larger than just for himself. Such belief provides positive influence to the life of believers. Even though the exact meaning of Kingdom of Heaven is not totally comprehensible, the methodology to connect to a Tree of Life is methodologically justified.

The fundamental reason for believing there is something higher than an individual human experience is the gestalt effect, that the whole is larger than the sum of the parts. Hence life is larger than the knowledge, and behavior of humanity as a whole is larger than the sum of individual behaviors. The whole is larger than the sum of the parts—the delta between the whole and the sum of the parts is what emergence is about. We also explained earlier that the reason for this intrinsic flaw is that the separation of the whole into parts causes loss of information. The delta is the lost information. The emergence effect is the result of recovery of the lost information. The reality corresponding to the lost information is termed metareality. It can influence its components but cannot be fully understood. For human group behavior, the constituent is any individual. The same logic applies here: the individual, living within the limited boundary of the material world, only knows the local information and can't understand or be aware of the additional reality arising from the emergence effect of group behavior. On one hand, it exists and can influence our lives; on the other hand, it cannot be fully comprehended. Because of this open-ended situation, it leaves room for imagination about such metareality. Furthermore, because it is abstract and not easily understood, a lot of religious doctrines use more imaginative language to manifest this additional information due to the emergence effect. From this regard, *we can consider that religious language, through introduction of the supernatural, is equivalent to using imagined language to describe nonlinear principles. There is truth behind it.*

Let's reexamine the objectivity of the concept of the fourth world that was introduced in Chapter 4. Human interaction can come from the conscious or unconscious parts of our minds. The fourth world is the delta between the aggregate of whole mind activities and the aggregate of conscious mind activities (i.e., the third world). By definition, the fourth world includes some components that are undetected and there incomprehensible, and the source of this incomprehensibility is due to the unconscious of the human mind and the emergence effect of human group behaviors. Although no one can tell the exact makeup of the fourth world, its existence can be justified by the following factors:

- The definition itself. Since the third world, the aggregate of conscious mind activities, is objective, it is natural to conclude that the aggregate of whole mind activities is also objective. Therefore the delta, the fourth world, is also an objective existence.
- The emergence effect of a group of human minds allows recovery of additional information. This information was lost when the conscious mind was separated from the whole.
- If the makeup of the fourth world is information, what is the reality that the information is reflecting? It must be the principles and laws behind how things are developing, how the human mind functions as a whole, and how human beings interact as a group. It must be the deepest laws that govern the world, but it cannot be fully expressed. This is similar to the concept of *Tao* in Chinese Taoism, or the Word in the Bible (John 1:1).

Therefore, even though the exact makeup of the fourth world may be indescribable, its existence is still justified. It is because of this justification that one can claim belief in the fourth world as a rational one, rather than mere superstition or pure fantasy. Even if one may not believe in the fourth world, it still exists—meaning the trend, direction, and goal of human group behavior can exist objectively. The difference between a believer and a nonbeliever is that for the believer, a sense of transcendence and meaning becomes conscious in the mind, and that person can thus voluntarily act in accordance with the trend and direction. From this perspective, the believer has an advantage for living a better life.

Methodology Justification—The Will of Belief

The argument made earlier that an initial belief is an accelerator for the spread of a hypothesis, and become less important once the hypothesis is established, is a pragmatic one. The use of pragmatic usefulness as a methodology to justify a belief system was popularized by William James. The truthfulness of a belief system, according to William James, comes from its outcome (Fuller, 11). Its proof is simply a man's life getting better and happier. For any theory on belief systems, the subject being studied is the human mind itself. To observe the outcome of a belief system, its impacts on the human mind, such as behaviors or attitudes, are measured. From an empirical point of view, if the mind gets happier and more harmonious due to interaction with a belief system, why is this not a proof? In fact, James declared that the value of any truth is dependent upon its use to the person who holds it. James pushed the understanding of empiricism to a limit that is beyond regular scientific empiricism. He asserts that the human experience cannot be objectively observed, because the mind of the observer and the act of observation will affect the outcome (Fuller, 7). In essence, the mind and the experience are inseparable.

James's philosophy of "will to believe" is a pragmatic way to interpret religious belief (Fuller, 2). He tried to lay the foundation for the lawfulness of belief, regardless of the content of a belief. Although James's pragmatic argument is quite convincing, one open issue is the criteria: for whatever belief, if it can influence human behavior, it is real. There must be stronger argument than that. Behind his philosophy, there is analogy to the methodology of megastatistics. By exploring the methodological analogy, his theory will be more complete. For example, James's goal is to defend the right of an individual, in the absence of final proof, to voluntarily adopt a "believing attitude" (Fuller, 2–6). The logic is very similar to the logic of Bayesian inference, discussed in the previous section on metastatistics. The statement that a truthfulness of a faith cannot be separated from the faith itself is also similar to the nonlinear methodology of goal and process are inseparable. Below we will do a comparison of James's arguments and the methodologies presented before:

- A hypothesis is anything proposed to explain our belief. Basically, it is a hypothesis that has a sufficiently high probability of being true that one accepts and acts on it without doubt.

- A belief must be neither skeptical, claiming zero possibility of attaining the truth, nor absolutist, claiming one hundred percent certainty of truth. Instead it should be empirical, with a probability of being true. This probability is achieved with evidence, which depends upon our judgment, and is expected for refinement in the future. This is exactly the Bayesian inference discussed earlier.

- The rationalist, in order to avoid believing a delusion, chooses to abstain from any belief. James thinks this is just another expression of fear of making mistakes. Rather than make an error, the skeptic holds his mind in suspense for his whole life. For science, this is acceptable, because the truth science is seeking has no great impact on normal life, so a decision on a hypothesis can be safely postponed. But real-life issues such as morality cannot be postponed (Fuller, 3). If one chooses not to believe it until seeing proof, the world would have a lower level of morality. Our will to believe is, indeed, crucial for making a difference in real life.

- Faith in practice is a major determinant of its own success. Faith influences the result itself. *This is exactly the methodology found in nonlinearity that goal and process are inseparable. Faith itself is both the goal and the process.*

- It is unreasonable to rule out faith as a path to truth due to lack of objective scientific evidence, particularly when the truth depends on our personal actions, and faith itself is part of truth's creation. This is a very fundamental thought. Without the initial input—faith, the system will not start to evolve to its true potential. This can be proven through Bayesian inference—if the initial probability of a hypothesis is zero, the subsequent probability, even with more evidence, will still be zero, forever.

- Putting off the decision till the evidence is available is itself a choice. However, such choice has its own risk: "the decision that it is better to risk losing truth than to possibly be in error" (Fuller, 5). The fundamental problem here for the skeptic is that it paints intellect as larger than life. There are two choices here: 1) Take the risk of error, but have a life of hope. 2) Take no risk of error, but risk loss of truth. Unless the religious hypothesis has a zero probability of truth, there is simply no proof that the first choice is worse than the second. If we recall the discussion on the fourth world earlier, the possibility of its objective existence is not zero. It is an individual's right to choose his own risks in life, such as the willingness to believe. Human courage and value are demonstrated here precisely.

In conclusion, we have a right to believe, at our own risk, any hypothesis that has a nonzero probability of truth and positive impact on our lives. However, such freedom to believe doesn't extend to matters the intellect can adequately resolve on its own. As mentioned before, one of the criteria for distinguishing healthy faith from superstition is that faith should not conflict with the best of intellect. If it has zero probability of truth, then it should be discarded.

Even though James's pragmatic interpretation of religious belief is solely philosophical, there are many analogies with the methodologies we have discussed so far, such as metareality, Bayesian inference, and emergence. As time moves on, it is possible more and more methodologies from scientific research will support James's philosophy of religion, making his seemingly pragmatic argument more rational and rigorous.

6.6 Behind the Symbols and Rituals

As we have discussed regarding the origin of belief and religion, there are intrinsic human needs that are benefited from a genuine belief system or the practice of a healthy religion. It is critical to separate the content of belief and the rationality of belief as an approach to life. However, religion normally convolutes methodology and content. It is unfortunate to see people reject the approach of belief altogether due to the fact that the content of a particular belief does not make sense to them. In the previous section, the methodological foundations of typical belief systems were extensively examined, and they are not really in conflict with many methodologies found in scientific research. In this section, the focus turns to the implementation of a belief or religion, i.e., the contents. Religious content is comprised of ritual, symbols, and the messages behind them. One should look beneath the surface of religious ritual and symbols instead of focusing on the messages.

To understand this difference, let's revisit the roots for human belief and religion. A belief system or religion is a complementary in remedying the disconnect within individual human minds and in human group life.

- The disconnect in human psychological development. Many religions and psychological theories seem to reveal the same phenomenon—the human mind's development goes in multiple phases. The early phase is driven by biological instinct and material desires; it is self-centric, governed by secular interests. This can be called the first mind. Actualizing potentiality is the central theme of this mind. The later phase is driven by an awakening of the inner voice and wholeness of the mind. This is the third phase and beyond the mind's development process discussed in Chapter 4. The first mind yields its dominance and the mind is tuned to integrate as a bigger self, with a new view that others, nature, and the universe are all interconnected and interdependent. Reconciliation is the central theme of this mind. The yielding of the first mind is the precondition for entering the second mind. Here, yielding just means giving up dominant status. The turning point of such psychological growth is not an easy step, and many people may not be able to reach this, leaving the disconnect to continue for their lifetimes.

- The disconnect between an individual human experience and the potential group behavior due to the emergence effect. The human psyche has a powerful need to attach to an external transcending existence. Typical psychology attempts to explain everything within the human psyche. From Jung's archetypes, to Maslow's self-actualization, to Bayesian inference, psychologists are exploring understanding of the psyche, and ignoring the objective and transcendent aspects of human minds due to emergence. Such disconnect leaves room for belief and religions.

These disconnects are the subject of religion, psychology, and related philosophies. A religion typically develops its own symbolism and rituals to explain the above principle of mind development, to foster a mechanism to execute the principle, and to justify the objectivity of this principle. But these symbols and rituals are fairly subjective. The end result is that even though the goals to link the disconnected are similar, the ways of manifesting truth are different.

For example, psychologists have developed many concepts, be it Jung's archetypes, Maslow's self-actualization, Fromm's humanism, etc., trying to reveal the importance of the second mind. They attempt to show that giving up the dominance of the first mind can uncover the potential of an individual, reconcile the conflict, reveal the intrinsic nature of values and morals, and lead to a harmonious and happy life. In the view of these psychologists, these attempts are without the need for a supernatural agent. On the other hand, in Christianity, sin is a state where a person is solely dominated by the first mind. Only when the person wakes up spiritually and accepts Jesus Christ as his or her savior, can he or she give up the dominant status of first mind and start the newborn life of the second mind. Furthermore, Christianity believes that Jesus represents the light (the higher level of laws), and the higher level of laws are coming from God, an objective, superior, supernatural entity of higher dimension. An individual can connect to the transcendent existence through Jesus Christ.

We need to penetrate the rituals and symbols of various religions to find the truth behind them. When we find that, at a deep level, the messages of many religions are actually trying to achieve the same outcome, we should put away the differences, allowing religions to coexist as different approaches to the same goal. This is similar to the polymorphism discussed in Chapter 5. Different theories describe the same laws. One can then come back to choose a religious practice that is most effective for himself, but he won't bear the mind-set anymore that his religion is the exclusive way to the truth. The question of "Can this be an effective belief, even knowing my religion is not the only way to truth?" is similar to asking "Can I believe Schrödinger's equation is true given that it is not the only method of describing the laws of quantum mechanics?" One should abandon the perception that only when a religion or belief is the exclusive truth can it be effective, because such a religion does not exist, though most of them claim to be. The root cause of such problems is that by definition, metareality cannot be completely understood and is open to many interpretations. So how can you believe your religion is the truth? The only way is through practice, observing its effects on your daily life, and finding it to be consistent. By definition, metareality is wordless; there is no single way to explain it, and therefore it is acceptable to have different method trying to approach it. We should penetrate symbols such as God, Tao, and Buddha to focus on the truth behind the scenes, believing that these symbols, in the end, point to the same incomprehensible object. Eventually, one should select the best method to repair the disconnect but should not exclude other methods, given it is impossible to comprehend the object through human knowledge.

Even if we accept the necessity of introducing a concept of metareality in dealing with the disconnects mentioned earlier, there must be certain laws that govern how the human mind interacts with such a metareality and how the unconscious interacts with the conscious. Such laws, again, may not be fully comprehensible, but we believe they exist. Such laws determine whether a belief or religion is legitimate or not. The philosophy of religion should be devoted to revealing such a law as much as possible. Although fully understanding is not possible, we nevertheless should define boundaries separating legitimate belief and religion from superstition. A believer should not accept a hypothesis that is known to be untrue. And because the unconscious is only part of the mind's activity, it cannot be overemphasized. It is equally dangerous to be totally idealistic and follow no objective criteria when dealing with metareality. At a minimum, it is possible to define what a belief and religion should *not* do, even if it is impossible to define what it should do. This is the subject of the following section.

The separation of religious content into ritual and symbolism and the truth behind them also allows the belief and the religion to evolve naturally. Rituals and symbols are means to manifest the underlying truth. The truth will not change over time, but the means to manifest the truth can change. Belief is an intuitive extension after rational thinking has been exhausted in the pursuit of truth. This intuitive extension involves symbols as agents of metareality. As time goes by, the level of understanding the self or the external world increases and deepens. When someone is one step closer to the truth, the symbols of a belief system and rituals of a religion can be changed to adapt to the new level of understanding of truth. In the meantime, humans will not be able to reach the absolute truth, so the intuitive extension after exhausting rational thought is always needed. In other words, The methodology of relying on the agent of metareality is always needed, but the actual contents, particularly the interpretation of the symbolism and ritual, can be adjusted over time.

6.7 The Mechanism of Believing

Because the root of a belief involves psychological and rational unknowns, and because the methodology of a belief framework introduces agent and proxy to metareality, which by definition is not fully comprehensible, there is plenty of room and flexibility for implementation and realization of a belief system. In order to manifest the underlying truth and attempt to make the unknown more accessible to normal individuals, symbols, agents, rituals, and others are introduced in an implementation. Obviously, there can be many interpretations of these symbols, agents, and rituals.

Also obvious is that these symbols, agents, and rituals have man-made components and hence are subject to the same limitations as other human intellectual endeavors. On one hand, symbols, agents, and rituals are necessary to manifest seemingly incomprehensible truths; but on the other hand, these man-made components create the greatest risk for turning a belief into a superstition. It is a challenge to find a balance.

Furthermore, such balance depends on the status of an individual's psychological and rational development. In this regard, belief and religious practice are more valuable at the personal level. Diversity in the implementation of belief and religious practice is unavoidable, although the methodological foundation of belief and religious practice holds the same.

Belief is an intuitive extension of rational thinking. It is a balance of multiple factors, which is different for each person. Here intuitive extension means it is a natural extension with respect to the baseline of the most trusted knowledge and experience. Everyone has his own baseline knowledge and experience that has been scrutinized and trusted without challenge; they are psychologically safe and part of his view of the world. In order to achieve the state of belief, the content of a belief is intentionally or unintentionally deciphered with respect to the baseline knowledge and experience, i.e., the believer is convinced there are logical or emotional connections between the content of the belief and their own baseline knowledge and experience, thus it is psychologically safe. The purpose of symbols and rituals is to make the connections more effective. Since each individual has a different level of knowledge and different life experiences, the connections are therefore highly personal.

As discussed before, religion has two components: 1) The laws, truth, and principles represented by the symbol. 2) Symbol and ritual.

This is necessary because the laws and principles need to be personalized in order to effectively interact with an individual, as well as a group of people. A religion that only emphasizes the second component is an empty religion; it is just superstition. However, the first component alone cannot form a religion, as it is not humanized. It is just cold, objective principles governing the world. It cannot really touch an individual's daily life effectively. The first component is objective; the second component is subjective and personalized. It serves as a subjective connection to the objective truth. Although we really cannot call the second component truth itself, it does help to reach the state of believing. The state of believing in turn helps one reach the highest level of wholeness and the truth.

There is a dilemma in reaching the state of belief. The more personalized or humanized a symbol, the more effective the belief will be in influencing daily life. But the more personalized or humanized the symbol, the less obvious or direct the connection between the symbol and the truth it represents. This will lead to a less authentic belief. Deviation too far from the first component will lead to superstition and to fooling oneself, eventually losing effectiveness. The balance depends on the individual's baseline knowledge and experience, and is specific to the individual.

6.8 Exclusivity in Religion

Although there are obvious reasons why belief and religious practice are diverse and highly personal experiences, in reality the majority of religions demand exclusivity, claiming it is the only path to truth. Why is this? The reason is related to the demand for objectivity of the metareality, which is the central piece of a belief. Objectivity, by definition, demands exclusivity.

This can be explained with the model for the mind's development process. In order for the ego and the conscious to completely surrender, and for the intellect to give in, the metareality should contain some element of objectivity; it cannot be completely subjective. In other words, metareality should objectively exist, regardless of an individual's will. An objective truth must be out there transcending an individual's life cycle; it is the fundamental element of a belief that can make the intellect completely surrender. Objectivity leads to exclusivity; it is logical in a linear rationality.

However, one must distinguish the metareality itself from the proxy or agent for it. It is potentially true that the metareality is an objective entity, but the agent, the symbol, is just proxy to the reality. The objectivity of a metareality doesn't lead to objectivity of the agent or symbol associated with it. When a believer states that God is the exclusive divine in the world, the actual meaning is that the truth represented by the concept of God is exclusive. However, God is referred to by different names, even in the Bible. There is really no need to demand exclusivity of agents and symbols.

Misunderstanding of exclusivity leads to conflict among religions. If a believer thinks the belief is an absolute truth and hence exclusive, he doesn't need to denounce other religions, since an absolute truth will ultimately be self-evident. There is no need to be defensive. Defensiveness of a belief just shows lack of confidence in it.

There are many risks like this in the realm of belief and religion. It is very important to call them out so that belief and religious practice can be truly healthy and serve their original purpose.

6.9 Is Religion Just a Personal Experience?

People have their own rational and psychological thresholds to entering the state of believing, because it really depends on the mix of an individual's reasoning capability, experience, and emotions. However, existing religions have tightly coupled the two components of religion mentioned above; not everyone can distinguish the truth of religion. It is easy to take a polarized attitude toward the second component of religion, either as a superstition or as a complete denial. It is therefore crucial that an individual, based on his own level of understanding, searches and finds a balance between what can be handled with intelligent reasoning and what must rely on the realms of religion. The key here is to be honest with yourself. Honesty to self is, in any argument, the highest ethic of human beings.

To reach the balance, one should deeply decipher the first component. During this process, he should explore all the intellectual capacity he possesses, then explore the available knowledge and science to understand the world and the self. At the end, the remaining items that cannot be explained by the available knowledge should be the starting point of the search for a belief. The advance of science has itself pointed to its own limitations; the fact that there is something that is unexplainable is self-evident, as we have shown in Chapter 3. Once the limitations of the intellectual world are self-evident, the need for a belief (and, thus, the associated symbolism and agent) becomes a natural necessity. Only at this point can one develop the second component to make his personal religion effective. And because individuals have very different levels of knowledge, the path to a belief system will be very different, hence religious practice is a mainly personal experience, although the statistical average of personal religions can be generalized and collective, hence pointing to objective values.

Another reason why belief is a primarily personal experience has to do with the psychological root of belief and religion. As was extensively discussed in Chapter 4, human nature has a tendency of reaching its full potential—actualizing potentiality. When such a tendency is applied to certain aspects of human nature, it strengthens and grows that aspect. One has to temporarily ignore the opposite aspect in order to reach full potential of the emphasized aspect. As the individual grows, the need for reconciliation becomes obvious to deal with the impacts of these unbalanced tendencies. The two tendencies of growth and reconciliation interact continuously and dynamically. How much an individual can actualize potentiality, and how much value he or she can unleash in life, depends on how much he or she can integrate the two tendencies into the wholeness harmoniously. The more of the oneness reached, the more difficult the integration, but also the happier the individual, with a stronger sense of achievement, relief, and of the eternal. A person can just stay in a small oneness that is harmoniously integrated and he or she will live a happy life, even though the sense of achievement is relatively weak, and the spectrum of mind activities is relatively narrow. On the other hand, a person can push hard to reach maximum potential but be unable to integrate with the whole self. He or she may have good sense of achievement but not a happy life; or in Christianity, he or she is stuck in original sin, unable to reconcile with God. When a person actualizes his potential and also successfully integrates the self, he will experience a great sense of achievement, relief, and awareness of the eternal. But to reach this stage first requires struggle and suffering from the separation. The process of growing is painful, and there is no guarantee of success. It is with this difficulty that many psychologists suggested religion as a complementary mechanism to help one reconcile the opposing forces in a harmonious way.

Such integration is a highly personal experience. Experiencing the opposite and insufficient state is the precondition for integration with the bigger wholeness. Such process and experience cannot by substituted with any other means. That's why for most of us, regardless of how much teaching or advice we've received, we will not believe or understand something until we experience it. We must respect this. When an individual goes through the process and experiences the difficulty, his or her chance of experiencing the truth is increased. Truth cannot just be taught. One must actively pursue it and tune to it. Even though everyone has the potential to gain knowledge of it, it is not automatic. If a person simply acknowledges and accepts all the teachings without thinking, challenging, and trying to experience it, it is simply superstition. It is for this reason that religious practice must be personal. In Christianity, this is expressed as the need for evil, or that evil is needed in order to reveal the glory of God. When facing difficulty in life is unavoidable, the attitude on how to experience it will make a big difference. The pain may not be in facing the difficulty itself, but in experiencing it without understanding the meaning.

Since the implementation of any belief and religion is intrinsically personalized; the path to a belief is different for different individuals. But is religious practice solely a personal experience? We cannot claim that either. The psychological development process is common and the methodological framework is common. It is true the religious experience is personal, but it is not the only aspect of religion. One of the roots of religion is the connection to the fourth world, which represents the collective output of human intellectual activity as a whole, subtracting the collective output of activities from the conscious mind. Religious practice seeks a connection to a transcendent existence, which by definition is collective. Therefore, most religious practices are group activities. If a religion is approached solely as a personal experience, it cannot address the need for connection to a collective transcendent existence, and hence it is an incomplete religion. The risk of group practice is it is easy for man-made factors to hijack the true messages behind a belief system. It is more difficult to separate the symbol, rituals, and the true underlying message from each other. It is easier to be misled. There are many critics of institutionalized religion. To be more fair, we need to look deeper into what a mature and healthy religion should be.

6.10 What Defines a Mature Religion?

Even though there are intrinsic needs for belief and religion, and there are strong justifications for their fundamental methodology, religious practice can nevertheless be easily misused or misguided, which indeed had occurred in history. Because of this high risk, when a religious practice turns into a superstition, it becomes a hindrance to the freedom and potential of an individual.

What is a healthy religious practice, and what is an unhealthy one? What are the criteria to make the distinction? These questions are not easy to answer. Based on the discussion in this chapter, some guidelines can be extracted to make the distinction and call out misleading practices.

Incorrect Root and Motivation

People start to engage a belief or religious practice for many different reasons: family tradition, wanting to enter a social circle, seeking help, facing a life disaster, political reasons, and many more. These are trigger points for engaging in a religious practice. Ultimately, the roots for engaging in a belief or religious practice come from internal psychological development and the spiritual search for a transcendent connection, which must come only after exhausting all rational thought. It can take time to realize this, but if one's motivation for a belief or religious practice stays on the initial reasons mentioned earlier, it is most likely a superstition. Furthermore, as religious practice is a highly personal experience, it is a spiritual journey that cannot be substituted with someone else's experience. No one can be forced into believing something. Religion based on fear or external force is plainly wrong.

The existence of institutionalized religion also complicates the situation. Institutionalized religion has a set of rituals. If one follows it strictly, one seemingly starts the religious practice. But as long as the individual does not go through the spiritual journey to realize the true root of belief and religion, he is not yet truly in a belief state. The reality is that not everyone can reach the belief state (see the discussion of unification in Chapter 4). As a result, there is likely a considerable number of people who join an institutionalized religious organization without being truly in the belief state. This poses a challenge to the image of institutionalized religious organizations.

Consider another risk that religious organizations can mislead those who try to believe. Religious practice indeed brings benefits to an individual's psychological development and a sense of connection to something that is perceived as transcendent. But it is possible that even if an individual has not yet gone through the spiritual or mental journey to reach a true belief state, he has already experienced the benefits and therefore ignores or pays less attention to the true belief state. This is the typical pragmatic methodology in religious practices. But it poses a risk for manipulation: after experiencing the benefit but before actually going through the spiritual journey, a believer can be guided to base his belief on religious doctrine. This may not be a problem if the religious doctrine is healthy and consistent with the actual roots of belief and religion. Otherwise, the believer may not be able to recover from the connection between the benefits versus the religious doctrine, and he will deviate from the true roots of belief and religion. In this case, believing is hijacked by the religious doctrine.

Inability to Separate Symbol and Metareality

The most fundamental problem of many religions is that they cannot separate the symbols and rituals from the underlying truth. Treating the symbols and rituals as reality is the most common mistake. There is a lot of discussion in this book regarding metareality. It is needed methodologically to introduce the concept of proxy to a reality that is not and cannot be fully understood. This methodology is also observed in scientific research. In the religious context, metareality refers to two components:

1. The self, which is the wholeness of the psyche that is larger than the ego.
2. The fourth world that arises from the emergence effect of a complex system and is beyond our current intelligence.

These exist but the exact contents are unknown. Concepts and proxies are introduced to supplement our regular reasoning to deal with metareality. In religious practice they are represented by symbols and rituals to manifest the underlying complex reality. There are subjective components in these symbols and agents. Therefore, it is a mistake to treat the symbols and agents as absolute reality.

The debate of whether God exists, whether there is an intelligent designer, is an example. The concept of God is a symbol, an agent to the incomprehensible metareality. It is a useful and necessary concept for assisting human understanding of the world. But it is just a proxy agent to reality. The reality represented by God likely exists, particularly the wholeness in the psyche. But the interpretation has a subjective component.

Recognizing the symbol and agent is proxy to metareality avoids the unnecessary claim of exclusivity. Claiming exclusivity is another problem of many religions. Because symbols and agents are just proxies to metareality, there can be many versions of them, and there is no need for exclusivity. Religions that claim their divine is the only true divine simply equate the symbol to the absolute truth behind the metareality. There isn't only one path to truth, nor only one proxy to metareality, but there can be a best path, a best proxy to the truth. Religions that claim their doctrine is the only path to truth are either mixing up symbol versus truth, or lack confidence. A religion that puts too much emphasis on exclusivity is not a healthy one. A religion should base confidence not on believing it is the *only* way, but believing it is the *best* way to attain the underlying truth. Furthermore, because religious practice is a highly personal experience, it can well be that different individuals find different religions are best for them. That is a key reason that modern society allows religious freedom.

The same argument applies with respect to rituals and miracles found in most religions. Miracles are rituals or sets of symbols representing the true underlying message. Believers should distinguish them and not place too much emphasis on obeying rituals and believing miracles. Judging the beliefs of a religion based on its rituals is certainly wrong.

Unbalanced Reconciliation and Growth Tendencies

A common characteristic of religions is overemphasis of the reconciliation process. This seems quite natural. Religion is rooted in helping the reconciliation process of the human mind. In order to achieve that, the ego and the human intellect need to give up the dominant position. Religious doctrine typically emphasizes the dark side of the secular world, the tragedy of ignoring the voice of the heart, the disconnection from the divine. The death of ego is the precondition for reconciliation. But here "death" does not really mean that the ego is destroyed; it just means the dominant position must be given up. The force representing actuating potential must work together with the force representing reconciliation. Together, they reflect the finest of the human mind, and their dynamic determines the spectrum of life. However, most religions downplay the force representing actuation of human potential too much.

If a religious practice implies a detachment from the routine life, from the secular world, from manifesting humanity, it is a questionable religion. Such a religion is not a mature one. The goal of religious practice is supposed to be living out the bigger wholeness, maximizing values as a human being. It therefore should encompass every important aspect of humanity, rather than ignoring, avoiding, or even condemning it.

Not Exhausting Rationality

Similarly, most religions tend to overemphasize the mythical aspects of the practice, and reduce or avoid necessary rational thinking. Again, it is seemingly natural for religion to have this kind of attitude. Belief is the intuitive extension of human intellect after rationality is exhausted. At that stage, myth becomes valuable to help people probe the underlying truth. But it is on the condition of exhausting human intellect first.

If the myth clearly contradicts our rationality, bluntly accepting the myth and ignoring rationality seems to be an assault on human intellect. It will not reach a harmonious state of reconciliation. When a religion tries to convey the message of hope and love, but builds upon some mythical assumptions that clearly contradict rationality, it is really a brutal experience. On one hand, believers have devoted emotion to the belief doctrine and are emotionally attached to it; on the other hand, the mythical assumptions conflict with rationality, so they constantly question whether what they believe is true or false. The struggle can be a painful experience. As discussed earlier on the mechanism of belief, to genuinely believe a hypothesis, an individual needs to accept it to a stage of psychological and rational safety, i.e., it is compatible with his or her psychology and rational mind. Otherwise, it is a struggle. To reach the compatible stage with his or her psychology and rational mind, rationality and intellect need to be exhausted first.

It is true that, by definition, a religion needs myth to convey certain messages that cannot be conveyed through rational logic. But it doesn't mean it should turn to the opposite of rationality. *The goal of religious practice is supposed to be to live out the bigger wholeness, to maximize values as a human being. It therefore should encompass every important aspect of humanity, including rationality and intellect, rather than reducing, avoiding, or even condemning it.* Inclusion and unification are the key words here, not contradiction and ignorance. This criteria is crucial to distinguish whether a religion is a mature one. A religion that places too much emphasis on myth and miracles, and ignores and avoids rationality, is not a healthy one.

Additional Criteria for a Good Belief System

We have called out the potential mistakes a belief system or religion can make. What would be the characteristics of a prudent belief system? Some characteristics of such a belief system include:

- Truly based on human nature, addressing the roots of the need for religion. It should be consistent with the mind's development cycle, providing a channel to facilitate the reconciliation process.
- Compliant with the fundamental methodology, especially accurately grasping the meaning of metareality and the relationship between agents and symbols with the underlying truth.
- Belief in the creativity, adaptability, and survival of human beings. Instead of blaming the ethics of the secular world as degrading, endorse efforts to extend survivability as a whole. This can include: a) better knowledge and understanding of nature, the self, and better capability to cooperate with nature (not control it); b) better relationships among mankind; c) that there is a life flow of human history, and one should attach or contribute to it to make oneself more valuable.
- A belief system should be constantly checked to see if it is an open-ended belief instead of one believing in some fixed content. It should acknowledge that there is a limitation on brain power and capabilities of mankind. We constantly seek for hints and guidance.
- Genuinely believing. One should ask herself if she truly believes something. A belief that is not genuine will not work. As discussed earlier, the belief threshold depends on whether the perception of a hypothesis is consistent with

the individual's intellectual knowledge and personal experience, consistent to a level that there is feeling of psychological safety. One should exhaust rationality before reaching such a state. Furthermore, if you believe something exists or will happen, there must be a probability it does exist or will happen, however small the probability is. If such probability is *zero*, it for sure cannot form a belief. This is the reality grounds for a belief. It may not be able to be confirmed, but it is also not total nonsense.

- Addressing the phenomenon of megastatistics. A belief may depend on the time scale of the content of the hypothesis. If the time scale is short, say within one's life-span, then it can be experienced. A belief is easy to affirm if one actually experiences it and applies it to influence his own life. However, if the time span is tremendously long, such as the destiny of human beings, it is then extremely hard to affirm. It is at this point one has to make a choice: yes, no, or avoid. Most people will avoid it because it is too far away from normal life. That's why only a small percentage of people are interested in these questions. A belief system should be able to answer this issue.

- Addressing concerns about the final destiny of human beings and the goal of life. It is not necessary to connect the goal of life to the final destiny of human beings. The goal of life can be derived even though the answer of humanity's final destiny is yet to be known. The goals for our current life-span can be derived, but beyond that, and how it connects to the destiny of humankind, is an evolving process, and the evolutionary path is incomprehensible.

Case Study: Truth versus Exclusivity

It is too abstract to discuss the truth behind religion without a concrete example. We will conclude this chapter with a case study on the topic "Who is Jesus?" in Christianity. It is by no means to be a bias toward accepting or rejecting Christianity. It is just a case study to see how the discussion of religion in this chapter can be applied.

According to the Bible, Jesus was crucified because he was accused of being dangerous to the Jewish religion. He forced everyone to face the question of who he was. The event was too mysterious, too profound, and it took mankind thousands of years of striving to understand it. Because Jesus drew attention to the cruel aspects of human nature when separated from God so deeply, he accepted such an extreme act as being crucified to reveal the "sin" of mankind. From that point on, whoever thought of this event would hopefully remember why it had happened and acknowledge the sin, changing his or her attitude to life. For thousands of years, theists did their best to reveal the meaning of the crucifixion of Jesus.

Jesus said, "I am the truth, I am the path." The truth here refers more to the truth of reconciliation ("salvation" in Christian terminology), truth for interpersonal relationships ("love" in Christian terminology). The path refers to the path toward reconciliation, the path to the transcendent life river ("Kingdom of Heaven" in Christian terminology). When one believes in the truth of love, he may appear weak due to the softer aspects of love. When the tendency of reconciliation dominates, an individual appears to be a weak person. In facing conflict with the secular world or from other immature religions, he feels helpless and in pain. He thus has more understanding of the pain of Jesus on the cross. Jesus represents the truth of reconciliation, the truth of love, but when faced with a society dominated by the force of just actualizing potential, he was crucified. This really posed a profound dilemma, not only on how individual minds developed, but also how human history unfolded.

- On one hand, it is quite acceptable to believe that the reconciliation tendency will eventually successfully integrate with the tendency of growth when an individual is more mature. People caring, respecting, and loving others will become the norm of society, regardless of race, geography, and cultural differences (the vision Jesus described as the Kingdom of Heaven). It is a universal standard and foundation for individuals to mature and for human beings to live together harmoniously.
- On the other hand, before the above vision becomes fact, before the ethics of caring, respecting, and loving become dominant values, whoever believes in it are the minority. They also appear to be a weak minority because they practice those values. From a secular point of view, mercy toward others and forgiveness given to enemies are the characteristics of weakness and even seem ridiculous. But these values will eventually dominate. It just needs thousands of years—not a generation but many generations. The methodology of megastatistics really applies here. During the process, generation after generation must continue passing the messages and practicing the values; it requires countless lives to attach to the value, which is what Christianity refers to as the eternal life.
- Because of this dilemma, before these values become dominant, Christian believers long for the resurrection of Jesus Christ. His resurrection would

show that the values of reconciliation and love will eventually win, regardless of how weak they initially appear. It provides strength and hope for them to continue their practices. However, the resurrection is not necessarily bodily resurrection; it is a resurrection of a new life representing universal values (2 Corinthians 4:18).

The key message the Christian religion conveys is that the reconciliation of the separation caused by human potentiality and intellectual evolution will eventually dominate. The means to realize such vision and influence others is through love, forgiveness, and mercy to everyone, including enemies. This effort is transcendent and needs thousands of years. Before that, whoever believes in and practices it may be considered weak and may even be persecuted by the secular world, which is dominated by the force of actualizing human potential. Jesus was the one who first called out and practiced such values, but he got crucified. It was a wake-up call and a turning point for human history with regard to the dynamics of reconciliation and growth tendencies. It forced the renewal of human ethical values to a new height. Christians believe that the vision described by Jesus will dominate in the end, which represents a resurrection of Jesus.

The above message is certainly profound and valuable. Modern people should not find much difficulty in accepting the message itself. However, Christian theists have proposed some confusing explanations. Trinity is one such thing. As mentioned earlier many times, metareality is something we believe exists but are unable to fully comprehend. It needs a concept of agent and proxy to it, such as God. But such a concept is very abstract and difficult to connect to daily life, hence the theists described Jesus as yet another proxy to metareality. Furthermore, one of the roots of religion is in the human psyche, the concept of self for unification of the conscious with the wholeness of mind. The self is yet another proxy to metareality. Christian theists named this the Holy Spirit. By attaching the self to the transcendent value of unification and love for others, the individual life is said to have eternal meaning. Hence the concept of the Holy Spirit and the concept of God are connected. By putting these three concepts together and making them equally important, theists came up with the doctrine of the trinity in an attempt to unify the different symbols into one.

As many other religions do, Christian theists claimed exclusivity of the above doctrine. Exclusivity, as explained before, is due to the fact that the doctrine equates the proxy and symbol with the metareality itself. It helps to enforce authority. The exclusivity issue has caused a lot of debate and conflict with many other cultures.

This is unnecessary. Jesus said, "I am the truth, I am the way." But he didn't say, "I am the *only* way." Indeed, there is probably no need for saying it is the *only* way, because confidence in a belief is not necessarily built on exclusivity but on its being the *best* way. The problem of exclusivity is as follows: for one to have a new life, a life with love, mercy, and forgiveness, the only way is to believe in Jesus. However, other cultures and religions say that such quality of life can be attained their way as well, and those cannot be excluded. Is the way Jesus taught the best or only way? Was the crucifixion of Jesus the *only* way to awaken the world to the dilemma of reconciliation? The doctrines of physical resurrection and trinity are extremely difficult to explain and interpret, causing many people to reject Christianity. It is an unfortunate thing that the precious message from Christianity cannot get through to many people due to its own methodological difficulty. How Christian believers can work through this difficulty and spread their message in a more effective way is a challenge, but at least the challenge should be recognized instead of ignored.

Reference

- Chuang-tzu. "Chi Wu Lun."
- Fuller, Andrew R. *Psychology and Religion: Classical Theorists and Contemporary Developments* (Lanham, Maryland: Rowman & Littlefield Publishers, Inc., 2008, fourth edition).
- Fung, Yu-lan. *A Short History of Chinese Philosophy* (New York: Free Press, 1997).
- Russell, Bertrand. "Why I Am Not a Christian" (lecture, National Secular Society, South London Branch, London, England, March 6, 1927).

CHAPTER 7

Comparison
of Cultures

7.1 What is Culture?

The previous chapter focused on beliefs and religions that deal with the deepest part of the human mind, including the unconscious. A belief system and religion are built on systematic philosophy and rituals. However, there are other byproducts of human consciousness that nurture the development of the human mind, regulating an individual's routine life, social interactions, etc. These more loosely defined byproducts of human activities are collectively called culture. A more rigorous definition can be found from a dictionary; Culture can refer to (*Webster*):

- The integrated pattern of human knowledge, belief, and behavior that depends upon the capacity for learning and transmitting knowledge to succeeding generations;
- The set of shared attitudes, values, goals, and practices that characterizes an institution or organization;
- The set of values, conventions, or social practices associated with a particular field, activity, or societal characteristic.

Either culture or religion can address the needs of psychological development and the search for the goal of life. Most people actually just rely on the culture they live in to provide values and norms to follow, without religious ritual. An individual's maturation process is like a scaled-down version of the evolutionary process of culture and religion, from preliminary level to mature level. But not everyone can reach the most current level, consequently everyone has different demands for culture and religion. This is why, at any given time, a society needs to offer different levels and variations of culture and religion to meet the diverse needs of individuals in the society. This is also why it is important to examine different cultures around the world. Religion is not the only platform that humans look to for answers and nurturing of the spirit. It cannot cover the whole spectrum of human mental activity. Many components of a culture other than religion, such as philosophy, music, art, literature, and traditions, are other forms of the byproduct of the search for meaning. By understanding how different cultures address the needs of human nature and build ethical value systems, we gain more insight into human nature and ethical value systems. By comparing different cultures, we gain better understanding of the strengths and weaknesses of each culture, which in turn helps us understand each culture.

The starting point to examine a culture is no different from that for any belief system or religion. It must be based on the understanding of human nature. A culture that can more completely and precisely cover the spectrum of human minds and everyday life, and more successfully put it into experience and practice, will be the more widely accepted culture, and hence have a longer life cycle. There are many ways to characterize the nature of human beings. In Chapter 4, we discussed the different phases of the human mental development cycle, and the two fundamental tendencies (growth and reconciliation) that drive development of the human mind. Another angle is to categorize human life into different levels: 1) Biological level: survival and reproduction. 2) Social level: social status and recognition, group life. 3) Spiritual level: transcending the biological life, living a bigger life.

Regardless of the method used to characterize the human life and mind, we need to pay attention to the following interrelationships between culture and individuals:

- A culture or religion is supposed to nurture and connect different levels of life and different phases of mental development, rather than emphasizing one particular level, or denouncing one level in order to endorse another.
- Just like any scientific model, a philosophy on life is just an approximation of reality. We ought to remember that the ultimate driver comes from real life—it evolves as time goes by, and the philosophy on life must be adaptive to it, not the other way around.

- A complete life should go through all the phases, otherwise it is incomplete. Further, the earlier phase must be completed before one is able to enter the next phase. It is better to remain incomplete, i.e., not experience more advanced phases, than to bypass (for whatever reason) an earlier phase in order to experience more advanced phases.

Culture is just an aggregation of individual thoughts and experience over a long time. The two tendencies discussed in Chapter 4 that influence the individual's development of the mind, actualizing potentiality and reconciliation, naturally influence how a culture is shaped through its dynamics and interactions. In other words, how a culture reflects the dynamics of these two tendencies influences how the culture evolves over its history. The following two questions are of particular importance when looking inside a culture: 1) Which tendency is more emphasized, consciousness and intellectual development or reconciliation? 2) How does a culture address the interaction between the conscious and the wholeness of self? Different answers to these questions can be found in different cultures. Many cultures rely on a religious approach to address them.

In this chapter, we will compare Chinese culture and Western culture. The goal is to apply the principles in Chapters 2 through 5 to better understand the cultural difference. The reason for choosing Chinese culture as the study subject is that it is less connected to a religion. It attempts to answer fundamental humanity questions based on philosophical reasoning rather than religion. Western culture places great emphasis on the differentiation of things. The ability to differentiate is the origin for generating knowledge; it is the force that unleashes human potential. Science, philosophy, and rational thinking are examples of the products from this powerful Western approach. Chinese culture, on the other hand, places much emphasis on the unification tendency without connecting it to religious approaches, which is quite unique. It is extremely valuable to know that a nonreligious approach can also address the reconciliation of the fourth world. The attitude of keeping unification as a starting point hinders the desire to zoom out the reality and generate more detailed, precise knowledge. Science, math, and logic remained in preliminary forms and were not well advanced. However, Chinese philosophy contributed a great deal on how to cultivate the heart and maintain the view of wholeness without relying on a religious approach.

There is a lot of literature on Chinese philosophy. This chapter will briefly survey only the major Chinese philosophies. Then the focus will shift to the comparison between Chinese culture and Western culture, what the differences are, and how they can learn from each other.

7.2 Taoism

The first major stream of Chinese philosophy is Taoism. The two most famous Taoist philosophers were Lao-tzu and Chuang-tzu. The key ideas of Lao-tzu are highlighted below:

- The concept of Tao cannot be named and cannot be described in our language. It is a concept of metaphysics. Tao is the origin of all things, which is why it cannot be expressed in our language. We can communicate with it, yet we cannot describe it. Therefore it is named Tao as a placeholder. Since Tao is the origin of all things, it cannot be one of the things. Everything has a name, but Tao is not one of the things, so it cannot be named. This is similar to the concept of metareality described in Chapter 5. But there are more important implications here: Lao-tzu emphasizes that Tao cannot be explained or separated into parts to gain understanding. The development of intelligence simply leads to a false understanding of reality (Lao-tzu, Ch. 18). The starting point is more focused on the cohesiveness and wholeness of Tao. Any knowledge of it gained through breaking it down into parts and differentiation is not recommended, even condemnable.

- Although Tao cannot be named and explained, its action and influence on the world can be observed. The world can change, but the laws that govern the changes are unchanged. These laws are simply the manifestation of Tao, and they are called *Chang*, or in English, invariable, eternal. Among the observed invariables, the following two are most fundamental: 1) "The movement of return is the action of Tao" (Lao-tzu, Ch. 40). The movement of any force cannot go on forever. When it reaches an extreme, it will return. This is simply the law of Tao. Lao-tzu didn't tell us the reason, but we can infer that it is due to the fact everything is connected—there is no single isolated object. For movement of any force, there is always a counterforce to get it to come back when the first force moves too far. Lao-tzu also didn't tell us where the limit is or when it will return. This law is in fact at a metaphysical level. It doesn't specify the actual limit, because the limit itself is relative, depending on subjective and objective conditions. 2) Thing exists because its opposite side also exists. In other words, everything has an opposite side, otherwise it doesn't exist. To preserve one thing, one should acknowledge and preserve its opposite. This is precisely consistent with the idea that any knowledge is generated by differentiation. An existence can be differentiated only because there is an opposite, otherwise it cannot be described. Lao-tzu said, "Knowing why it is beautiful means it is ugly; knowing why it needs to be nice means it is not nice; being and void are born together; difficulty and ease exist together" (Lao-tzu, Ch. 2), which is very similar to the idea from dialect.

- No intentional action. Lao-tzu considers human intellect as a stumbling block to grasping the deep truth of reality. Therefore, his advice to us is to follow nature and not play in the realm of intentional action. Human action should be confined to only what is necessary and in keeping with nature. Humans should carefully refrain from the use of intellect to attempt to outsmart nature. To Lao-tzu, it is better not to have too much human-generated knowledge, and instead follow nature to grasp the meaning of wholeness of the world.

- Virtue, or *De*, refers to the intrinsic nature of things, or the thing as it is. Having virtue means respecting and following the nature of things. There is no need to invent ethics and values to regulate human behavior. Ethics, values, and laws are needed because we have lost De. This is why Laozi doesn't like Confucian theory (Lao-tzu, Ch. 38). But what Lao-tzu missed here is that human desires and intellect are themselves part of human nature. We cannot totally ignore them, and instead need to accept and guide them.

In general, Taoism views knowledge as being the product of human intellect. The more knowledge one has, the more one wants to know more. Furthermore, the limited knowledge is a distorted understanding of nature. The more one attempts to consolidate and generalize knowledge, the more their understanding of nature is distorted. Ironically, if one applies the concept of, "The movement of return is the action of Tao," one should not worry about the expansion of knowledge, because at some point, the knowledge itself will realize its own limitations. But at the time of Lao-tzu, accumulated knowledge was not sufficient yet to have reached its turning point of awareness that limitation was self-evident.

The next most-famous Taoist philosopher was Chuang-tzu. Chuang-tzu continued the thought that things are inseparable and that the separation of self from the outside world is the source of unhappiness. Even though there was little knowledge of psychology at the time of Chuang-tzu, his ideas regarding the boundary of self were profound and influenced generations of Chinese philosophers after him.

- There are two levels of happiness for human beings. The first level is freedom and development of human nature (Fung, Ch. 10). Every life in nature has its own characteristics and personality, but they all have the same need—only when their potential has been freely developed and unleashed will they feel happiness. But this level of happiness is relative, because it depends on the physical body and the self; there is still a boundary between self and others.

- The next level of happiness comes from the elimination of the boundary between the self and others. "The Heaven, the Earth, and the Self are born together; the Self and everything else are the same One" (Chuang-tzu, "Ch'i Wu Lun"). When one is able to blur the boundary between the self and the rest of the world, he reaches the state of unifying self with nature, the Tao. Chuang-tzu described a very interesting experience: he dreamed he became a butterfly, flying happily. He was not sure if it was Chuang-tzu becoming a butterfly in the dream, or the butterfly becoming Chuang-tzu in a dream. When the boundary of separation is blurred, one experiences a high level of Tao and reaches the ultimate happiness.

- Building on the above understanding, Chuang-tzu continued to explore the meaning of life. Since everything in the universe is connected, when an individual reaches the state of blurring the boundary of self and the nature of oneness he becomes a saint, and the physical body is simply dust (the chemical components, in modern language). Life and death are just as day and night. They are a natural continuation and won't bother the state of mind of a saint. When unifying the self as part of the One, the One is transcendent with the universe, therefore the mind of the saint is transcendent. "The Saint's mind can live in the same environment of all things and therefore all are transcending" (Chuang-tzu, "Da Zhong Shi").

Chuang-tzu's idea of the two levels of happiness goes one step further than Lao-tzu's idea. Though both acknowledged that human intellect and knowledge create more separation and should be reduced, Chuang-tzu accepted that freedom of mind and the unleashing of human potential are a level of happiness one should pursue. It is simply part of human nature that no one can deny. This was an advancement on Lao-tzu's philosophy.

Similar to Lao-tzu's idea on Tao, One is incomprehensible, indescribable. Since knowledge introduced differentiation and separation, one should eliminate knowledge step by step and reverse back to the state of only experiencing the One. But we should note that such state of mind is different from the state of no knowledge at all. Instead, it is an "unwiring" process of the acquired knowledge, because it is the output from our intellect at the current level. Chuang-tzu had deep insight on the limitations of human knowledge. He said, "My life is limited, and knowledge is unlimited. Letting the limited life pursue unlimited knowledge is sure to fail" (Chuang-tzu, "Yang Sheng Zhu"). In reaching for higher-level experience, knowledge at the lower level becomes a burden, and hence it should be "unwired" so that the secular ethics, the separations, will be eliminated. The mind is then free to transcend to the next level.

Chuang-tzu's description is similar to the self-organization theory of society. There is no need to impose rules or laws—just let people enjoy the freedom to explore and actualize their potential. The next level of experience and understanding exists in parallel with the secular world. By cultivating the mind and listening to the heart, one may be able to take a higher-level view that is different from the secular world. It is possible that two levels of worlds coexist, but at the time of Chuang-tzu, people didn't have the knowledge of nonlinearity of complex systems, so his description of "eliminating knowledge and intelligence" sounded very radical at the time.

Taoism had a profound influence on Chinese culture. It shows that more than two thousand years ago, Chinese philosophers already had a deep understanding of the two levels of the mind: 1) Freedom of development and unleashing of human potential. 2) Reconciling the self with the rest of the world by eliminating the boundary and giving up the dominance of human intellect in order to enter the higher level of life.

More profoundly, the philosophy was developed in a nonreligious context. The nonreligious context had both an advantage and a disadvantage. The advantage is that it is easier to further develop and refine, and thus it integrates with later advancements in the culture. The disadvantage is that it is hard to put into practice. Typically, only a small portion of the population, the most intelligent group, can understand and practice it. The majority of the population at that time would not understood such profound thought. This was different from religions, which have symbols and rituals to manifest the deeper message (see Chapter 6) and is more easily understood and practiced by a majority of the population.

Although Chuang-tzu's idea was one step closer to accepting the importance of freely developing human nature and proposed a view of the world from a higher level to unify the self with the rest of the world, his treatment of human nature was still too simplistic. It neglected the complexity of exploring potential and instead emphasized the return to nature. Confucian philosopher Xun-tzu criticized, "Chuang-tzu overemphasized the understanding of Heaven, but did not know well about human beings" (Xun-tze). This meant Taoist philosophy neglects the complexity of human nature and doesn't establish a value system to address the complexity of development of human nature, human behavior in social life, etc. These issues were the main subjects of Confucianism.

The human mind is always occupied with something. It is impossible to organize or control the living flow of the mind, because mind itself is an autonomous entity. To empty these preoccupations, the mind should open itself up, let everything be as it is, and live itself in its nature to feel the oneness. When in this state, the mind feels the world as it is, without imposing any individual ideas. This is the state of mind Taoism pursues. But such state of mind is not the primary state, and it cannot be held for a long time. Instead, it is momentary. The mind still keeps reaching, floating, and exploring. One cannot ignore this nature. Another natural characteristic of human beings is the desire to reach maximum potential. All these intrinsic natures cannot be dealt with by simply emptying the mind so natural law can run as it is, because actualizing potential itself is a part of natural law. The result is that one will search for goals, meanings, and values, consequently resulting in complex social structures. For addressing these requirements, Taoism is insufficient. Instead Confucianism filled up the gap and became the mainstream philosophy in Chinese culture.

7.3 Confucianism

In Chinese philosophy, Confucianism was the mainstream for more than two thousand years. It embraced the nature of the human mind, building up a value system that supported the growth tendency, human intellect (relative to Taoism), and a complex social life. However, in Confucian philosophy, values and meanings are relative. The starting point of Confucianism is that humankind is the center of the world. The statement "Man is the measure of all things" probably best describes the core value of Confucianism. Although Confucius (K'ung-tzu in Chinese) and Mencius (Meng-tzu in Chinese) proposed certain concepts that cannot be derived from human nature, such as Heaven, fate, Hao-Ran-Zhi-Qi (the Great Supreme Morale (Fung, 78)), and "Union of Heaven and Man," these words were fairly elementary and not developed into a religious form. There is no concept of eternal life. Heaven sounds like a supernatural idea, but it is just a static concept and not personalized. The idea of transcending beyond human nature was not in the mainstream of Confucianism and had weak influence. Essentially, the starting and central points of Confucianism are human beings themselves.

Confucius (K'ung-tzu) was the founder of this most important Chinese philosophy. The key concepts from Confucius can be summarized as below (Fung, Ch. 4):

- *Jen*, meaning love others as they are. This concept was later extended to cover a much broader meaning. *Jen* is essentially the sympathy connection of life, between human beings, or even between a human and another life in nature. *Jen* is the most basic emotional connection in life. Loving others is just a concrete outcome of *Jen*. In Chinese characters, *Jen* simply means "two persons together." Since *Jen* is the most basic connection based on the relationship between two people, it echoes the core value of Confucianism: that man is the measure of all things.

- *Chung* and *shu*. Chung means conscientiousness toward others. "Desiring to sustain himself, sustain others; desiring to develop himself, develop others"(Fung, 43). It means do to others what you wish for yourself. This is the positive aspect of practicing *Jen*. Shu means altruism: "Do not do to others what you do not wish done to yourself" (Analects, XII 2). It is the other side of practicing *Jen* (Fung, 43). Putting the two together, it means we measure others based on our own standard. This is the basic approach to practice *Jen*, extending the meaning of man is the measure of all things. It is a fundamental idea that can be found in many other cultures.

- *Yi*, righteousness, means "oughtness" (Fung, 42). Anyone in a society must do what morally ought to be done, and do it as the end goal, not as a means for other purposes. When a person does things according to the morality instead of his own interests, it is the action of righteousness.

- *Ming* (fate). Taoism taught us not doing intentional things because human intellect can distort the understanding of true nature. It is rather passive. Confucius, on the other hand, was more proactive and proposed, "doing the best, but not demanding the outcome" (Fung, 44–45). The attitude of doing the best is at the hand of human beings, but the result is at the hand of Heaven. One cannot really passively do nothing as proposed by Taoism. Instead, one should continue to strive for the best, even though there is no definite guarantee of the results. The value is in the process itself, not the results. *Ming*, fate in English, means the external conditions and other forces that are beyond one's control. We do our best even though the outcome may be beyond our control. We know that this is nonlinear thinking in modern language. It acknowledges the limits of the human intellect, but doesn't give it up. There is force we don't know even though it exists. This is positive thinking. It points out the basic human nature of striving toward our best potential in given external conditions. It is because of this difference that we say Confucianism was more supportive of actualizing human potential, while Taoism was more focused on the tendency of unification.

Confucius's teaching touched many aspects of human nature and established a social and ethical system that helped stabilize the society. It was much more widely accepted—it dominated Chinese culture for more than two thousand years.

Later, other Confucian philosophers continued to refine and develop these basic ideas. Xun-tzu emphasized the importance of human intellect. He proposed that the Heaven, the earth, and the human being are equally important in the universe. Xun-tzu believed that "men are born with evilness" (Xun-tzu, Ch. 23), that men are born with the desire for profit and sensual pleasure. It is the human intellect that can help them become good. "The nature of man is evil, his goodness is acquired through training" (Xun-tzu, Ch. 23). Conscience and values are created by human beings. Values are embedded in a culture, and culture is the creation of human intellect, which is equally important as Heaven and Earth.

Another Confucian philosopher, Tung Chung-shu continued to develop Xun-tzu's ideas. He believed "The Heaven, the Earth, and the human being are the foundation of all things. Everything is born by the Heaven, cultivated by the Earth, and realized by the human being" (Tung). But how is it realized? Through culture and cultivation. The reason that human beings can stand in parallel with Heaven and Earth, is that they have intellect and generate knowledge and culture. Heaven and Earth comprise yin and yang, and human beings are the replicas of Heaven and Earth. Therefore, the human mind also possesses these two components that manifest as the virtues (*Jen*, righteousness, wisdom, etc.) and emotions.

Mencius (Meng-tzu) believed "Men are born with the seeds of four goodness (*Jen*, righteousness, propriety, and wisdom)" (Fung, 70). Fully developing these seeds, anyone can become a sage. Mencius said, "Whoever knows everything at the bottom of heart, knows the mind; whoever knows everything in the mind, knows the Heaven" (Meng-tze). So according to Mencius, virtue and conscience are in the original nature of men. If not hindered by external conditions, they will develop into full virtues from within, like a tree grown from its seed. This view was very different from Taoism and some of the other Confucian philosophers, who believed men are neither good nor bad, and morality is artificially added through training. But why should humans develop these virtues in full instead of just following the lower-level instincts? Mencius answered that these virtues differentiate human beings from animals. Only when these virtues are fully developed is that person a fully developed human. Humanity is the core value. *The notable tradition of Confucianism here is that the teaching is not based on religious context and does not assume benefit from an afterlife or next cycle of life, or penalty for developing the virtues or not. Instead, these questions are answered consistently within the context of current life and within the scope of human beings themselves.*

Even though Confucianism was not developed in a religious context, it did enjoy wide acceptance and spread across the region due to its official status bestowed by the government. The disadvantage of this was that the government support hindered its natural development. For a long period of time, since the Han Dynasty, there weren't many new ideas until the spread of Buddhism into China. In the meantime, other folk religions were popular in rural areas of China. Confucianism was largely understood and practiced by intellectuals and the elite class of Chinese society. The needs for religion were there only for a lower class of people. Since Confucianism and Taoism were not really religions, folk religions were popular in rural areas to supplement them.

7.4 Neo-Confucianism

Origin of Neo-Confucianism

According to Fung Yu-lan, Neo-Confucianism originated from three sources (Fung, 268): traditional Confucianism, Taoism, and Buddhism. It is an effort to blend multiple philosophies into a cohesive theory. For hundreds of years after Buddhism spread into

China, it influenced the Chinese culture in several ways. There was tremendous similarity between Buddhism and Taoism on the understanding of *wu*, or void in English. At the highest levels of the human mind, reality was indescribable. Both Buddhism and Taoism proposed a method of eliminating secular knowledge and intelligence in order to unify with the Buddha (or nature in Taoism).

One of the most profound contributions of Buddhism to Confucianism was the introduction of the Universal Mind (Fung, 254). Buddhism suggested that everyone can become a Buddha if he realizes everything is in the end associated with *wu* (nonexistence), and can "see" the Buddha in his own heart. The concept of *wu* was at the metaphysical level and can be translated as the Universal Mind. As mentioned before, traditional Confucianism put human beings at the center of the world. Man is the measure of all things. The Universal Mind does not only exist in the human psyche, but at the metaphysical level. But lack of a systematic metaphysical foundation was an issue for traditional Confucianism. Furthermore, the descriptions of how human beings interact with the Universal Mind in Buddhism also reached a level that was beyond traditional Confucianism. Neo-Confucianism was developed partly in response to such deficiency. But there is a big difference. Buddhism teaches everyone to become a Buddha through meditation as a monk, while Neo-Confucianism teaches everyone to become a sage but in the secular world.

First, Neo-Confucianism goes one step further regarding how to cultivate one's heart. A person can cultivate the heart to a certain level so his heart becomes like a mirror. He acts purely based on the reality of the particular moment and particular environment, rather than mixing it with his own desires or selfish motivations. When the heart is not filled with any personal desire, its response to the external world is natural, and its reflection of nature is authentic and trustful. He is happy or sad with the true reality, true situation, but such feeling will fade away when the situation changes. Wang Bi said, "The sage shows the emotion, but does not obsess about it" (Wang). Chuang-tzu had a similar statement as well, "The sage treats the heart as a mirror...it can reflect things but not get hurt" (Chuang-tzu, "Ying Di Wang"). This is very similar to modern psychological theories, such as Maslow's being-cognition (Fuller, 138). Although still unable to address the complexity of the mind-nature interaction, it is one step further in refining how to cultivate the heart in the context of Confucianism. However, it did not yet address the feeling of transcendence and still lacked completeness in covering the spectrum of the human mind's development cycle.

The Chinese Version of Plato's Form

The second, but more important, development of Neo-Confucianism was the meta-physical theory of *Lixue* (or theory of *Li*) from Cheng Yi and Zhu Xi. The concept of *Li* is similar to Plato's concept of Form. Basically, everything has *Li* inside. *Li* exists before any concrete realization of it. *Li* is an abstract form of truth and can have many forms of actualization. *Li* is a more basic concept than heart, because everything in the world has its own characteristics and *Li*, but not necessarily heart (or emotion).

Generalizing the same logic, it was assumed that the entire universe must have its own Li. It is the ultimate truth, which is called Tai Chi. Tai Chi contains the *Li* of all things. More importantly, everything in the world also contains or connects to Tai Chi (Zhu Xi, "Recorded Saying," Vol. 1). This seems difficult to comprehend at the time Zhu Xi lived. In modern language it can be explained through the self-similarity phenom-enon shown in Figure 1 for the Mandelbrot set. The implication here is that everything in the world not only has its own unique characteristics (its own *Li*), but also has char-acteristics from the universe (the Tai Chi). This idea is similar to the ideas in many other religions, such as the Holy Spirit in Christianity.

After constructing the metaphysical concepts, Zhu Xi went on to develop the theory of developing the human mind. Because everyone has Tai Chi inside their heart, theoretically speaking then, "the *Li* of everything are all inside myself." But not everyone is aware and makes use of them. Instead, they are shielded from awareness due to many different kinds of defects or shortcomings. It is like a pearl in dirty water—it cannot shine. What one needs to do is try to reveal the pearl inside. The methods of revealing the Li inside are through "strict investigation and research of things" and "the attentive-ness of mind" (Fung, 305). Through strict research and investigation of things, one can attain the ultimate truth—the *Li* of things. This method is to search the truth at the metaphysical level through the physical world. In the meantime, since *Li* is inside the human mind, by revealing the *Li*, we also better know our minds. The more knowledge of *Li*, the more knowledge of the nature of the mind, which is mostly concealed due to lack of knowledge and awareness of *Li*. The second method of "attentiveness of mind" is to emphasize that the endeavor of revealing *Li* is for the purpose of knowing the nature of the mind, not just a simple intellectual activity (Fung, 306).

The *Li* for the human mind is common. Yet everyone is different because an in-dividual is a concrete actualization of the common *Li*. Therefore, the nature of the individual human mind is the generic *Li* of mankind that is living and actualized in an individual. *This concept seems similar to the archetypes described by Carl Jung. It is also similar to Plato's ideas.* Plato said, "Before we are born, we already have the intuitive knowledge of the truth and value of everything" (Phaedo, 75). A human being can learn to realize the beauty of truth gradually, from the outside in, from realizing to experiencing, and from experiencing to sudden enlightenment.

In Zhu Xi's philosophy, *Li* is at the metaphysical level, while *Chi* is another concept that forms the physical world.[5] The two coexist and it is impossible to explain which one existed first. There is sophisticated explanation of how *Li* and *Chi* are related to each other. When they are applied to understanding the human mind, *Li* is the abstract part that is the nature of the human mind, i.e., the laws that influence the human mind; *Chi* is the concrete part of the mind, i.e., the concrete activity of the human mind. When we refer to the concept of the human mind, it basically refers to the abstract *Li* actualizing in the concrete activities of mind. Hence, to understand the nature of the mind—the *Li* of mind—one needs to go through the concrete mind's activity—the *Chi* of mind.

The separation of *Li* and *Chi* makes Zhu Xi's philosophy very unique. *Li* can exist independent of the human mind even though the human mind also contains *Li* of all things—the Tai Chi. As mentioned earlier, traditional Confucianism put human beings at the center of its philosophical foundation, man is the measure of all things. But Zhu Xi's philosophy went an important step further by introducing the metaphysical concept of *Li*, and proposing both *Li* and Chi are equally important in explaining the world. Furthermore, Zhu Xi emphasized the need for "strict research and investigation of things." This logically leads to the importance of the differentiation of things, which is the drive behind the expansion of knowledge. But historically this idea didn't contribute much to the development of science in China. One reason for this is that Zhu Xi's philosophy was not the only dominant school of Neo-Confucian philosophies. Instead, there was another school of Neo-Confucianism, the idealism, that developed in parallel and sparked much debate between the two schools of thought.

The Idealism

This school of Neo-Confucianism, led by Lu Chiu-yuan, and Wang Shou-jen, proposed that "The universe is my mind, and my mind is the universe" (Lu, Vol. 36). The universe

---

5 In Neo-Confucianism, the meaning of key concepts can be translated as following: *Li* (理)—the principle behind the physical world; *Chi* (气) —the matter that forms the physical world; *Xing* (性) —the nature of thing, which Chu-Hsi believed is the same as Li; Heart （心） —the mind of a human being, which Lu and Wang believe is the same as Li.

is a self-contained spiritual wholeness, in which there is only one world. This world is the concrete world we ourselves experience. There is no other world of abstract *Li*, which Zhu Xi had heavily emphasized. Wang Shou-jen claimed, "If the mind is *Li*, how can there be objects and *Li* outside the mind?" (Record of Instruction, pt. 1; Fung, 309). *Li* cannot exist without the mind. This was contrary to Zhu Xi's belief that *Li* is an objective entity, independent of the mind. We would think such a debate is a classical one of mind and reality, nothing special from a modern philosophical point of view. But what was significant was that Wang Shou-jen's argument dove deeper into the psychological root of the conscience. Wang Shou-jen carefully examined the typical human being's first reaction to a baby falling into a well. He found that human conscience is rooted deep in the mind but not in the conscious (Fung, 310). The root, where humans know what is wrong and what is right, is at the subconscious level (in modern psychological terms). Because the conscience is not rooted from the conscious or from knowledge that is learned after birth, the nature of the mind itself is *Li*. It is more real than the abstract *Li* that Zhu Xi envisioned. Because of this, Wang argued that "everyone can become a sage" by sincerely following the nature of the mind and intuitive knowledge (Fung, 312–313). Although this is oversimplifying human nature and doesn't address how hard it is to curb the dark side of human nature, it was so concise and easy to follow that it gained wide acceptance in China in the time Wang Shou-jen lived.

In other words, while Zhu Xi believed there is a world of abstract *Li* that is independent of the mind, Wang Shou-jen believed that the mind and *Li* are inseparable. They are simply the same. While Zhu Xi proposed the method to reveal *Li* is through "strict investigation of things" and focus of the mind (meditation), Wang Shou-jen suggested that since *Li* and the mind are the same, the method to reveal the true nature of the mind is to follow it naturally, instead of interfering with willfulness or intellect. Conscience is revealed when one follows the deep mind sincerely, instead of calculating and overthinking. In modern language, Zhu Xi believed there is a rational world, and the conscious part of the mind can learn about it through research and investigation. When knowledge is expanded, we know more about ourselves. Wang Shou-jen, on the other hand, believed that the mind is inseparable, that the conscious and the unconscious are in the same wholeness. The unconscious is the root of wholeness. To follow the voice from the unconscious, one should avoid interference from the knowledge and intelligence of the conscious.

Wang Shou-jen's ideas were more consistent with traditional Chinese Taoism. That is why it was also quite popular and could coexisted with Zhu Xi's philosophy under the Neo-Confucianist umbrella. If we consider the model for the development process of the human mind discussed in Chapter 4, Zhu Xi's philosophy more emphasized differentiation and the unleashing of human potential since it endorsed human intelligence and provided for strict research of things. Wang Shou-jen's philosophy more emphasized the reconciliation process, since it proposed to bypass knowledge and intelligence and simply follow the conscience in our hearts. Zhu Xi's philosophy helped to explain the second phase of the mind development model, while Wang Shou-jen's philosophy helped to explain the third phase of the model. But ultimately the goal of both schools of thought was to get the human mind into the fourth phase of the model.

In modern philosophical terms, Wang Shou-jen's philosophy was close to idealism. Idealism believes that reality only exists in the mind. Outside the mind, there is no reality. The debate between the two major Neo-Confucian schools was similar to the classical debate between materialism and idealism. It is true that knowledge and intellect are products of the human mind. However, claiming knowledge is meaningless outside the mind is not true either. After knowledge is created, it has its own life and gains objectivity due to the filter of the mass populace. This is the third world. Here objectivity means it is independent of a particular individual's mind. It can be recorded and passed on from generation to generation. Zhu Xi used the concept of *Li* in attempting to describe the objectivity of laws outside the human mind.

Another reconciliation of the debate about *Li* and the mind can be explained through the source and receiver model in Chapter 2. In wireless communications, without a handset tuned to the right frequency, the information transmitted in the spectrum cannot be decoded and understood. Idealism insists everything should go through a tuned device—the mind in Wang Shou-jen's theory. However, Zhu Xi insists that even without a tuned device, the information and coding are still transmitted in the spectrum, so the law still exists in space-time. Both theories only capture one aspect of the meaning of knowledge. Knowledge is about information of relationship, a connection between the human mind and external objects. After transmission, information exists independently but can only be decoded by a tuned device. There can also be other encoded information existing in nature that our minds are not yet ready to tune into.

But Lu Chiu-yuan and Wang Shou-jen's philosophy did have its own value by pointing out that regardless of the knowledge generated by human beings, the human mind is still the source of everything. This is particularly important when the upper layer knowledge started to distort reality. When this occurs, going back to the source—the human mind—is the only way to correct the distortion. Lu Chiu-yuan had a famous statement, "What book did ancient sages read?" (Lu, "Shun Yao") What he meant was that the original wisdom of ancient sages didn't come from books, as there were no books before the first sages. Instead, the initial wisdom came from deep reflection and meditation of the mind. Hence, seeking truth through intuition and through the mind is more reliable than through others' knowledge.

Another contribution Wang Shou-jen made was extending the meaning of *Jen* in Confucianism. He believed that "*Jen* is the law of the life in nature, it flows around the world everywhere...When seeing a baby falling into a well, one must have the feeling of sympathy; this means his *Jen* is connecting with the baby as a whole. When hearing the mournful call of a bird and feeling the sadness, this means his *Jen* is connecting with the bird. When seeing the tree is broken down and feeling sorry, this means his *Jen* is connecting with the tree" (Wang, Vol. 26, 373). *Jen* is invisible but can be experienced as a connection between one's heart and everything in the universe that has life. In short, *Jen* is about the law behind life. This idea teaches us that one should cherish precious life and share it among every life, including human beings.

Comment on Neo-Confucianism

Neo-Confucianist philosophies put too much emphasis on constructing a systematic theory based on certain concepts and assumptions. It did push theoretical development to a new level, but it lacked the original Confucianism's exploration of human nature itself. It focused more on integrating different concepts (such as *Li, Chi*, and the mind) into a cohesive theory, but less on deep understanding of the nature of the human mind. This also indicated the difficulty of having a comprehensive understanding of the nature of the human mind. Even modern psychology and science still cannot understand it completely. Integrating a philosophical system to cover the complex nature of the human mind was not as fruitful as could be expected. Rather, traditional Confucianism focused on exploring different aspects of the human mind, not caring much about the integration of them into a systematic theory, which seemed to be more fruitful.

Life itself is more important that the theory on life. As human knowledge advanced, we gained better understanding of human psychology, complex systems, and the methodologies behind them. The philosophy on top of these foundations, such as Neo-Confucianism, shall evolve and possibly find new life in modern times.

7.5 Comparing Chinese and Western Cultures

There are many angles to comparing two different cultures. The purpose of this chapter is to examine cultures based on the principles discussed in Part I, i.e., looking at a culture from the angle of the two fundamental tendencies behind the development of the human mind, and how a culture covers the spectrum of complex activities from the human mind. Therefore, we compare Chinese and Western culture from this same angle.

Different Starting Point: Unification Versus Differentiation

The first question to ask is whether there is a difference between these two cultures with respect to the two tendencies in the human mind. It appears that Chinese philosophy emphasized more the wisdom of reconciliation. What are the starting points of Chinese culture when it comes to the most basic view of human beings?

- First, one of the ultimate goals of cultivation in Chinese culture is the "unification of Heaven and human being." Its starting point is that any object always has two sides: yin and yang. The dynamics of yin and yang are the result of action from Tao: "The movement of return is the action of Tao." The world is comprised of two sides, Heaven (yang) and Earth (yin). The interaction with Heaven and Earth is where human beings derive the value. "Born from Heaven, nurtured by the Earth, and realized by the human being." Therefore, a human being is a very unique creature; even though he lives on Earth, he possesses spirit from Heaven. The values of human beings include cultivating the heart and realizing the spirit from Heaven. It is important to note that in Chinese cultural tradition, humans were always connected to Heaven and Earth, to the environment, and to other people, rather than being isolated individuals. It is a starting point and a precondition for most of Chinese philosophy; therefore the reconciliation issue discussed in Chapter 4 is a much less difficult issue.
- Next, Chinese culture placed human beings as the central point of everything. Understanding the human mind is a precondition to understanding everything else. "Understanding the self leads to understanding human beings. Understanding human beings leads to understanding the objective world. Understanding the objective world leads to understanding the cultivation

of nature" (the Middle Way). Meng-tzu also said, "Understanding the mind leads to understanding the human being. Understanding the human being leads to understanding Heaven." Because of such belief, the classical teaching from Confucianism for the development of an individual, step by step, is as follows: "Cultivate the heart, then raise and nurture the family, then serve the nation, and then make the world peaceful" ("The Great Learning"). The Chinese culture never put human beings as isolated individuals in the context of studying or pondering. However, human beings are the central point connected to everything else.

- Lastly, the emphasis on unification of Heaven and human beings is much more important than developing the intellect itself. This was most articulated in Taoism. Lao-tzu said, "Knowledge will increase every day if learning knowledge, but it will decrease every day if learning Tao" (Lao-tzu, Ch. 48). He sees knowledge as a hindrance to understanding the meaning of Tao.

While human beings are the central point and their connection with the rest of world is the starting point in Chinese culture, differentiation and separation are the central point in Western culture. Knowledge is generated through differentiating reality, separating the whole into parts. However, by doing that, certain information about reality as a whole is lost. Theoretical models were created, refined, and the process repeated, infinitely. This Western approach is a better fit for the actualization and expansion of human potential. The evolution of human history already selected this path. More and more, the human intellect is developed, and it is an irreversible process. Because of the loss of information about wholeness during this process, more advancement of the differentiation results in a larger gap between the acquired knowledge and the actual reality. Western culture struggles in unifying the fragmented knowledge with true nature, in unifying the conscious mind with the wholeness of self. To remedy this deficiency, Western culture needs the concept of the supernatural in order to unify the developed intelligence and the knowledge being generated. This is because the conscious and the intellect have to surrender to a bigger reality to achieve unification, and the easy way to solve the problem is through a mythical, personalized, supernatural entity. This level of integration was not seen in Chinese culture because the development of differentiation was not evolved to an advanced level that demanded such an extreme approach to ease the dominance of the conscious and the intellect. Chinese philosophers always kept in mind the need for unification; hence in a daily secular world, they promoted the Middle Way. They cared more about knowledge of the wholeness than knowledge of the parts, and keeping the whole rather than separating it.

However, the development of the intellect is part of human nature. Human history shows progressive development of intelligence and hence more and more awareness of the conscious. As pointed out in Chapter 4, failure to fully develop the conscious and the human intellect will leave the mind's development incomplete. Furthermore, there is no need to overemphasize the unification tendency. When the intellect comes to realize its own limitations, surrendering to the bigger wholeness becomes voluntarily. The evolution of culture follows a similar pattern.

The attitude of keeping humans as the central point and connected to everything else hinders the desire to zoom out the reality and generate more detailed, precise knowledge about the objective world. In the traditional Chinese culture, science, math, and logic were not developed to an advanced form. The lack of drive to separate the whole into parts, to differentiate reality, also led to lack of deep and systematic rational reasoning and abstract thought. Rational reasoning and abstract thought help to induce knowledge that cannot be intuitively understood.

"What can be said" versus "What cannot be said"

Because the starting point is to zoom in on the parts and differentiate them, a Western methodology would explore a subject or concept systematically, with great detail, to the widest and deepest possible extent. In short, "what can possibly be said" on a subject. Fung called it the positive approach (Fung, 341). But Chinese methodology, on the other hand, focused on "what cannot possibly be said" on a subject, which Fung called the negative approach (Fung, 341). By doing that, the truth of an object is revealed in a way that preserves the integrity of the whole, and you're not falling into the limitation of the sum of the parts is not equal to the whole.

The negative approach is spelled out most explicitly in Taoism. "The Tao that can be described in words is not the eternal Tao; the name that can be named is not the abiding name" (Lao-tze, Ch. 1). In Western philosophy, Kant termed the unknowable the noumenon. Since one cannot know the thing with absolute accuracy, the wisest way is to keep silent. This is odd and unacceptable to Western thinkers. But to Chinese thinkers who were used to the negative approach, it is very natural. Knowing and accepting the unknowable, one actually knows the most important aspect of it. It is a realization of the limitations of rational thinking.

The negative approach most likely ends up in mysticism. But the great Western philosophers, who explored the positive approach to the extreme, seemed to also end in myth as well. The list of these philosophers includes Plato, Aristotle, and Spinoza. Fung proposed that a complete philosophical system should start with the positive approach but end up with the negative approach (Fung, 342). Myth is not a contradiction of rationalism but a complementary approach to it. The Chinese philosophical lack of positive approach and focus on the negative approach seems naïve from a rationalist point of view. Their statements are simple and concise, not attempting to tear the whole into every bit and instead providing a perspective that Western metaphysical methodology lacks.

I tend to agree with Fung's analysis. This is similar to human nature's dual characteristics: growth and unification, or differentiation and reconciliation. When a person is young, the growing process dominates. It helps him to get strong and mature. The positive approach is dominant. If the negative approach dominates at this stage, one will not fully grow and become mature. However, at some point, when potentiality reaches a limit, the reconciliation process starts to dominate. At this stage, the negative approach is critical. These two characteristics are complementary; they are two phases of an integrated process.

The Ultimate Reference

As the mainstream value system in Chinese culture, Confucianism based its core values on the belief that man is the measure of all things. Ethical values were derived by reference to other human beings. Values outside the reach of humans were not emphasized. A person who can reach the highest standard of ethics was called a sage and became the ultimate ethical reference for regular people. In Western culture, on the other hand, the concept of God was deeply rooted. The values coming from God have much higher standards than those from human beings. God is the ultimate reference. The standard is higher, and consequently it imposes stricter disciplines.

The teaching from Confucianism is to start the cultivation with the individual, to do your best to reach the highest ethical standard until you reach the level of sage. In this model, the ultimate goal is that humans and Heaven are unified as the One. Humans were considered to be at the same level as Heaven. There wasn't much restriction on human limitation. While in Western culture, with the root from religion, there was a clear separation between a man and God. The limit, the sin, and the evil side of human-ity were acknowledged first. That was the starting point to build ethical values.

The difference of the ultimate ethical reference may not be as obvious as for per-sonal cultivation of the mind. But when it comes to social implications, the difference is important. In Chinese culture, personal relationships are the foundation of social structure. Confucianism placed great emphasis on relationships between king and servant, father and son, husband and wife, brother and sister, friends, etc. The Chinese character of *Jen* is simply written as "two persons together." In such a social structure, ethical value very much depends on the other persons you interact with; in other words, it is very subjective. It is difficult to have a set of objective values that everyone will follow voluntarily regardless of whether there is personal relationship with other persons underlying the interaction. *Jen* is a concept easy to understand and easy to follow. But when it comes to constructing advanced social structures, it has a problem building a social structure based on a set of objective laws. Instead, the Chinese social system typically ended up with family-style leadership. In Western culture, since it is easier to have a set of objective values that everyone will follow, society can be gov-erned by a set of laws. Whether a society is ruled by laws or by family-style leadership, heavily dependents on where the ultimate ethical reference point lies for that society.

For mainstream Chinese culture, the starting point of searching for understanding of the world is human beings, the measure is based on human beings, and the ultimate reference is also from human beings. There is no limitation being set for humanity's capability to do this searching. It is assumed that human beings can ultimately unify with Heaven as the One. In such a framework, intellectual individuals would feel the freedom of soul searching and intellectual activities. He could feel he was empowered, could cultivate personal virtues without limit. They were searching for perfect virtues, a perfect society, and a perfect world. But the reality was that the limits of human be-ings were not fully recognized and addressed, and the wishes for perfect virtues were just a bubble. When the bubble burst, it would be painful. When that happened, most Chinese intellectual individuals chose to follow Taoism and Buddhism. Hence main-stream Confucianism only addressed a limited portion of the spectrum of human minds. Taoism and Buddhism are supplementary to cover other parts of the spectrum of human minds. Taoism and Buddhism were equally important as Confucianism for Chinese culture. However, they were not the mainstream because religion in general was not well accepted as a dominant force in Chinese culture. We will discuss deeper why this was the case.

7.6 Why Was Religion in Chinese Culture Not Mainstream?

There were religious practices throughout the history of Chinese culture, but mostly among the lower classes of the population. For the upper class, particularly the intellectual class, religious practice was not mainstream culture. To understand this, we need to start from the origins of religion. In Chapter 6, three main roots of religion were identified. Let's see how they were addressed differently in Chinese culture. This also provides an opportunity to see whether the origins of religion can be addressed in other nonreligious ways.

The first root of religion is psychologically based. It is an intrinsic need when the human mind develops to a stage that the conscious realizes its limitations and its root to the whole self. At this stage, the conscious concedes its dominant status and gives in to the whole self. The old mind must be transformed to the new mind, and thereafter reach a new level of unification. By returning to the root of the intellect's source, one will reconnect to the inner voice of heart, reviving feelings of love and caring, and restoring the conscience. In Western culture, the process was addressed with religion. In Christianity, the separation between humans and God can be restored by believing in Jesus. The sense of separation is so strong and it is so difficult for the conscious to cede its dominance that the concession was symbolized by the crucifixion of Jesus. However, in Chinese culture, the separation of the conscious/intellect and the rest of world was not a central issue. The starting point of Chinese culture was about the unification of the individual with the wholeness. The separation of self and the external world was never emphasized in the major Chinese philosophies. Instead, there was plenty of wisdom to smooth out the separation, such as Chuang-tzu's dream of a flying butterfly. Confucianism also offered much wisdom to cultivate the mind and unify the individual with others, particularly the concept of *Jen*. This is why when a typical Chinese person learns about the concept of sin in Christianity, which means the separation of human beings from God, he finds it very strange because the separation is not a central issue in Chinese culture.

However, the fact that there was no clear separation between human beings and supreme nature in Chinese culture posed a problem. The ancient Chinese scholars believed that an individual, by cultivation of the mind and virtues, could ultimately unify with Heaven as the One. This, unfortunately, is unrealistic. Separation and isolation are an irreversible development of the human mind. The deficiency of self-reliance is always there, and the distance between the conscious and the mind as a whole is always there. It might be possible that an individual can cultivate deeply and become a sage, but only an extremely small number of people get to that stage. The teaching of Chinese wisdom is "to cultivate as a sage internally, and to act as a king externally" (Chuang-tzu, "Tian Xia"). The majority of the population won't get to that stage and likely will overlook the deficiency of human beings. It leads to an overestimation of human capability. This is a problem. At the individual level, a person can behave without respect to a superior authority, can mistakenly think he can be at the same level as Heaven. At the social level, it also leads to the inclination to believe in dictatorship and superheroes. Western religion, on the other hand, explicitly acknowledged the separation of human beings from God and the intrinsic limitations of humans. One outcome of such belief is that in the social and political system, there must be ways to limit the power of any individual, or have checks and balances of the government.

The second root of religion is the realization of the limitations of human intellect and rational reasoning. The fundamental limitation of human cognitive capability, the dilemma of actor and observer, and the need for a megastatistical method for ethical law, all imply that solely relying on rational reasoning is insufficient to address the needs of individuals as a whole, or to address relationships of a society as a whole. Religion and a belief system as a supplementary approach are needed. Introduction of a metareality agent is one of the solutions. It is an intuitive extension beyond the limits of rational reasoning. In Chinese culture, the limitations of rational reasoning and human cognitive capability were clearly addressed by Taoism, particularly Chuang-tzu. The idealists of Confucianism, such as Wang Shou-jen, also understood and articulated this very well. Following a nature other than intellect and knowledge is a better way to understand the Tao. However, they seemed to go too far by undervaluing rational reasoning. The limitation of rational reasoning doesn't mean it is not needed anymore. Belief and religion are intuitive extensions of rational reasoning, not replacement for it. Undervaluing of rational reasoning means a major portion of the spectrum of the human mind is not covered, and hence the philosophical system is incomplete and at risk of falling into superstition.

The third root of religion comes from humans seeking transcendent connection and the meaning of life. It also comes from the belief that there are laws higher than what we have seen in the secular world. In Western religion, this is addressed by believing in the existence of God and the Kingdom of Heaven. The meaning of life is to connect to the Tree of Life, to live out the image of God in oneself, and to glorify the creator. Chuang-tzu's idea is that there is a higher level of happiness that can be attained through blurring the boundary of self and the rest of the world. Confucianism, particularly its idealism branch, however, didn't accept that there are laws beyond the grasp of the human mind. Confucius himself mentioned, "Not yet knowing the meaning of living, how can I know the meaning of death?" (Analects, "Xian Jin"). He refused to discuss the topics of the supernatural and God. Basically, Confucius tried to ignore topics about future life and focus only on current life. This was progress at the time of Confucius. Later, Confucian philosophy continued this tradition of not discussing concepts of the supernatural and God, except the concept of Heaven, which was a static, nonpersonalized entity, similar to nature. Religion was not an option for Confucianism, because its primary interest was to establish an ethical system that was practicable in a society. The starting point was human beings themselves, and the ultimate reference of ethical values was human beings as well. Confucianism chose to cover only a portion of the spectrum of the human mind, and hence would not contain the power and risks of a religion.

Taoism was a true philosophy because it attempted to answer the origin of the universe, to seek the ultimate truth. Tao is a timeless and formless unknowable force that governs the cosmos, including the human mind. This was close to the concept of God but without personalization. Lao-tzu didn't offer a concrete approach on how to connect with Tao—maybe he was smart enough and purposely neglected it. Both Lao-tzu and Chuang-tzu believed that human rationality (the conscious part of mind) is insufficient to comprehend Tao. Tao exists there, governing the universe, but it is cold and nonpersonalized. Tao is unknowable and unspeakable. It is very hard for ordinary people to engage it for daily guidance. From a methodological point of view, Taoism covered another end of the spectrum of the human mind but is incomplete as well. Confucianism, on the other hand, offered a concrete approach of how to guide daily behavior; that's why both are complementary in Chinese culture.

Buddhism entered China from India and was developed into many Chinese specific variants. The most famous one is probably Zen Buddhism. Most monks practiced Buddhism in remote places away from society. Buddhism proposes that everything essentially is empty; the difficulty, pain, and hustle in everyone's life are due to the fact the person is not aware of the causes. Once one realizes the causes eventually belong to the emptiness, pain and difficulty do not exist anymore. Buddhism believes in reincarnation, using the next life to motivate the current life, similar to Christianity's concept of eternal life. These ideas are incompatible with mainstream Confucianism.

Chinese culture, especially Taoism, believes that ultimate truth (Tao, God, Buddha, etc.) is indescribable—it can only be experienced. Talking too much about the ultimate truth is simply insane. Modern philosophers such as Alan Watts believe the same concept. Watts said that belief in all ideas, concepts, and words of God must be abandoned. God in his infiniteness is not a speculation but an experience of realization. Various religions could get together if they came to realize their shared basis in experience.

In summary, the most important obstacle for the Chinese intellectual class to accept religion is that the mainstream philosophy, the Confucianism, considered human beings as the central point of concern, and built ethical systems with humans as the ultimate reference. Human beings as the center of everything, including methodology. It was extremely difficult for Chinese intellectuals to accept the abstract concept of metareality, as it is experienced mostly through induction, instead of personal feeling. The Chinese philosophies addressed the roots of religion in different ways so that the intellectual class felt less need for a religion. However, the less educated population didn't understand the philosophies well, hence felt more need for a religion. The result was that religion in China was accepted more widely for the lower-class population but didn't become a mainstream acceptance.

Confucianism developed a detailed value system addressing the ethical and social portions of the human mind. It put human beings as the center of everything, even able to reach the same level of Heaven. This confined itself within the human mental domain and neglected the need for a higher level of unification. Taoism acknowledges that the wisdom of human intelligence and ethics are insufficient to understand Tao, but it was insufficient to guide the daily behavior of normal people. Therefore, the typical Chinese intellectual embraced both philosophies to have a complete philosophical system.

Even though Taoism and Confucianism coexisted well, they were not really integrated into a single complete philosophy. Instead, they just complementarily coexisted. The Chinese culture accepted the concept of two complementary components coexisting, as demonstrated by the theory of yin and yang. The human mind is so complex and the spectrum is so broad, that when cultures around the world attempt to understand it, different philosophies, techniques, and methodologies were developed. A truth can be approached from different angles, and therefore these different approaches should coexist. There is no need to argue which one is right or wrong. Right and wrong, good and evil, can be mutually exclusive, but methodologies are not. Taoism and Confucianism approached the understanding of humans and nature from two different ends of the spectrum. This satisfied the spiritual needs for most Chinese for a long period of history. But, as will be discussed later, there is an intrinsic shortcoming of such coexisting yet not integrated philosophical systems.

7.7 Cultural Synergy

Western culture encompasses three major sources: 1) Greek philosophy, which leads to science. 2) Hebrew religion, especially Christianity. 3) Roman law, which leads to a law-based, democratic society.

But Chinese culture is relatively uniform and mostly focused on the central theme of ethics and value systems. Western and Chinese cultures are seemingly orthogonal on the starting point and the ultimate reference. If the starting point is so different, is there any synergy that can occur between these two cultures? Is there anything Western culture can learn from it? To answer this, we need to know if there are challenges in the Western culture itself. Later, we will look at what Chinese culture can learn from Western culture as well.

Challenges of Western Culture

First, Western culture tends to study the parts in great detail and put them together, differentiating reality and generating mighty amounts of scientific knowledge. This manifests in the advancement of human intelligence. Yet in doing so, it is difficult to find ways to unify the conscious self with wholeness and nature, unless a God exists. Certainly, Western culture, especially in recent history since the Renaissance, helped humans release creativity and productivity, producing science and the industrial revolution, but in the meantime consuming the natural resources of the earth to a point where this model is unsustainable—one example is global warming. The endless expansion of human intelligence and productivity needs to be confined in a framework that is sustainable. A different view from a different culture may be able to help, and one such different view is rooted from the Chinese cultural stance that the *unification of human and Heaven, the wholeness of human beings, is the starting point, instead of just a remedy for something else.*

Secondly, in Western culture, the need for God is intrinsic. It is essential to derive the meaning of life clearly. Without the existence of God, the culture's foundation is at risk. One school of thought in Western philosophy is existentialism. It assumes there is no God and that society is not reliable either. Your existence is the only thing you can rely on. Yet mankind is "condemned to be free" (Satre, 28), meaning freedom is not a blessing but a curse, because you have burdens and responsibilities. Self-reliance is essential to be truly alive. Sartre said of what he called authentic existence that conformity and the comfort of being subsumed by a structured society is a refuge for the cowardly, because it is an illusion (Sartre, "Existentialism Is Humanism"). It is only the brave hearts that have the courage to live an authentic life. The meaning of their lives is to maintain human dignity in a world of bureaucrats, automatons, and nothingness. This seems very difficult to understand and be followed by regular people. In Western tradition and culture, how to live a meaningful life without God is hardly imagined.

Because of this, it is crucial to justify the existence of a supernatural in Western culture. The traditional ways in Christianity or related religions based on the Bible may not be sufficient in modern times. The advancement of scientific knowledge, especially study of the origin of orders, the nonlinearity theory for complex systems, and emergence will provide more and more hints. Modern physics also shows that the limitations of science are self-evident. There continues to be challenge and debate in the Western world on the meaning of God, on whether there exists an intelligent designer.

The most fundamental problem of introducing a supernatural is it automatically puts such concept as a separate entity from a human being. But in fact part of such entity is in the psyche of the human himself, which is an inseparable part of oneself. Great confusion and struggle occur when one is trying to unify with it. The famous story of Job in the Bible manifests such struggle. Job complained that God examined him every morning and tested him every moment, saying "Will you never look away from me, or let me alone for an instant?" (Job 7:18–19). Job thought of God as a separate entity watching him every instant. But in fact, the concept of metareality comprises two components. One component is part of the psyche, and the other component is external to the psyche. In the language of Western religion, it means God is inside yourself (or dissolved in yourself), and also connects you to an external existence. Focusing only on the second element causes puzzlement and struggle when unifying with it, as described in the Bible story of Job. But only focusing on the first element will leave the belief entity solely inside the psyche and lose the objectiveness of the truth behind religion. In the Eastern philosophy, the separation is less an issue since the starting point of Eastern philosophy is the wholeness, not the separation of self and consciousness.

What Chinese Culture Can Bring to Western Culture?

One of the major foundations of Western culture is religion, and if such foundation is at risk, an alternative view is needed. Chinese philosophy, particularly Confucianism, on the other hand, worked hard to develop a system of wisdom without religion. The system had successfully dominated Chinese culture for thousands of years. This is exactly what the Chinese culture can bring to the world—assuming it is an improved version that has addressed the issues just listed.

One central theme of Chinese philosophy is that to reach the stage of total unification of human being and Heaven, one doesn't need to do anything special, certainly there's no need for magical supernatural action. Instead, he does the exact same daily routine as other normal people, but with a totally different attitude. He realizes any action he does is part of the connected natural universe. He lives in this world, but his spirit does not belong to the secular world. Everything is related and there is intrinsic Tao and order for everything. Experiencing the moment with a sense of complete integration is the end of the fulfillment. There is no need to further seek the purpose. In Western culture, the complete integration will occur in the future (the second coming of Jesus Christ, for example), so the purpose of life is tied to the future. As such, people tend to live in the future and experience more separation.

Methodological contribution from Chinese culture is the negative approach described earlier (Fung, 342). This means at some point it is important to research what *not* to say, instead of what to say, about a reality. Chinese philosophy lacks a positive approach but is rich in its negative approach. It seems naïve from a rationalist point of view, but it is simple and concise, not attempting to tear the whole into every bit. It provides a perception that Western methodology lacks. Taoism proposed that "reversion is the action of Tao." There is always a strong doubt in pushing things to an extreme; hence the central approach in Chinese culture is the Middle Way, the emphasis to balance relevant factors.

As mentioned earlier, Western culture tends to believe there is a universal value system, due to the religious root. The benefit of this is that people within the culture will be more likely to follow the value system and establish a law-based society. However, when such a culture meets other cultures with different (even slightly different) value systems, it will be difficult to accept these others. Instead, it tends to impose its own value system, which is believed to be universal, on other cultures. It always has a sense of superiority and a lack of respect for the specific characteristics of other cultures. This will cause conflict. The root cause is, as discussed in detail in Chapter 6, that religious belief is exclusive by nature. *A belief or philosophical system, when developed to a certain stage, starts to claim exclusivity. A culture based upon a religion tends to be exclusive as well, hence has difficulty accepting and integrating values from a different culture.* Furthermore, the Western reasoning style—rationalism—tends to generalize an idea. *Chinese culture, on the other hand, was not (at least the mainstream part of the culture) based on a religion. It was much more open to other cultures and other philosophies.* This was shown in history when Buddhism entered China. The Chinese culture didn't show exclusivity, instead gradually absorbing and integrating it. Zen Buddhism was a local branch of Buddhism as a result. Confucianism evolved to Neo-Confucianism after absorbing the finest description of the human mind from Buddhism (Fung, 254). However, Neo-Confucianism went too far when it developed itself as a systematic philosophical system. Traditional Confucianism, on the other hand, was more open-ended, thus a better starting point to integrate with other philosophies.

The only way to resolve exclusivity of a value system, a belief system, a religion, or a culture, is to unwind the face values, including religious symbols or rituals, and to look at the true underlying message. This was explained in Chapter 6. One needs to understand the roots of a belief and religion to understand the spectrum of the human mind. *In mainstream Chinese philosophy, the central interest is the human being. And because it wasn't evolved into a religion, it is open to any other cultures or philosophies that are addressing the same topics. The openness makes it a good starting point when consolidating the multiple cultures around the world. Confucianism taught that "Truth exists in parallel with other truth without conflict"* (the Middle Way).

As a specific example of the above point, we can compare the concept of *Jen* in Confucianism with the concept of love in Christianity. Love is supposed to be unconditional. Christianity even teaches people to love their enemies. Love means to respect the human being as he or she is, because everyone is created by God and has the image of God. Because we are connected through God, to love another even an enemy is just a natural extension of loving God. Hence love is not really unconditional—it is based on the precondition of loving God. The source of love comes from God, not human beings. Christians are enthusiastic to show the love to others, which is different from the Confucian concept of Jen. Jen is the connection among people who share the feeling of life. It is a resonation among people who share the preciousness, the subtleness of life. Both Christianity and Confucianism have the same teaching of treating others in the way you want to be treated. It is the bottom line for respecting others. Respect means to accept the individual as he or she is, not imposing preconditions, regardless of the individual's religious or philosophical belief. But there is a subtle difference here. Jen is the end purpose with no other precondition or purpose—for example, by showing the love, it attracts others to join the religion. Whether or not the other is ready to accept our offer of love is also respected. Therefore, the expression of Jen is through politeness. The enthusiasm of love is not explicitly expressed most of the time. Instead it is restricted by respecting others' readiness. This approach is very different from the Western approach. Typical Christians are eager to show their love to their neighbors and are eager to preach. They could have two motivations. One motivation can be that action is just a natural extension of knowing. Christians believe in the love of God so much that to them it is natural to preach. However, there is another possible motivation. Through converting others to Christianity, the Christian reaffirms his own belief. This second motivation would be problematic. Christianity is a religion, and there are many religions in the world. It is hard to convert each other. Religion in this case becomes a hurdle. Confucianism, on the other hand, is not based on religious philosophy. It is open to other thoughts that share the same interest of understanding the human mind. It will not become an enemy to any other religions.

Rational reasoning tends to look ahead and infer the future. Therefore, the arrow of time in Western culture tends to point to the future. It appears to overemphasize the movement of things. Everything seems to rush to the future. Although it is true that nothing is statically still in the world, there is a dynamic balance in this world that can be our starting point to understanding the world. The dynamic balance now is a miracle itself. It reflects the beauty and the myth of Mother Nature. The sense of eternal already exists when we completely put our hearts and minds to be in the moment. This was called the "eternal now" by Alan Watts. Such state was exactly what Chinese ancient philosophers tried to describe. Western culture tends to ignore the here and now, and overemphasizes the future. Dialectics is one methodology that overemphasizes the dynamics of opposites and doesn't focus on the state of dynamic balance.

Lastly, the rational reasoning in Western culture is good at studying the parts. It differentiates things at every possible angle. Yet it has a hard time consolidating them into a cohesive view. The Chinese reasoning style is more focused on the wholeness. Without the depth of inspecting things, it is harder to integrate them in a higher level or more accurately reflect reality. This is like looking at a mountain from hundreds of miles away; one gets a very rough impression and may not even know why it looks green. But when you get closer to the mountain, you see the trees, the bushes, and the trails, but you may not see the overall shape of the mountain. You will need to go back a distance in order to see the overall shape. But now you understand what is on the mountain and can explain why the color is green. Similarly, science and knowledge can greatly enrich our understanding of a complex world. But we need to step back and look at the world as a connected wholeness. We will have to combine both as complementary ways of understanding the world.

What Chinese Culture Can Learn from Western Culture?

The Confucian philosophers had developed a system of wisdom without religion and successfully dominated Chinese culture for thousands of years. But this was at the cost of only addressing the most practical portion of the spiritual spectrum. By ignoring the far end of the spiritual spectrum, human needs for that end of spectrum were not well addressed, and the depth of human emotion was not nurtured properly. For example, Confucianism didn't articulate in depth about the dynamics of the multiple stages of mind development, didn't address the meaning of life beyond death, rejected any concept of the supernatural (agent to metareality), and neglected the need to emotionally attach to something transcendent. People who have that spiritual need turn to other philosophies such as Taoism or Buddhism. They end up with a hybrid philosophy with multiple components that were not organically integrated. It was just multiple schools of thought mechanically coexisting; a person may take one of them depending on need instead of true belief. This resulted in a pragmatic attitude toward Confucianism, Taoism, or Buddhism. It was a big challenge for Chinese culture. Chinese culture could learn from Western culture on the following ideas and develop an alternative system to address these challenges:

- Place human beings in the right position. Clearly define the limitations of human beings (similar to the distinction between God and humans in Western culture). Even though Confucianism mentioned Heaven, and Taoism had the concept of Tao and others, there should be deeper and more clear articulation on what the distance is, and how these concepts influence the human mind spectrum.
- Consequently, derive an ultimate reference that is beyond individual human beings. The value system is not just relative to an individual human being or a certain group, but universal to mankind as a whole. It is not a closed-loop system within human beings. Instead, it should seek the objectivity of the value system transcending human individuals. The ideas of megastatistics or emergence from the synergy of human society provide potential hints for justifying the objectivity. By doing this, it would reduce the degree of pragmatic attitude that is quite common among the Chinese people. The bonding of a society needs to be based on laws rather than relationships. Refraining from doing wrong will come from the heart to align the value rather than from fear of losing face in front of others.

- More emphasis on the methodology of differentiation. This means to research a subject in great detail and depth, systematically, and to trust abstract reasoning. Modern China is catching up on this. But they should realize that in the Western culture, the expansion of human intelligence is at the same time bound by a deep and profound religious root. This is somewhat similar to the relationship between Confucianism and Taoism (or Buddhism), except that in the West, religion is more organically integrated and more mainstream compared to Taoism (or Buddhism) in China.
- Religion is a response to human needs as a whole from rational and irrational/emotional, conscious and unconscious. Since religion was not a mainstream practice in the upper class in China, there must be something else to nurture such needs. Since the message behind religion reflects the core value, the meaning of life, only when a person's response to this is as a whole will he follow those values from the heart, instead of from the head. In a pragmatic culture, finding holes in the laws is considered clever; following laws is not valued. This is a real challenge and there is no easy answer yet.

Summary

Western and Chinese cultures come from different angles. The Western culture starts from outside the human being, while the Chinese one starts from within the human being. Methodologically, the Western culture emphasizes differentiation, rational reasoning, and going from a part to the whole, while the Chinese one emphasizes unification and wholeness. The arrow of time in Western culture points to the future, while in Chinese culture it points to the here and now. The ultimate reference of the value system is the external God in Western culture, while it is human beings themselves in Chinese culture. Western culture more emphasizes the limitations of human beings and hence is more successful in confining the sin of human beings, while the Chinese tend to believe that the gap between Heaven and humans can be eliminated through cultivation of the mind. Western people believe that there is a universal value system, while the Chinese tend to think values are relative. Western culture tends to push its value system to others, believing it is beneficial for them, while the Chinese emphasize treating others with politeness and waiting for others' readiness to accept the values they believe. It is possible that in a cultural evolution for mankind as a whole both views are needed, depending on what stage the worldwide culture is at. *At a stage when society is still immature, human potentiality is actualizing and expanding, and a value system is being established, so religious Western culture meets the needs better. But when the endless expansion of human potentiality poses risk to the wholeness of the world, the wisdom from Chinese culture meets the needs better.* They are really complementary.

For Western culture, how to justify the existence of a supernatural? Or is it possible to keep and strengthen the value system without a religious symbol? For Chinese culture, how to solidify the objectivity of the value system without religion? They may point to the same question: how to explain and strengthen the value system, how to address the entire spectrum of the human mind without religion or with a new explanation of religious symbolism? The world will eventually evolve to a unified culture if these questions are answered. We will come back to this in the final chapter. But as a common denominator, an open-minded attitude to each other is particularly important when multiple cultures meet. It avoids unnecessary conflict, opens the possibility of synergy among cultures, and unleashes the best from each culture.

7.8 Attitude When Facing Different Cultures

As time passes, a regional culture sooner or later would be exposed to a different culture. Especially in modern times, the advancement of transportation and communication makes it very easy for people to experience different cultures. However, the physical convenience of experiencing different cultures doesn't automatically translate to an ease in understanding them. Instead, misunderstanding among cultures is the root for conflict and even wars we have seen frequently.

Western culture tends to believe there is a universal value system, and it is its responsibility to promote such a value system in other parts of the world. This belief introduces a sense of superiority and is problematic when meeting another culture with a long history and deep roots. When a culture has a sense of superiority, it is unwilling to listen objectively. When there is a difference of opinion from the other culture, it may argue that people in that culture are brainwashed. It is naturally biased toward a voice that fits into its own value reference. In the real world, cultural conflict is embedded in the political conflict between countries. Countries with a sense of superiority will tell other countries that as long as their value systems are different, their life standards are inferior to those of people with our value system. Their life standards should change.

Let's start to ask questions: 1) Is there a universal standard of life every country should follow? 2) Assuming the answer is yes, is that the right way to keep the sense of superiority?

On the first question, there were extensive discussions earlier. Because of the strong religious background, Western culture tends to believe that there is an absolute truth. Freedom and equality are the basic human rights. Even though not every country agrees, it is a reasonable belief to accept.

The difficult part is the second question on what approach should be used in truth-telling. The emotional support to get the message across effectively is very subtle here. Straightforward truth-telling or imposing a value system on other people can cause resistance and conflict, even though the message is true. An inappropriate truth-telling approach can backfire and hinder getting the message across. Chinese Confucianism preferred the middle way. The truth-telling process is very indirect. It may take a tremendous amount of time and effort to get one message across. The Western approach is much more straightforward. Truth is truth; there is no need to hide. The root of the Western sense of "truth authority" is it believes there is a universal value system. It externally and objectively exists, and everyone should follow it. Eastern culture (Confucianism or Buddhism), on the other hand, believes that ethical value exists inside the human mind. An individual needs to be awakened to be made aware of it. Hence the approaches are very different. Western culture tends to explicitly call out its value system and expect everyone to follow it. Not following the universal value system means not "civilized." The Eastern approach is to respect the individual, or the society, to gradually wake up and develop the value system at its own pace. This is more consistent with the meaning of "love." As explained before, love essentially means to respect and accept others as they are. Whatever stage of development the individual is at, whatever advancement of civilization the society is at, all deserve to be respected and accepted. Only when such respect is established can trust and dialogue start.

One might argue that putting respect before truth-telling is unacceptable. If you know the truth, you should tell it directly. Otherwise you don't have the courage to stand for the truth, or you don't really believe in it. Love versus truth, which one is more important to human life? In Christianity, Jesus taught people to love the enemy, to turn your face to the right when people slap the left. Confucianism taught *Jen*, which is the highest standard for interhuman relationships. Both teachings basically preach a fundamental principle of human life: that life is larger than knowledge—respect and love should take priority over knowledge and truth-telling. If one truly believes in a value, he or she lives out the value instead of just speaking about it.

Consider the following extreme case. A person believes he knows the truth, therefore looks down on people he thinks don't know the truth, and even sometimes humiliates them. Such a person doesn't deserve others' respect. When a person only has knowledge and intelligence, but lacks of respect and love, it is just another form of dictatorship. A righteous person is the one who knows the truth and also knows respect to others. He cares about other people's feelings and accepts other people as they are, even in an early developmental stage. Forcing others to accept a value system simply won't work. The better approach is to first build trust and respect, allow others to grow organically, and encourage their progress. Once the trust and respect are built, it is more effective to tell them what needs improvement. Listening, respect, and constructive dialogue are the basic principles to handle interpersonal relationships. This is no different to handle cultural difference. The reason one may escape from these principles is that she has her own interests. Similarly, in an international relationship, a country may escape from these principles due to its own interests, or due to fear of threats or of being unable to maintain superiority.

Building a constructive relationship with others, living out the values one believes in, and being open-minded to learning from others, are all a culture needs to do when facing a different culture. This is true for either well-developed or underdeveloped cultures. There is no need to be either offensive or defensive. As the world becomes more and more connected, the geographical boundary of different cultures will eventually disappear. Appropriate attitude towards a different culture is more and more important.

Reference

- "Analects, Wei Lin Gong." "己之不欲, 勿施于人",《论语·卫灵公》。
- "Analects, Xian Jin." "季路问事鬼神。子曰:'未能事人,焉能事鬼?'敢问死。曰:'未知生,焉知死?'"《论语·先进》。
- Chuang-tzu. "Ch'i Wu Lun.""天地与我并生, 万物与我为一", 庄子《齐物论》
- Chuang-tzu. "Da Zhong Shi." "圣人将游于物之所不得遁而皆存", 庄子《大宗师》。
- Chuang-tzu. "Tian Xia." "圣有所生, 王有所成, 皆原于一(道)" 庄子《天下》。

- Chuang-tzu. "Yang Sheng Zhu." "吾生也有涯, 而知也无涯, 以有涯随无涯, 殆已。", 庄子《养生主》。

- Chuang-tzu. "Ying Di Wang." "至人之用心若镜, 不将不迎, 应而不藏, 故能胜物而不伤。"庄子《应帝王》。

- Fuller, Andrew R. *Psychology and Religion: Classical Theorists and Contemporary Developments* (Lanham, Maryland: Rowman & Littlefield Publishers, Inc., 2008, fourth edition).

- Fung, Yu-lan. *A Short History of Chinese Philosophy* (New York: Free Press, 1997).

- Lao-tzu. "Tao Te Ching," Chapter 1. "道可道, 非常道; 名可名, 非常名。"老子《道德经》第一章。

- Lao-tzu. "Tao Te Ching," Chapter 2. "天下知美之为美, 斯恶已; 皆知善之为善, 斯不善已。故有无相生, 难易相成", 老子《道德经》第二章。

- Lao-tzu. "Tao Te Ching," Chapter 18. "大道废, 有仁义; 智慧出, 有大伪", 老子《道德经》第十八章。

- Lao-tzu. "Tao Te Ching," Chapter 38. "上德不德, 是以有德。。。失德而后仁", 老子《道德经》第三十八章。

- Lao-tzu. "Tao Te Ching," Chapter 40. "反者道之动", 老子《道德经》第四十章。

- Lao-tzu. "Tao Te Ching," Chapter 48. "为学日增, 为道日损" 老子《道德经》第二章。

- Lu, Jiu-yuan. "Collection Works of Xiang-Shan.""宇宙便是吾心, 吾心即宇宙。"陆九渊, 《象山全集》卷36

- Lu, Jiu-yuan. "Shun Yao." 陆九渊,"尧舜所读何书?"

- Meng-tzu. "尽其心者, 知其性也。知其性, 则知天矣。"《孟子。尽心章句上》

- Sartre, J. "Existentialism Is Humanism," Lecture in 1946.

- "The Great Learning." "修身, 齐家, 报国, 平天下", 《大学》

- "The Middle Way." "尽己之性, 可以尽人之性。尽人之性, 可以尽物之性。尽物之性, 然后可以赞天地之化育", 《中庸》。

- "The Middle Way." "万物并育而不相害, 道并行而不相悖", 《中庸》

- Tung, Chuang-shu. "天, 地, 人, 万物之本也。天生之, 地养之, 人成之", 董仲舒《春秋繁露。立元篇》。

- Wang, Bi. "圣人有情而无累"。王弼。

- Wang, Shou-jen. "Collection Works of Wang Ming Yang." "仁是造化生生不息之理, 虽尔漫周遍, 无处不是", "见孺子之入井而必有恻隐之心, 是其仁之与孺子而为一体也。见鸟兽之哀啼而必有不忍之心, 是其仁之与鸟兽而为一体也。见草木之摧折而必有悯恤之心, 是其仁之与才木而为一体也。"《王阳明全集。大学问》26卷373页

- Webster Dictionary, http://www.merriam-webster.com/dictionary/culture, Web. Jan. 15, 2015.

- Xu-tzu. "Jie Bi." "庄子蔽于天而不知人,"《吕氏春秋》荀子《解蔽》。

- Xun-tzu. "Xun-Tzu," Chapter 23. 《荀子》23章 "性恶"。

- Zhu Xi. "Recorded Saying" Vol. 1."在天地言, 则天地中有太极；在万物言, 则万物中各有太极", 朱熹《语类》卷1。

- Zhu Xi. "Recorded Saying" Vol. 94. "如月在天, 只一而已；及散在江湖, 则随处可见, 不可谓月已分也", 朱熹《语类》卷94。

CHAPTER 8

The Meanings of Life

n the introductory chapter, we asked the question of what the meaning of life is. In order to answer the question, we turned to the starting points of the understanding of human beings. We started by examining the origin of knowledge, the limitation of scientific knowledge, the complicated development process of the human psyche and the dynamics of the conscious and the unconscious mind, and finally, the methodology extracted from scientific research and philosophical reasoning. With these learnings as a foundation, the focus is turned to the justifications of belief and religion, and the common ground of different cultures. Belief systems, cultures, and religions are the outcome of spiritual activities. They reflect the spectrum of the human mind and in turn nurture a person's spiritual life. Searching for the meaning of life is closely connected to these spiritual outcomes. We attempted to decipher the underlying origins of a belief system and the messages behind religions. Subsequently, Chinese culture was reviewed in detail and compared to Western culture because it offers a different, and less religious, philosophy. It has been a long journey to reach here. Are we ready to answer the question on what the meaning of life is, and what the goal of life could be?

8.1 Why Seek Meaning?

Searching for the meaning of life is a natural step originating from the awakening of the human mind. It is an intrinsic force arising from the evolution of the human mind. First was the awareness of consciousness—the waking of consciousness is the start of humanity. This followed with the concept of self, and the awareness of what is right and what is wrong. Along the evolution, human being created languages and generated knowledge, science, culture, and religion. At the same time the sense of isolation increased, and the awareness of life-span (i.e., every life has a limited time) is associated with this sense. Human beings are no longer satisfied with just meeting physical needs. The spiritual part of a human being is searching for guidelines and meaning. This dilemma of isolation and limited life-span pushes humans to seek something that transcends beyond this life. The question is whether such a transcendent thing exists, or is it just a wish or a human invention?

Man is used to the thinking pattern that there is a reason behind anything that happens. This is particularly true for Western methodology. If life comes and goes, generation after generation, is there a goal and meaning behind this? Is life just a random, natural phenomenon? If there is a goal and meaning behind life, what is it? Is it knowable? With the current knowledge, we don't know the answer. There is a possibility that there is an underlying goal and meaning that is beyond our comprehension. If that is the case, what is the meaning of searching for the meaning of life?

Accordingly to Frankl, searching for the meaning of life is basically inexplicable. It is just one of the instincts of the human mind, and one of the most fundamental components of the human psyche (Fuller, 238). Such searching persists because the human mind is capable of inferring things that are higher than the human himself. Man is born with such capability; whether one is aware of it is a different issue. With such assumptions, the isolation is reconciled if one embraces the higher-level transcendent existence. The meaning of life is simply to live out such capability and connect to the higher-level world. The search for the meaning of life inevitably leads to the concept of transcending existence, if we insist there is a reason behind life. The concepts of the third world and fourth world discussed in Chapter 5 are tied with the transcendent media. There are many other philosophies or religions that share this similar idea:

- Jung suggested there are archetypes in a person's mind. These archetypes are born with a person. The goal of life is to live out such archetypes.
- Christianity believes humans were created in God's image. The meaning of life is to live out the image of God through loving others.
- The Neo-Confucian philosopher Zhu Xi believed *Li* is in everyone's mind. Particularly, the *Li* of the universe; Tai Chi is in everyone's mind. Tai Chi is the law that governs this world, and one should research and work hard to live out these laws.
- The Hindu philosophy believes that Brahman is the knowing self that cannot be known—the ego. The self here and now is the atman; the self in its infinity

is the Brahman. The goal of life is to realize the Brahman is inside you, to realize the relationship of self, atman, and Brahman (Fuller, 176–177).

- Buddhism believes that the Buddha is in everyone's heart. With the Great Awakening to realize it, anyone can become a Buddha.

However, not everyone in normal life is actively searching for the meaning of life. There are two different reasons for this. First, it depends on the individual's awareness of this internal search. The internal search can be buried by other secular activities. The second reason is more subtle. The goal of life and the process of it could actually be the same. They are convoluted together and inseparable. As such, unawareness of the meaning of life doesn't mean there is no meaning. The daily life routine itself is a meaning. We will discuss this further later.

8.2 Is the Meaning of Life Objective?

If there is a meaning of life, is it just a subjective feeling, or is there objective meaning? This question is one of the origins of religion. There are different levels of goals for a life.

- The basic-level goal is simply to meet physical needs, survival, and seeking happiness.
- Reproduction, and other ways of continuing the existence of self, such as a long-lasting enterprise, fame, social position.
- The spiritual meaning beyond the physical life. Physical life comes and goes. Spiritual meaning can be transcendent. This can be through science, knowledge, philosophy, culture, or through belief and religious practice.

The question on the objectivity of the meaning of life primarily refers to the third level, because the first and second levels of meaning are attainable and observable. The third level of meaning is connected to whether there is a transcending existence.

The question of objective life meaning is tied with the destiny of humanity. For example, there is a belief that the earth can be destroyed someday, and the knowledge and cultures generated by human beings (i.e., the third world) will be destroyed as well. How can we expect anything meaningful beyond the current life? It is certainly a gloomy picture to envision that in the end, human beings and all cultures will be destroyed and disappear. Fortunately the advance of science itself seems to veto such verdict. In nonlinear and chaos theories, the view that the future is deterministic is not held anymore (Prigogine, "The End of Certainty"). One cannot predict the future of a highly nonlinear system with current knowledge. Human society and the whole world are far more complex than a nonlinear system. It is prudent to conclude that we cannot predict the ultimate future of human beings and cultures with our current knowledge. Because the future is unpredictable, any vision of destiny will be linked to some sort of belief, i.e., cannot be inferred rationally. In other words, it is only possible to resolve the puzzle of human destiny through a belief system. Ironically, this is a scientific conclusion through the study of nonlinear and chaos systems. Then the question is, what to believe? There is no simple choice. No belief itself is a belief, which is equivalent to believing that only the current life matters. Most religions assume there is future life in order to foster belief. There should not be exclusivity to the beliefs. Instead, we offer some characteristics of a healthy belief on the destiny of mankind:

- First, there is really no need to envision a heaven or hell as the possible destiny of human beings in order to foster a belief. The foundation on a belief of current life should be self-reliance. It should be truly based on the understanding of human nature and address the deep desires for certainty, being loved, and survival, and at the same time the focus should be the current life.
- Second, the creativity, adaptability, and survival skill of humans will play an important role in determining our own destiny. There will be solutions to solve problems humans face or will face. Efforts to extend human survival ability as a whole should be encouraged. This includes: 1) Better knowledge and understanding of nature, the self, and better capability to cooperate with nature, instead of controlling and consuming. 2) Better relationship and connection among human beings. It will help us be stronger as a whole. From the pragmatic viewpoint, if a belief can increase the strength of humanity as a whole, the belief itself is objective. Particularly, as explained in megastatistical methodology, throughout multiple generations, there can be an observable flow of life passing from one generation to the next. Because there is an objective component of such life flow, attaching or contributing to strengthen it makes a human more valuable, and also partially answers what the meaning of life is.
- Lastly, such belief should be constantly checked that it is an open-ended belief instead of one believing in some fixed content. It should be aware that there are limitations of the human intellect. We constantly seek for hints and guidance. This is similar to the belief that there is a generic God, and one cannot predict the behavior and actions of God.

In other words, the destiny of human beings is somewhat in our own hands with the power of belief. We cannot control it, but we are part of it and can influence it. *The objectivity of the meaning of life is in our hands as well.* Inseparability between goal and process is a common characteristic for a complex nonlinear system. This principle is certainly finding its place in the search for the destiny of humanity. The traditional understanding of knowing the goal first, then devoting oneself to achieving the goal cannot explain the process of believing. The destiny depends on our action. Furthermore, the destiny can be good or bad. An example of good destiny is that humans enjoy a better life, more caring and respectful relationships, and better environmental conditions. An example of bad destiny can be cultural conflict, wars, and worse environmental conditions. If you want humanity to have a good destiny, and you can be part of influencing factors—no matter how small that part is—you will need to take the responsibility as a human being. *The responsibility of believing and acting to help human destiny as an objective goal is a responsibility associated with the fact that we have free will. No matter how small the helping effort is, when such effort is aggregated, the impact can be influential to the whole. Even though the individual cannot determine our destiny as a whole, it is the best option for us to take responsibility for helping the world get better, regardless of how small the helping effort is.* This can be and should be one of the purposes of life.

The objectivity of the meaning of life is also connected to the objectivity of the fourth world. We have extensively discussed the definition of the fourth world (see "Aggregation of Minds" in Chapter 4). In the fourth world, however, by definition, not all components are expressible by language. The human mind itself keeps evolving. The objectivity of the fourth world depends on how honestly our heart detects the signal from the wholeness and responds to it. It depends on how truthfully the experience is passed from generation to generation. The inexpressibility can be also due to the highly nonlinear interaction between the observer and the observed. Since the interactions between each individual are nonlinear, group behavior is unpredictable. There is no simple model to describe it. One may get hints from the self-organizing system that even though each individual may not be aware of the evolutionary path (therefore it is a myth), the system or society over time still exhibits an evolutionary path. It can take many generations to understand that. But at a given moment, these behaviors are not totally comprehensible by the conscious of an individual. In essence, the aggregation of mind is achieved through the media to carry the products of the minds from generation to generation. When we are searching the goal of life, these subtle relationships must be better understood and realized. They reveal profound hints of the meaning of life and hints on why human beings must take responsibility to influence our own destiny.

The Message of Life

How is the objectivity of the meaning of life different from the objectivity of other scientific laws? Certainly, the laws of physical nature, such as Newton's laws, are independent of the existence of human beings. On the other hand, it appears that the third world or fourth world will disappear without human beings. However, it is possible to believe that the principles that govern the nature of life, govern the human interactions (such as caring for and loving each other), or the principles that govern the psyche are concrete messages of more abstract laws that are actually independent of the existence of human beings. Human beings happen to be the best carrier, or interpreters, of these laws. Whenever or wherever there is life, such principles will prevail. We call them the message of life. The only thing that can exist and transcend independent of the material world is information, principles, or laws. However, it needs the material world, including human beings as carriers, to manifest these messages.

This viewpoint was echoed by the Neo-Confucian philosophy of Li, which is the law that governs the universe, including human ethics, and exists independent of human beings. The same belief can be found in the Bible (John 1:1–18), and also can be found in Taoism (Lao-tze, Ch. 25). The Li, the Tao, the Word existed before the world. The messages of life are among them. These messages are carried through human beings, since human minds happen to be able to resonate with them. If a person wants to seek any eternal connection, he has to align his life to these messages. This sounds very mystical, because no one can prove the messages of life existed before the existence of human being. At most, it is just a belief. It is an extension of intuitive reasoning after pushing rational reasoning to a limit. The goal of this book is to push the reasoning to a limit. The next step is up to the reader to choose: are there better answers to connect our lives to a transcending existence without the assumption of a supernatural entity or any eternal existence? One should not expect a rational answer, because it is beyond it. It is up to our courage and responsibility to make a choice.

There can be many forms of belief that claim to manifest the same messages of life as well. Then what is the criteria for distinguishing truth versus delusion among different manifestations? The criteria is the response from the human heart. If a belief is truth, the human heart responds with peace and happiness. The person will have harmonious human relationships and a peaceful mind. The belief must be tested generation after generation to see if it generates similar responses.

If we believe the objectivity of the fourth world, and believe that the destiny of the world is at least unpredictable, then we have an objective foundation for searching for the meaning of life.

8.3 What Defines the Meaning of Life?

The fact the meaning of life is connected to human destiny, and besides the belief of the objectivity of the fourth world, what other factors define the meaning of life?

"Life seeks completeness, not perfection"

From the psychological perspective, one goal of life is to go through the complete development cycle of the human mind described in Chapter 4. Jung stated that "Life seeks completeness, not perfection." It means that one should strive to complete the development cycle from stage one to stage five, although most of us cannot reach that. When one gets to the more advanced stage of the development cycle of the mind—for example at stage three, when the wholeness is awakening—the dark side of human potential is integrated and loses its destructive power. With this, the value of a human being is manifested more. One caution though, we should not misinterpret this statement. To seek completeness of life, one cannot choose any means that have negative impacts to others or to the society.

Jung reinterpreted the goal of life described in Christianity from the viewpoint of psychology. In his interpretation (Fuller, 93),

> A complete life is said to be the work of the Holy Spirit, who leads into all kinds of dangers and at the same time, into consciousness—the wider consciousness created by the Holy Spirit is the very goal of God's incarnation. Without error and sin, there is said to be no experience of union with God. To Jung, to serve God means: to be an active participant in the emergence of light out of darkness, to further God's becoming conscious of his creation and the human being's becoming conscious of his or her self. We meet the God yet to be transformed when we confront the unconscious. Jung finds in the progressive incarnation of God in human life the real history of the world.

The above quotation assumes one believes in the existence of the Holy Spirit and God. For those who still do not believe that, the message may not be easy to get through. At the minimum, one should believe there is some form of higher order of principles and laws that is transcending. This can be the Tao in Taoism, *Li* in Neo-Confucianism, and Buddha in Buddhism. After getting through stages one and two in the development cycle (see Chapter 4), an individual should work closely with these agents of metareality to go through stages three, four, and five. In the process of going through these stages, there is the possibility that one may suffer difficulty, hardship, and at the same time increase the awareness and consciousness of human experience. In the meantime, the human mind is more sensitive to probe deeper and wider, to gain deeper and wider understanding or experience of the truth that is unexperienced at the early stages of the mind. With deeper and wider understanding of the world, one can manifest the message through the concrete action of caring about others, deep respect for life, and a wider sense of responsibility.

"Life seeks completeness, not perfection." Equally important is that "life seeks depth, not only breadth." A person should realize that the depth of life experience cannot be substituted by breadth of life experience. If a person is always living in the "deficient" state, driven or dominated by material desires or intellectual curiosity, he or she will be stuck in stage two and unable to enter the next stage, unable to deepen the life experience, and hence missing important value as a human being. This is regardless of how much or how wide a life experience one has reached in the early stage, regardless of how much money one earns, how high a social position one achieves. The missing of deeper life experience is always a regret, since the individual is underachieved as a human being. In a society that is driven by materialism, one cannot easily realize this fact. Consequently, the society as a whole is underachieved as well.

Experiencing the Opposite

Why is there evil (or Satan in Western religious terminology) in the world? The reason is simple: experience of hardship is one way to understand the meaning of life. Experiencing difficulty and hardship can be one step toward the completion of the development cycle of the mind. This doesn't mean that one should voluntarily seek hardship and difficulty. By nature human beings tend to avoid them. What it means here is that when hardship and difficulty inevitably come, there is no need to panic. One should see the bright side of it.

The truth and messages for life are complex and subtle, and not every aspect can be easily known. Truth will not reveal itself unless you pursue it and tune to it. Even though everyone has the potential to know about it, it is not an automatic process. If a person simply acknowledges and accepts the teachings without thinking or challenging, it is unlikely that he truly understands it. True belief occurs only when one exhausts his rational thinking in the pursuit of truth to a state of looking up for intuitive guidance. That is the beginning of belief. The process of believing has been explained in depth in Chapter 6. The contents of belief can be adjusted as the level of understanding increases or deepens. Experiencing the opposite is part of such process.

If the hardship is man-made or caused by malicious human intent, one should avoid it. But if it is unavoidable, one should face it with courage. Going through it, one may gain precious experience about the truth of life. Attitude can change the value of such experience. There is pain when experiencing hardship and difficulty. But it is even more painful when one goes through such hardship but misses the opportunity to better understand the nature of human beings, to glorify the dignity of the wholeness of human beings, and to deepen the understanding of the meaning of life.

Human nature has both good and bad sides, both kind and evil. The psychic wholeness is achieved through enduring the opposites. The suffering of the opposites is a necessary step on the way to reconcile the differentiation in the unity and wholeness of the self (Fuller, 92). The path to psychological rebirth is through suffering and death of the old mind. When a human mind reaches stage four in the development cycle, the ego's isolation is overcome, the consciousness is broadened, and the conflict is reduced. The evil part of the mind is integrated into the psychic totality of the self. When this occurs, the evilness is put into a new and larger context, being understood at the higher level of integration, and thus "loses its destructive power" (Fuller, 93). For example, a person may have the intention to hurt others due to his own unhappiness. When he is able to understand the source of the unhappiness, he basically has stepped out of the previous mind-set and entered into a wider mind-set, thus the malicious intent loses its destructive power.

Scale of Time and Space

The meaning of life depends on a different scale of time and space. From the scale of time and space, the meaning of life can be zoomed in and out with the following levels: 1) Personal level: the meaning of life is straightforward and attainable—happiness, reproduction, wealth. 2) Societal level: social relationships, love, positive influence on others, social position, fame. 3) Mankind's history and Earth level: seeking meaning of life from intellect, knowledge, culture, religion. 4) Nature, universal level: here, what is not meaningful to human beings can be meaningful to other species. When a leaf falls from a tree, the value of the leaf ends for the tree. But it is still valuable to other plants, or to an ant or worm in the ground. Similarly, when a person dies, his own life-span ends. But there is still meaning for others in nature, at least freeing up of resources to others.

Some of the goals of life are universal. For example, survival and reaching maximum potential are universal to all species on the earth. When you see the new sprout in a plant, you feel the strength of life, even though the information comes from a plant. Similarly, the information radiated in your life-span may have certain meaning to others in nature that you are not even aware of. The cultural information transmitted from humankind as a whole may be in a form that has meaning to others in the universe, regardless of how the universe evolves. We have touched on this topic in the discussion of the destiny of human being and the objectivity of the meaning of life. There are messages in the universe that objectively exist; human beings are just one carrier of such messages. The meaning of life when manifested by such message is objective. This becomes one of our responsibilities.

The evolution and growth of an individual's mind at a given time is very much a miniature model of the evolutionary path of humankind's culture in history. The difference is that every individual is different; as such, each individual can reach different levels of understanding of the current state of the culture. Not everyone can grow mature enough to reach the front-line level of understanding of the culture. It is for this reason that at a given time and for a given society, there must be a wide variety of cultures, religions, and beliefs to meet the needs of different people. Particularly, even the rudimentary components (myth, rituals) in a religion can still be valuable in modern times, because they address an essential part of human nature that will not disappear no matter how advanced the modern society is. The proportion of this number of people, or the proportion of time in an individual's growth that needs the nurture of religious preaching, could be reduced when understanding and knowledge of human nature as a whole increases, but the portion will unlikely reach zero. Different people seek different levels of meaning, which should be respected.

In short, when searching for the meaning of life, we ought to be able to zoom in and out of different levels from the time scale or from the space scale. Different levels of scales can provide different views.

Clear Understanding of Self-Limitation

The meaning of life also depends on the understanding of self-limitation. As the person grows mature, he realizes his limitations. This can be physical health, family life, past history, experience, or emotion. Realizing the limitations from every aspect, now he can redefine what he can achieve with his capabilities and not feel deficient anymore. When the balance between achievement and realistic capability is reached and realized, the attitude toward life is different. He feels more rewards; everything around him is a privilege.

This self-discovery process is extremely subtle. It can be painful to accept self-limitations. One can have weak health conditions of the stomach or a minor mental problem that influences daily decisions. They are subtle to detect, but they influence the mind development to a degree. There can be a bad experience while a person is growing up that causes impacts they are not aware of until much later, as an adult. There can be cultural limitations (e.g., social relationships are based on family ties), or political limitations (e.g., no freedom of speech or religious practice). Since they are applied to everyone in the same society, you are not aware of it and even accept it as normal. These limitations can alter the perception of the meaning of life. Even if one eventually realizes these subtle limitations, it can be painful to accept.

Self-discovery is a journey that needs courage and wisdom. It is in this area that a belief can help to lift up the spirit. Deep soul-searching and meditation help. This is one necessary step to go through in the mind's development cycle. Since each individual is vastly different, each will have his or her own perception of the meaning of life. It is crucial to respect the diversity. Any attempt to have a uniform perception on the meaning of life is not practical, even unethical. When discussing the meaning of life, we must take account of the diversity and consider the meaning of life for different people.

Daily Routine in Normal Life

Life should be examined. But there is no need for a special or big event to actualize the goal of life. The meaning of life is embedded in the normal life routine—given that you know the meaning. If a person seeks the meaning of life from only big events or from social achievement, it just indicates that his spirit level is still in stage two. There is also no need to seek the meaning of life by living remotely from urban areas, isolating oneself from the secular world. When one's mind development cycle gets to stage four or five, the meaning of life is just here and now. One can find the meaning residing in every decision in daily life. Every second contains the subtlety of life and its beauty. However, this doesn't mean to completely ignore the meaning of life when the mind is at an earlier developmental stage. There are multiple levels of meaning at the same time. Together they help to achieve the completeness of life.

8.4 What Is the Meaning of Life After All?

After discussing the factors that influence and define the perception of the meaning of life, it is time to summarize what the meaning of life is after all. Obviously, there are different levels of meaning at the different periods of life, especially at the different stages of the mind development cycle. One of the purposes of life is to complete the developmental process of our minds in full, and it encompasses multiple levels.

At the very basic level, the goal of life is to survive. This is inherited from the most basic instinct of living creatures. Having enough food, a house to live in, marriage to form a family and raising children are some of these goals. Human desires should be satisfied within reasonable ethical boundaries. There is no point for religion or ethics to ignore basic human desires. These are the most bottom level of goals. There is a large number of people in this world who are just living for these goals. What is the meaning of it? Even with this level of goal, life has a meaning. *No matter how normal or how great a person is, in the end he or she is just a link of an evolving chain of human-kind's history. The most basic goal of a person's life, in essence, is simply to connect the past and the future in the self-evolving history of humankind, even if the person is not aware of it at all.* This meaning is applicable to any level of goals of life described below. We can name it *meaning of connecting*. A person may not be aware of it, just lives a regular life but still has this level of meaning.

The next-level goal of life is to fully actualize a person's potential. When the potential is unleashed, one should feel his talent has been explored and utilized. This is on the condition that he knows what his unique talent is. Different people have different talents and capabilities. It can be intellectual talent, it can be skills for notable achievement in science, social position, finance, entrepreneurship, etc. Eventually, the outcome is an achievement in the material world. This corresponds to stage two in the development cycle of the human mind. Unleashing of human potential is an intrinsic force of civilization. There is no good or bad ethics associated with it since the ethical value is derived from the other force of unification. It should be supported since it is unavoidable, but it must be within the ethical boundary as well. Not everyone can have notable achievement in the material world. Hence, there is pride associated it once a person obtains such achievement. What is the meaning of this level of life goals besides the *meaning of connecting*? It strengthens the connection between the past, the present, and the future. The connection is stronger because the span, the dimension of life, is expanded due to the actualization of human potential. Unleashing of human potentials advances the development of science and technology. As a consequence, the survivability of mankind is stronger due to advancement of knowledge and technology.

Next of the goals of life is at the spiritual level. An awakening of wholeness of self occurs. A person realizes the limitations of the intellect, the limitations of the conscious mind, and begins the reconciliation of the conscious and the unconscious. He listens to the inner voice from the heart, and starts to perceive the world very differently. This is corresponding to stage three of the mind development cycle. Achievement at this level is unrelated to achievements from the material world. A person at this stage would more easily follow the heart, not the brain. He would be more comfortable with the dynamics of nonlinear thinking (e.g., the future is unpredictable, but there is still a meaning associated with it, similar to self-organization). He would know that life is larger than knowledge and intelligence, and action is more important than deep thinking. The end result is that such an individual will have a more peaceful mind, will enjoy the inner peace that results in happier interpersonal relationships. The spiritual integration should not conflict with the previous level of goals of exploring and actualizing the potential. A person with higher capability, better achievement, and also successful integration with the spirit will have a life experience bigger and deeper in scope than others. At stage two, a person who is seeking achievement in the material world may pursue the goal without considering an ethical bottom line, i.e., one may seek the achievement by all means. But at stage three, the individual is serious about the ethical bottom line, because he is more caring of the integrity and totality of the wholeness. In fact, this is not a pure ethical self-control issue, there is actual benefit to it. There are always hurdles and conflicts when a person pursues achievements in the material world. But since the perception of life at his level is deeper, one is able to view these hurdles and conflicts as temporary and not the most important issues in life. This attitude in turn helps a person be more patient, more peaceful in dealing with the hurdles and difficulty, which is more likely to end up with successful results as a byproduct. *In stage two, there is a dilemma. One must believe that actualizing human potentiality is the center of life in order to reach its maximization. In stage three, on the other hand, the maximum level of potentiality is achieved as a byproduct. It is a byproduct of shifting the center of life from the reconciliation of ego to the wholeness of self. It results in a new level of integrity of self.*

What is the meaning of life at this level beyond the meaning of connection? The key difference at this level is the awareness of the connection itself. In the previous two levels, the meaning of connection is involuntary and the person is unaware of it. Now he or she is aware. A person starts to consciously seek connection to a transcending media that is not obviously tangible and tries to contribute to it. Examples of such contribution include a scientific discovery that widens or deepens our knowledge of a certain area, a masterpiece of music that people enjoy, or a spiritual inspiration of a religious leader who inspires people's souls. A person at this stage not only does his or her best to live out potentiality but also consciously strives to contribute to the connection media at the spiritual level. However, one should not expect such contribution is everlasting. Instead, a contribution is always one step in an ever-evolving chain.

The last level of goals of life is a continuation of the previous level: a person seeks completeness of life. The mind development is at its possible maximum extent. One is looking beyond limitations and unnecessary boundaries of the existing cultures and religions, reaching the messages and the foundation behind existing beliefs, religions, and cultures. Such individual is consciously contributing to the connection media at the level of whole self. The boundary between oneself and the nature of the universe is not a burden in the perception of life anymore. Instead, one is part of the transcendent flow of life, part of the world. Every second in human life is a miracle. Depth and width of the total life experience are expanded. Such spiritual connection is not an escape from the routine life. Instead, it enables one to cherish every second, every bit of the routine life. With the correct spiritual integration, the love for life is intensified and manifested, instead of weakened or hidden. The original ego is less and less important, and the larger self, with characteristics of caring and love of others, increases. He is able to experience the messages of life. Effectively, when one approaches his death, he has no regret, because his talent is unleashed, his biological and spiritual connections are addressed. *The length of life is transformed through the depth and breadth of life, so that the total life experience is expanded. A person at this stage with a finite life-span can experience much more than a normal person. Even if one lives much longer, what can be experienced has been experienced at the current moment, because of the vision he sees. Hence living longer doesn't increase the meaning. The fear of death is managed.*

The whole purpose of exploring the meaning of life eventually is to appreciate the preciousness of life. An individual who realizes the beauty, the complexity, the unspeakable awesomeness of human life shall cherish every second of living. Consequently, respect and love of others shall naturally flow from his or her heart. Indeed there is no need to rely on religion to reach such seemingly religious feeling. The route to reach the feeling is long and needs deep soul-searching. Religion can shortcut this process by relying on a certain divinity and making the feeling more personal, but at the risk of introducing potential side effects such as becoming superstitious or extremist.

In summary, the meaning of life encompasses several levels:

- As the common denominator, we are just part of an evolutionary chain. No matter how normal or how great a person is, in the end, he or she is just a link of an evolving chain of humankind's history. The goal of a person's life, in essence, is simply to connect the past, the present, and the future in a self-evolving river of life for mankind as a whole. Aware or not, everyone has this level of meaning as long as he or she lives a normal life, takes the responsibility of helping the previous generation, and raises the next generation. The objectivity of such an evolutionary chain cannot be explained in linear logic, which has been discussed in the section of "Is the Meaning of Life Objective?"

- Next, a person is looking at exploring his or her talent, seeking all sorts of goals in the material world. Actualizing potentiality is a neutral force with respect to the meaning of life. It is the natural force of human beings that influences the evolutionary path. A person may not be aware of the meaning of connection at this level, but just seeks to maximize the potentiality. Doing so expands and strengthens the connection.

- At the next level, a person is not only an actor but also an observer, with respect to the meaning of connection. Because of the increase of awareness, a person starts to consciously seek connection to a transcending media that is not obviously tangible. He also strives to make contributions to knowledge, science, religion, culture, and be more caring and loving to other people. Everyone is benefited by the education and nurture of these outputs of the third world or fourth world evolution, and therefore everyone bears the responsibility to give something back, even though we don't know exactly how the evolution will end up. We don't know because of the scale of time and scope and nature of self-organization. This awareness and voluntary contribution makes a person's life more meaningful.

- The final level is to transform the length of life through the depth of life. It is a continuation of the previous level. One looks beyond the boundary and limitation of existing culture and religion, and looks for the messages behind the scenes. The boundary between oneself and the nature of the universe is not a burden in the perception of life. Every second in life is a miracle; the depth and breadth of life experience are expanded. The person is able to live out the truth of life that is hidden. He makes aware of it through his deep perception of the message of life. The scope and experience of life is expanded through the depth of understanding. The sense of connection to a transcending media is strong and obvious. When a person comes to this experience and then goes back to the daily life routine, the meaning of every tiny thing in daily life is fundamentally different. The perception of interpersonal relationships is also transformed to be more loving and forgiving.

Because there are different levels of meaning, in reality not everyone can reach the same level. There are different types of people with very different attitudes toward the meaning of life, and a person can be one of the following:

- Not able to complete the development of intelligence, or not able to maximize his potentiality, due to internal or external constraints.
- Not aware of the force of searching for meaning. But it doesn't mean it doesn't exist, just that he is not aware of it.
- Aware of it and relies on religion to address the issue.
- Aware of it, searching religion, but discards it due to the symbols and rituals, considering those as superstition.
- Able to look beyond religion and total human knowledge, searching for the meaning behind the scene and realizing the real meaning of the search.

8.5 Life and Death

Frankl thinks everything has a meaning, including death (Fuller, 232). The meaning of death is so that one shall have a sense of urgency to do something meaningful. Without death, anything can be postponed infinitely, and nothing will be done effectively. It is the destiny of death for everyone that pushes each of us to live out the best quality of life, to live out the deepest possible dignity as a human being. Death is like a set boundary of an equation, so that there is concrete solution, therefore concrete meaning of life can be found.

Another meaning of death is to release resources consumed and occupied by the current generation to the next generation. The earth has limited resources for living creatures. If everyone can live forever, the resources will be depleted. From the perception of the material world, death for an individual is a sad thing, but for the species as a whole, it is a good thing.

So death is not a choice but a destiny. For human beings, the period of life is so short that we can consider death as a normal state and living as an abnormal state.

No one can describe the feeling when he or she is dying; instead, one can only imagine the feeling of dying. Therefore, the issue here is not about death itself but the fear of death when one is still alive. One cannot avoid death but can defeat the fear of death. Physical death is unavoidable, but a human being is not just physical. We have a spiritual mind. Therefore to manage the fear of death, one cannot count on the physical body, but has to look into the unique part of human beings—the spiritual mind. This is one reason that people seek the spiritual meaning of life. Fear of physical death is nonsense since it is a destiny. Fear of spiritual death, on the other hand, is manageable. The question then is how you manage and use the precious time when you are alive. When a person defeats the fear of death, there is no regret when he or she has to face death today.

How do you achieve such state of defeating the fear of death? Obviously, this depends on the perception of life, on the understanding of the meaning of life. If a person doesn't have a clear understanding of the potential and limitations of human beings, he will nevertheless fear death, as death means the termination of possibility and potentiality. A person may look for a connection to a transcendent media as a way to manage the fear, but there is no guarantee such a transcendent media is an objective existence, the attempt will fail and won't result in defeating the fear. A person may count on life after death as proposed by many religions, but there is no proof that life after death does exist; there is no connection between the current life and the eternal life, or eternal life is a myth, hence the fear of death is not really addressed.

Confucius said, "I don't even know the meaning of living—how can I know the meaning of death?" This is a very practical approach. However, the management of the fear of death reveals the fundamental meaning of current life. Without addressing it means missing the coverage of an important portion of the spectrum of the human mind.

To manage the fear of death, there are two components to consider: 1) Is your life potential maximized? This includes the material and spiritual potentials, and both must be balanced. 2) Is your spirit connecting to something transcend? Is there a connection to a transcendent media? Is that media an objective entity?

In the previous section "Is the Meaning of Life Objective?" it is pointed out that the answer depends on our own responsibility. The choice of influence on the destiny to a better world is our responsibility. The first component tries to manage the fear in the current life, which is more tangible. But the first component is not self-sufficient because if there is no direction on human destiny, many attempts in the current life are not worth trying. The second component is at the higher level and less tangible, but it assures there is continuity of the current values. The root cause of the second component is that we human beings have spirits, we have the capabilities to perceive laws at the higher level, i.e., laws derived from the principle that the whole is larger than the sum of the parts.

When one faces the question of death, there is a checklist one can go through to see if there is a regret left behind. If what is expected and can be expected has been met, there is minimized reason to regret. Do I have the normal life with the most basic human needs addressed? i.e., basic food, a house to live, established family. Do I take care of the elderly, the children in the family? Do I connect to the society in some way—a job, being associated with a group, or even a group of close friends? If these answers are positive, a person has achieved the most basic goals of life. If this person is not aware of other potentiality, or the knowledge level limits him to reach more potentiality, then what he has experienced in life and what he is capable of are matched. He can leave this world without regret. It is not a reasonable thought to see such a person pass away and state that his life is meaningless. There are other goals that he may not be aware of, but by living a normal life he still meet those goals involuntarily. The next checklist is for a person who has more awareness of the spiritual needs, a person who cares about what is left over after death. Do you leave anything behind? At the smaller scale of impact, this could be a piece of music people enjoy, a book, a painting, and a sculpture that touches others' lives, or a good reputation. At the larger scale of impact, this can be a scientific discovery, an engineering breakthrough, a powerful politician, a successful entrepreneur who built a long-lasting company, or an influential religious leader who inspires many people. People will remember them after they die. This feeling helps to manage the fear of death.

However, for a number of people who are seeking roots and origins of everything, there is one more checkpoint to go through. If in the end, maybe a billion years later, the earth will be destroyed, human beings will disappear, nothing is really forever-lasting, then what is the point of leaving something behind? The answer to this is that such perception is not really scientific. It is a religion based on current scientific knowledge. Science itself has self-evidence about its own limitation. No one can really predict the future a billion years later. The future is uncertain by nature. To search for certainty, a natural answer is to look beyond the material world, to believe there is absolute unchanged existence. This can be information, principles that are independent of the material world. These were named as Tao, *Li*, Buddha, or symbolized by Western religion as God. It cannot be proved or explained clearly. Having the answer for ultimate destiny, one can manage the fear of death on top of it and find a satisfied solution.

Another Eastern wisdom to manage the fear of death is to trade the length of life with the quality and width of life. If for every second, spiritual-wise, one experiences much more and better quality, say ten times more and better, there is no difference for one to live one hundred years or one thousand years. What can be experienced for living one thousand years has been experienced in one hundred years, then what is the regret of death? This is perhaps why Confucius said, "If I know the Tao in the morning, I have no regret to die in the evening." How to reach such state? It is through cultivation, meditation, connecting to nature—the Tao. Such a perception also resolves the ethics question: if nothing lasts forever, is there still a meaning to following certain ethical values in the current life? The answer is yes. The ethical value to following has benefited the current life already by maximizing the experience in quality and in width. Hence the wisdom system itself is self-consistent without counting on an everlasting existence or relying on a promise of after-death life. The only catch is that it should show the moral direction: good moral improves the quality and completeness of life experience while bad moral blocks it. A good moral increases the quality of life, increases the joy of life. Why? A good moral keeps a person honest to his heart to the best degree. This allows one to experience the message that is transcending time and space. Hence it is like "living in heaven." A bad moral, on the other hand, blocks such possibility. Therefore living with a bad ethical value is like "living in hell." These are real-time states of mind in current life, and there's no need to wait till after death. The Western and Eastern wisdoms probably are complementary each other. The absolute God provides better guidance on moral direction, and the here-and-now approach reduces the reliance on life after death for moral direction.

In a more plain language, the central themes of life are growth, joy, responsibility, understanding and sharing. An ideal life should experience all these components. Growth means the physical body, intelligence, and any special talent are strengthened. The individual enjoys life as a gift from Mother Nature; he not only takes care of the family, takes responsibility in society, but also takes the responsibility as a human being to influence the moral direction and hence the destiny of human beings. He is capable of digesting the message of life. And finally, when he thoroughly understands the meaning of life, he is able to share the message with others. When a life has accomplished all this, there is really no regret in life.

At the very end, the most precious quality of a life is from the spirit, the holy feeling from the heart about the admiration of life, the admiration of the magnificent complexity and subtleness of life, and the respect of other life and the seeking of equality. *The respect of life results in a sense that confidence and self-respect are of basic face value and need no explanation or reason.* Instead it is a given. This sense is probably the most transcending message of life. It could be across any living creature, and human beings just happened to be one of the carriers of such message. This sense is similar to the concept of *Jen* in Confucianism. It is echoed in the Bible that "there is word before any life." When a person's mind is able to resonate with this message, the light shines forth from a person's mind. Throughout a person's life, the goal is to reveal this message and share this light by resonating with others on the same message. There can be many ways of doing this depending on a person's talent, e.g., just living an inspiring life, supporting and caring for others, being a religious leader, writing a book to convoy the message, etc. When the light of life shines and is shared, the mission of life is accomplished. It is the innermost relief of life. Physically or materially one can either have a normal life or can still suffer difficulty, but spiritually he is "entering heaven." The rest of life is just a leftover, a gift to enjoy. One basically can die any time without regret. In this sense, the fear of death is defeated.

When I look back on our predecessors who have passed away, they could be very normal people. They could live just for the meaning of connection or could live lives to reveal and share the message of life. A life is really not judged by the length but by the quality, by the fact that one can reveal and share of the message of life. There is no good or bad criterion which life is more meaningful. It depends on the talent a person was born with and developed; it also depends on the level of awareness. If a person is unaware of the message of life, or unable to explicitly express it, the meaning of life is limited to the meaning of connection. If a person has higher awareness of the message of life, he should find a way to share and reveal it; otherwise it is a regret. When Christianity mentions the Final Judgment, that is the meaning of it. When a person is about to face death and goes through the checklist discussed in this section, it is similar to a "final judgment." And if a person can face death comfortably, he or she basically passes the judgment. When a person is strong and alive, this seems not a concern. But when a person is approaching death, he is weak and in a collapsed state, this can be a terrible question to face. A person who has clearly understood and shared the message of life has no fear to face this question, therefore will pass the final judgment. But this is just a guess, no one can really explicitly tell the real experience in the moment of dying.

In conclusion, the understanding of death is tightly coupled with understanding the meaning of life. The statement from Confucius, "I don't know the meaning of life, how can I know the meaning of death?" may be changed to "If I don't know the meaning of death, how I can know the meaning of life?" The only rational way to justify the statement from Confucius is that we cannot completely understand the meaning of death, as there are emotional and unconscious parts of the meaning. As such, we cannot completely defeat the fear of death just relying on rational thinking. Support from a belief system is needed here. It is up to each person's courage and responsibility to make a choice.

<u>Reference</u>

- Fuller, Andrew R. *Psychology and Religion: Classical Theorists and Contemporary Developments* (Lanham, Maryland: Rowman & Littlefield Publishers, Inc., 2008, fourth edition).
- Lao-tzu. *Tao Te Ching*. Chapter 25. "有物混成, 先天地生, 。。。吾不知其名, 字之曰道。" 老子《道德经》25.
- Prigogine, I., and I. Stengers. *The End of Certainty*. (Free Press, 1997).

CHAPTER 9

Looking into the Future

We start the journey of understanding the meaning of human life from looking into the origins of knowledge and the limitations of our cognition capability, seeking hints from scientific advancements and its self-revealed limitations, and more importantly, examining the understanding of our psyche and human mind. The central piece of foundation is the understanding of the nature of the human mind, its evolution and development cycle. An integrated model is developed to help the thinking process. With these building blocks, in Part II of the book, we attempt to decipher the meaning of belief and religion, particularly the message behind the symbols and rituals of a belief system and religion. We found that some of the justifications of a belief and religion can be derived from the building blocks described earlier. Belief and religion are at the far end of spectrum of the human spirit, while the near end of spectrum is mostly reflected in culture, a more loose and easy form of product from mankind's civilization. As an example, the Chinese culture was briefly surveyed, and the comparison of Chinese culture and Western culture is discussed. The key point is to show that different cultures have different presentations of the building blocks described in Part I of the book. Finally, we go back to answer the initial question of the meaning of life and particularly to explore the meaning of death. Both questions are tightly coupled together. The answer is related to aligning one's life to the message of life, which in turn cannot be proved scientifically. That is one root for the need of a belief system and religion. It is a person's own courage and responsibility to influence his or her own destiny.

Seemingly the journey ends at this point. That is not the case though. What part of the discussion so far will be truly lasting? Would what we know or believe to be true today be found too rough in understanding reality, or just delusional? I believe that some of the principles or methodologies shall stay true in the future. Furthermore, there are currently unnecessary distortions or boundaries in our understanding of human life, due to the historical evolutionary path, and these could be improved in the future. This chapter will discuss these issues and call out the key assumptions to be further examined in the future.

9.1 Key Assumptions and Future Validations

The starting point of understanding life and human beings is science and psychology. Religious people typically think that is the wrong starting point. Instead the starting point should be the belief in God. However, such path poses unnecessary boundary between religion and science, when in fact both can be consolidated in the future. The key thing is to wait till science and psychology are developed to a level that their limitation becomes self-evident, and hence the need for a metareality becomes self-proved and better understood. At that point, the gap between religion and scientific research can be consolidated. In this book, there are several assumptions made based on the current understanding of science and psychology advancement, and these assumptions are heavily used to justify the origins of belief and religion, to justify the foundation of the meaning of life. They are so crucial that they will be highlighted here again. Hopefully in the future, they are better explained and better understood.

The first assumption to mention is the emergence effect of a complex system. Emergence effect refers to the property of a complex system that cannot be explained from the properties of the components in the complex system. Principles observed at the larger system level cannot be induced from the principles at the component levels. Such phenomena have been observed in micro and macro complex systems. For example, at the micro level, the irreversibility of thermodynamics, the phase transition in statistical physics, the quantum entanglement effect; at the macro level, the ant colony phenomenon, the evolution of life. The idea is that there is higher-level order that cannot be derived or understood from the order at the component level. Furthermore, the component-level element is not aware of the higher-order principle, even though they can be involuntarily contributing to it, as has been observed in the ant colony behavior. If the emergence phenomena exist quite universally in complex systems, there is no reason to reject the idea that for human life as a whole, there are higher orders that we are not aware of, but in fact we involuntarily are part of the contributions. The information loss when breaking down the whole into part cannot be recovered by simply putting together the knowledge of the parts. It is this method-ological induction that can be used to justify the concept of metareality. Metareality refers to a reality that exists but is unable to be fully comprehended with our current knowledge and experience, it ties with the lost information mentioned earlier. Such assumption is the basis for many religions. If there is a breakthrough in the future that emergence order can be explained from the component level, it will definitely change a lot of philosophical views and the foundations of many religions. The origin of order in a complex system, chemical organism, simple form of life, or even advanced form of life, will be one of the most fascinating areas of research in the future.

The idea of megastatistics is the second reason for believing there could be a metareality that is beyond our current knowledge to comprehend. If a law can only be shown in a scale of hundreds of years, or thousands of years, a person cannot fully experience but only be part of it. In Chapter 5, we use Bayes's theorem to model such phenomenon. A more strict mathematical treatment can be helpful. The implication can be quite profound: if an individual can influence a long-term trend, even an ex-tremely small influence, aggregately the influence is substantial. This means that in seeking the meaning of life, we human beings with the free will bear the responsibility of influencing our own destiny. It would be awesome to mathematically model this assumption.

The next assumption is related to the first one. If a metareality cannot be com-prehended with our current knowledge and experience, we can pretty much ignore it since there is no influence on our daily lives. However, the human mind seems to have the capability to sense such higher order momentarily. To formalize the process, symbols are introduced and facilitate the process of interaction with the metareal-ity. The scientific similarity to such process is the introduction of wave function in quantum mechanics. The physical meaning of wave function is still a debating subject in modern physics. But it doesn't stop the usefulness of such concept, as it helps to solve tremendous physics problems at the quantum level. The pragmatic approach of quantum mechanics echoes the pragmatic view of religion from William James. The concept of God is a symbol to a metareality. One cannot prove it is right or wrong. But pragmatically it has influenced the lives of many people who believe in it. It remains interesting to monitor in the future how quantum physicists continue to interpret cohesively the meaning of wave function.

The third item is not really an assumption because it is certain to be true. Reality is indivisible. Any concept human beings defined for building up knowledge is in a way just a simplification or abstraction of part of the reality. Dividing the wholeness of the reality introduces the loss of information. Therefore the knowledge built on top of it is incomplete. The true reality can only be experienced but not completely explained. This principle was well articulated in ancient Chinese Taoism. But why are we human beings still so fascinated in the discovery of laws of nature to advance our accumulation of knowledge? This is a tradeoff. First the advance of human intelligence is irreversible. After the awakening of the human conscious and intelligence, the power of human cognition cannot be stopped, and more and more knowledge was and will be accumulated. Secondly, human beings are better off acquiring such knowledge, even if it is incomplete, than just simply experiencing the reality in chaotic understanding. This knowledge increases their ability to utilize and cooperate with nature, which increases the survivability for human beings as a whole. The well-being is also increased as people know better about themselves and how to get along with others. However, we should always keep a humble mind-set. Knowledge is the result of the human mind's capability for differentiating the reality, and differentiation is always associated with isolation. They are two sides of the same coin. No matter how intelligent we are, how advanced the knowledge we accumulate, it is just the approximation of the true reality. We should always keep our minds open to adjust the knowledge acquired, and potentially completely redefine current successful theory when it reaches a breaking point.

The next foundation of our journey is the understanding of the human mind. Recent advancement of psychology, even maybe still in preliminary status, has proved to be very important in the understanding of the human mind. The relationship of the conscious and unconscious parts of the mind are crucial. Intellect is the outcome of the conscious mind. However, the human mind cannot fully become conscious; therefore the implication is that intellect cannot fully understand the human mind as a whole. This is similar to saying that the mouth cannot eat the whole head since the mouth is just a part of it. It is this fundamental limitation that religion becomes a necessary complementary process for us to cope with the need of integrating the mind as a whole. Dividing the mind into the conscious and unconscious parts is probably too simple, but it reflects a certain level of truth. Moreover, the conscious mind has this intrinsic tendency of growth and expansion. The tendency advances its intelligence, increases the survivability, and maximizes its own interest. In the meantime, the conscious part of mind is nevertheless always part of the wholeness of mind. It cannot exist without its own root, and therefore another hidden intrinsic tendency is to pull back the conscious mind to unify with its mother roots. These two tendencies are equally important, and the dynamic between them is exactly the growth history of an individual. It is very subtle to understand this process. In Chapter 4, we attempted to develop a model to facilitate the discussion. The model is by no means proven scientifically. But the key message in the model is quite obvious: an individual's psychological maturity comes in two phases. In the first phase, the tendency of growth dominates, the individual has less concern about spiritual integration. In the second phase, the tendency of reconciliation dominates, or at least has the same priority as the potentiality. In this phase, a person strives to live more than the conscious self but live with the integrated larger self, and strives to align the spirit with the messages of life. The transition from phase one to phase two is an awakening of the inner voice, a giving in of the intelligence, and a death of the old self. Looking into the future, I believe more refinements on the psychology will be described. There can be more states to describe the conscious and the unconscious. There will be more phases to describe the development process of our minds. Although we know there is a limit, it remains interesting to see how far human intelligence can go and how much of our minds can become conscious.

In resolving the classical debate between idealism and materialism regarding which is the first determining factor, the external object or the internal mind, a simple receiver and transmitter model is introduced in Chapter 2 to explain that the dilemma is essentially unnecessary. The existence of external objects is independent of the human mind. They transmit information regardless of whether there is a receiver that can decipher the information. The human mind, on the other hand, is a receiver to such information. Only when the receiver is tuned to the resonating frequency can the information be deciphered and understood by human beings. Otherwise, the information is just noise being ignored since it is meaningless to human beings, and the objects are as if nonexistent. This model is used to support the objectivity of the meaning of life. *There is a belief that there is information, principles, and laws that guide the functioning of life. Life is not only about survival and meeting physical needs, but also about being able to detect information, principles, and laws, even at the higher level. We call these messages of life.* Such messages exist regardless of the existence of human beings. Human beings are an ideal carrier to express such messages. Other living creatures on Earth may carry portions of such messages as well, such as survival and caring for each other. But the ability to spiritually listen and detect these messages is a unique characteristic of human beings. The evolution of human consciousness enables human beings to not only live for survival, but also exercise self-control on instinct, and have a spiritual level of life that is different from the physical world. *Human spiritual activities mimic some objective message from the universe.* This statement is just an assumption and remains to be further examined.

Lastly, there is a belief that human ethical values are consistent with the best interests of oneself, biologically or spiritually. More importantly, the consistency benefits the current life. There is no need to assume an afterlife benefit or penalty in order to follow ethical values. Ethical values are the natural flow when a person is tuned to the messages of life. By doing that, a person feels the maximum of spiritual happiness and a sense of attachment to the eternal existence. Religions relying on afterlife benefit or penalty do not really convey the truth regarding how human beings align and follow the message of life voluntarily. Instead, it either introduces fear or causes desperation for believers, as it is hard for them to convince themselves that the afterlife is a reality. It also causes distraction from maximizing the value of life here and now. Historically, most major religions used the afterlife to influence the current life, as it provides relief from uncertainty and justification for living an ethical life. This was a necessary step in the process of civilization before. Now, with the progress of science and psychology, we understand better the actual rewards of ethical behavior in the current life. The assumption of an afterlife is unnecessary. As for the statement that ethical value is consistent with the best interests of oneself biologically or spiritually, I would expect that research in the future will provide more and more relevant proof.

9.2 Potential Evolution of Culture and Religion

There are different levels of goals for human life: biological, social, and spiritual. The human mind, in its development process, also has different phases. Cultures and religions are supposed to nurture and connect these different levels and cover the entire spectrum. They should not emphasize one particular level, or denounce one level in order to endorse another level. Culture and religion typically have their own philosophies about human life. Like any scientific model, a philosophy is just an approximation of wisdom about real life. We ought to remember that the ultimate driver comes from real life. It evolves as time goes by. A philosophy must be adaptive to it, not the other way around. The earlier phase of mind development should be completed first before entering the next phase. A complete ideal life should go through all the phases, if possible, but it is also important to follow the order of the phases. It is better to remain incomplete than bypass (for whatever reason) an earlier phase in order to experience more advanced phases. As time goes by, I would expect a culture or a religion will more and more cover the spectrum of the human mind, and be more and more consistent with the dynamics of the human mind. The geographic boundary of different cultures and religions around the world will be blurred and gradually ignored.

But the exact evolutionary path of society cannot be predicted. At a given moment, society is just a snapshot of an evolutionary chain. The ultimate picture of the evolutionary path is not predictable by us. All we can do is make sure the next step is in the right direction. The right direction means it evolves toward a state that is more reflective of the truth of human nature, more gearing toward unlocking human potential while also supporting harmonious reconciliation. An ideology or societal endeavor can influence only the next step, but it cannot predict the whole course of evolution. It is a different level of law beyond control with current knowledge. I don't believe any ideology that claims to predict the social evolutionary path. Such claim is dangerous and can cause social conflicts if the ideology is enforced with intentional effort.

Cultural evolution is a similar situation. Culture is the synergy of the mind-sets from the whole society. Just as the individual human mind needs to go through the development cycle from growth to reconciliation, from full control to following self-organization, and from linear to nonlinear thinking, the cultural evolutionary path likely demonstrates a similar pattern. A culture that provides a living environment that is more reflective of the true human nature, more gearing toward unlocking human potential while supporting harmonious unification is a healthier culture that lasts longer. Many cultures, regardless of the regional boundary, exhibit similar ethical value systems.

Even though there is much commonality among different cultures around the world, the difference also needs to be respected. One should be fully aware that each culture has its own unique evolutionary path. Interaction among cultures is realized through the interaction among people from these different cultures, as human beings are the carriers of the culture. The principles for the interaction among people discussed in Chapter 4 apply here. The most important one is to respect an individual as a whole, not to simply judge him. An individual growing up in a culture has total attachment to that culture, regardless of whether it is better or worse. This fact must be fully respected. When the individual is exposed to a new or better culture, one should respect his own organic process to absorb and reconcile, instead of enforcing the new value into him and believing that it is better. This is true even if the new culture is a truly better one. Unfortunately, this is not the case in the current world. Lots of conflicts among countries are due to not following this principle.

As modern society enters the information era, the interactions among different cultures are getting more and more frequent and intensive. The aggregation and synergy among cultures and among religions will become more and more powerful. It is easier to digest thoughts from other thinkers before us, easier to expand or add one step on top of existing thoughts. A person's contribution is just a drop of water in the river of human history. With help from information technology, the aggregation and synergy effect can speed up the knowledge acquisition and cultural evolution at the global scale. It is reasonable to believe that such globalization of cultural evolution will enable us to get along much more harmoniously. The world is definitely getting smaller.

9.3 New Wisdom System

Wisdom systems around the world share many of the same principles: encouragement of growth, love, respect, and reconciliation, and alignment to the message of life. They all describe the peak of spiritual experience, such as the feeling of awesomeness of the universe, the littleness of oneself, the eternal, the indescribable, the blurring of the boundary between self and nature, the disappearance of the fear of death, and the resonation with the messages that will last beyond life and beyond humankind. The respect and love of others naturally flow out with such experience. However, it is difficult to reach such a state. The approaches to reach such a state are different from different wisdom systems around the world. The religious method calls out an agent (even a personalized agent) explicitly and elevates it to a divine status. It is easier to follow a personalized agent. The nonreligious approach is more moderate, more tolerant, but more difficult to follow by the mass population. However, these differences between religion and nonreligious approaches are not an essential one. In the future, these differences could be smoothed out, and only the primary message behind them will prevail. Human beings will get along better at that stage. We should anticipate a new wisdom system will emerge from the evolution and synergy of existing knowledge, cultures, and religions around the world.

Consolidation of science and religion, synergy of the Western and Eastern cultures, will be key to the evolution of the future wisdom system. *Science and religion represent the two fundamental forces that drive the evolution of the human mind, i.e., the conscious and the wholeness, the growth and the reconciliation. Western and Eastern cultures represent different reasoning styles, i.e., starting from the parts to the whole, or starting from the wholeness.* We have discussed the consolidation of science and religion earlier. When science advances to a certain level that its own limitation is self-evident, for example, the emergence effect, the interpretation of quantum wave function and quantum entanglement, the nonlinear behavior of complex systems, it is clearer that there is hidden order that cannot be fully understood by those at the lower-level order. At that point it is easier to consolidate. This is similar to the human mind's development cycle. When the human intellect realizes its own limitation, it is the turning point for reconciliation. *The ultimate question here is whether such "hidden order" does exist. If it does exist, how do we human beings interact with it?* While science assumes nothing to start with and may reveal such existence in the future, religions, on the other hand, believe the higher-level order is a given to start with. A religion can even call out explicitly the agent, proxy, or symbol in order to make it easy, or even possible to follow the underlying message. Without the religious approach, the myth is just a myth, very difficult to follow in routine life. Why? To understand the message (i.e., fully in a state that can interact with the hidden order momentarily), one needs to be an observer of the self. But in daily life, one needs to be an actor (fully in the normal state); one cannot be in these two states at the same time. Hence we need a symbol to represent the hidden and higher state so that we can be fully in the normal state. This helps to keep the dialogue open. Since it is also personalized, it can be a total response not only rationally but also emotionally.

Western and Eastern cultures in their evolutionary histories presented two reasoning approaches. Explicitly calling out this symbol is the tradition of Western reasoning style. Eastern reasoning would rather keep the myth as it is, insisting that it can only be experienced and is indescribable. But for normal people, this is hard to follow. More concretely, Western religions call out a God explicitly. Laws come from an external God. One needs to connect the mind to God. Eastern culture believes that the mind itself contains the *Li*, the Buddha, and the Tai Chi. The human mind has the potential to know these laws but needs to be awakened. The modern interpretation of God seems to be closer in connecting God to the Eastern concept of *Li*, Buddha, and Tai Chi. For example, Jung suggested that God exists inside the human psyche. Although both cultures approach the hidden and higher-level order differently, they share the same issue: how to prove that God, *Li*, Tai Chi, Buddha are objective entities? The question is similar to the objectivity of the third and fourth worlds, as discussed in Chapter 4. Such worlds are *not* purely subjective, they have elements of objectivity.

The third world is the output of the conscious mind. Its objectivity is due to the following two factors, both serving as a remedy of the human mind's deficiency:

- The human mind is changing constantly, like a river's flow. A mind cannot do rational reasoning all the time. It is interrupted by emotion and other random thoughts frequently. When the rational reasoning and ideas are written down, it has its own logic and direction, no more depending on the ever-changing mind. When the content in the mind is written down, it is consistent. It connects thoughts at many different moments but in a consistent way.
- An individual human mind is always limited and subjected to his own experience and knowledge capacity. But when the ideas are written down and shared, it can be criticized, modified, enhanced, and thus become more and more independent of any individual mind.

The remedy is also true for the unconscious mind, emotions, etc., that are the elements of the fourth world. By definition, the content of the fourth world is undetected and cannot be written down. However they can be shared, can be felt, unintentionally. Consistency and independence can be attained through sharing. The human mind can only grasp a glimpse of the light of the hidden order momentarily. Such a moment needs to be shared and expressed in some way in order to be sustainable. Religion tried to symbolize this, making it easier to understand.[6] However, what has been written down and shared must be evolving when our minds detect more hidden truth. Updating what has been written down when the human mind detects more hidden truth also ensures its objectivity. One can believe there is absolute truth, but the understanding of it is deepened and widened over time. Eastern wisdom even suggests that the fourth world can only be experienced unintentionally. Writing down or symbolizing is a risky attempt, anyway. On one hand, calling out explicitly the details of what the human mind is reasoning is a remedy to the subjectivity of the human mind; on the other hand, the symbol and scripture are just proxy and agent to the metareality in the fourth world. We need better methodology to describe the interactions between our minds and the metareality. The future development of nonlinear science and psychology may provide more methodological hints. Advancement in the

---

6 For example, according to the Bible, Jesus only taught in the secular world for three years, because as an image of God living in this world, he cannot live for long. This symbolized that the truth of the higher state could be only grasped by human beings momentarily.

understanding of the internal composition of the human mind, the dynamic growth of the human mind, the interactions between human minds, the evolution of the collective mind over a long time scale, and applying nonlinear methodology, may make it possible for us to better understand the complexity of how the human mind interacts with the hidden order (i.e., the metareality). We can gain more insights from the hints from nonlinear science and psychology and reinterpret the meaning of the many different religious symbols. We may find these symbols share a large portion of meaning that they represent. There is more commonality than difference.

The advancement of human intelligence is in an accelerated scale. For example, how many people understood algebra and calculus several hundred years ago? Nowadays typical high school students understand them. The difficult concept or theory hundreds of years ago can now become easy to grasp. Similarly those difficult theories such as general relativity, quantum entanglement, or thinking in a fourth (or higher) dimensional world, will become easy not long in the future. The wiring of the human brain advanced at an acceleratory speed as our knowledge accumulated. Therefore, at the current moment, even though we can only have spotty understandings of a higher-order world (e.g., a 4-D world) based on its projections to our regular world (e.g., a 3-D world), it is possible that such spotty understanding can be better connected in the future and have a more comprehensive understanding.

In the future wisdom system, what is the most important ethical value an individual should follow? The answer is as usual: honesty. It is the most single important wisdom of life. It ensures one's mind is tuned to the inner voice, to the message of life. It is the most basic practice to live as a true human being. As long as such channel is not blocked, ethical values flow naturally. Conscience, sympathy, caring about others the way we want to be cared for—these ethical values are a natural flow of the message of life, as long as our minds are not blocked to them. Honesty is sufficient to induce other morals or values. Honesty itself summarizes all the needed values in directing our moral system. I believe conscience itself has a biological foundation, hence it is intrinsic in our nature. However, we may ignore it due to many other conscious engagements. Life must have been formed (or, "created") with the code that living an honest life will maximize the happiness of life and the benefits of being alive. An honest person is in the most harmonious state between soul and body, between conscious and unconscious, and between ego and wholeness, even though such state can be shadowed or superimposed by other suboptimal states. Such message of life cannot be explained by simply understanding the parts and then summing them up. An honest person will be natural and restless to probe truth, will listen to the heart and maintain the conscience when dealing with others, will eventually realize the preciousness of life and hence respect and care for others, will be open-minded to avoid unnecessary conflict due to an incomplete understanding of life.

The next important ethical value is responsibility. Freedom means responsibility. In the beginning, human beings had little conscious awareness and knowledge, just followed instinct. This could be the optimal way for self-interest, since there are natural laws that guide them to behave, even if they were not aware of it. Therefore there is no need to make any choice. Later when human consciousness was awakening, we started to gain knowledge, to define concepts and ethical values. People did not simply follow instinct; instead they tried to use the derived ethical value to guide life. However, due to the deficiency of these concepts, theories, and values because they were just an approximation to the reality, by following them we may actually live in a suboptimal state. Now we have freedom and many choices, but there could be a disconnection between the choice picked by our free will and what is the optimal thing to do. That is why we need responsibility to direct our choices to align with the optimal state.

We should distinguish two things here: 1) The action of aligning to a direction is a responsibility. This responsibility is tied with the will to believe. It can be derived from megastatistics as well. 2) What direction to align with. The direction is tied with the destiny of human beings, the goals of life. However, the fact that we are both actor and observer means the goal and the process cannot be separated. If we care about our destiny (the goal), the daily-routine decision (the process) is part of the destiny already. As long as one keeps the high standard of being an honest person, the responsibility of making the right choice is a natural act, instead of a forceful one. By doing that, we may head to a better destiny, even if at a given time and in a certain environment, we don't know exactly what it is. Not knowing the destiny exactly is less crucial now, since we have carried out our responsibility already.

9.4 Back to Here and Now

Philosophy is a type of preknowledge, meaning it is not yet approved. Therefore it can be correct or can be proved to be wrong. Lots of statements in this book fall into such a category. The human mind tends to think ahead of what can be proved right or wrong. It is the nature of our intellect.

The human mind is such a complex and miraculous creation in the universe. The biological components are nothing special, but it is amazing how much information the mind can absorb, process, and reflect back to the outside. The biological parts will be aging and dying at some point, but the information it transmits can be lasting. The spectrum of the mind is broad. If the information from our mind is transmitted at the right frequency, it can be detected and digested in the future. Theoretically, such information can even last beyond the existence of human beings and the earth. Perhaps some other forms of life can decipher the information, as long as such information is embedded in a physical carrier. We cannot imagine what form other physical carriers can be. Even at present, the DNA and genes that carry the information of human life have not been fully understood yet. DNA and genes carry the biological codes for human life. But the spirit information of human life is passed through knowledge, culture, or religion. Physical life can be ceased, but the spectrum of mind that carries the information about life will transcend. Human life is most meaningful and respectful when life is aligned with the message of life. This seems to be mythical. The purpose of this book is to try not to rely on mythical symbols but to push rational reasoning to the limit. The intuitive concepts beyond the limit are also described explicitly. Those concepts, including the fourth world, metareality, and the message of life, are some of these intuitive concepts. They are left to the readers to choose to accept or reject.

As scientific knowledge advances, the journey to understanding the human mind and the meaning of life will be more exciting, and the evolution of human history, the culture, and the wisdom system will continue. But for now, we need to pull our mind back to the here and now. There are always unknowns, the future is uncertain, and there are many different cultures and religions that provide different perceptions; some of them even conflict with each other. But they won't hinder our appreciation of the magnificence of life; they won't stop us from being honest people who listen to our hearts or take our part of the responsibility to choose and share the message of life and connect to each other. We may speak different languages and believe different wisdom systems, but the messages behind them are likely similar.

On a sunny Saturday afternoon in Southern California, I was jogging around a lake near my house as my weekly routine. The sky was clear and blue with a few white clouds floating around. The sunlight was warm on the shoulders, and the wind was blowing softly. Thousands of light reflections were on the water surface of the lake, which was surrounded by trees and bushes. It was such a beautiful and tranquil scene. I felt there was nothing in my mind. I totally enjoyed the peace and merged myself into this beautiful nature. This was very similar to the scene described in the beginning of the book. As I walked toward the end of the hiking trail around the lake, I spotted an old man a few steps away, sitting quietly on a bench near the lake. His eyes gazed at the lake. He was very calm and peaceful. I thought he might be enjoying the same feeling as I was. Suddenly, when I passed by him, I heard a greeting uttered from this old man's mouth, gently and nicely, "God bless you." Without a thought I replied, "Thank you." It was a simple exchange of two sentences, but it was an amazing moment to me at the right time and at the right place. I felt blessed and appreciative. We may have different understandings of what God means, but the power of sharing outweighs the difference.

At that moment, the spectra of two minds overlap. And the meaning of life is revealed.